Anonymous

Historical Papers and Addresses

Of the Lancaster County Historical Society. Vol. I

Anonymous

Historical Papers and Addresses
Of the Lancaster County Historical Society. Vol. I

ISBN/EAN: 9783744686075

Printed in Europe, USA, Canada, Australia, Japan

Cover: Foto ©ninafisch / pixelio.de

More available books at **www.hansebooks.com**

HISTORICAL PAPERS AND ADDRESSES

OF THE

LANCASTER COUNTY

HISTORICAL SOCIETY.

VOLUME I. ILLUSTRATED.

1896–7.

LANCASTER, PA.
1897.

CONTENTS OF VOLUME I.

	PAGE.
The Names of the Townships, by JOSEPH H. DUBBS, D.D.,	3–14
The Chickies Furnace, by H. L. HALDEMAN,	14–24
Reminiscences of Conestoga Township, by CASPER HILLER,	24–27
The Hero of the Christiana Riot, by THOMAS WHITSON, Esq.,	27–35
The Acadians in Lancaster County, by S. M. SENER, Esq.,	35–44
Baron Henry William Stiegel, by J. H. SEILING, M.D.,	44–69
Ann Henry, Lanc. Co.'s Woman Treasurer, by GEORGE STEINMAN,	69–72
The Oldest Daily Paper of Lancaster County, by F. R. DIFFENDERFFER,	72–85
Indian Tribes of Lancaster County, by F. R. DIFFENDERFFER,	85–89
Address, by HON. W. U. HENSEL,	89–92
Constitution,	92–94
Reminiscences of Strasburg, by JACOB HILDEBRAND, Esq.,	94–109
Irish Occupation of Lancaster Land, by R. M. REILLY, Esq.,	109–111
Proposed Location of State Capital on the Susquehanna, by HON. W. U. HENSEL,	111–114
Coroner's Verdict in Christiana Riot Case, by HON. W. U. HENSEL,	114–117
A William Penn Deed, by HON. W. U. HENSEL,	117–119
Reuben Chambers, by R. J. HOUSTON,	119–133
Samuel Bowman, Founder of Bowmansville, by HON. A. G. SEYFERT,	133–141
Committees,	141
When Was Strasburg Erected Into a Borough, by SAMUEL EVANS, Esq.,	146–150
Reminiscences of Paradise Township, by A. E. WITMER,	150–160
An Old Martic Township Petition, by SAMUEL EVANS, Esq.,	160–167
Early County Mills, by SAMUEL EVANS, Esq.,	167–176
Officers for 1896–7,	176
The People Who Made Lancaster County, by W. M. FRANKLIN, Esq.,	181–204
Early Industries of the Octorara, by J. W. HOUSTON, M.D.,	204–218; 245–361
Some Helfenstein Letters, by REV. J. H. DUBBS,	218–226
The Early Telegraph, by W. B. WILSON, Esq.,	226–251
A Prominent Scotch-Irishman, by R. J. HOUSTON,	251–258
History of Donegal Church, by J. L. ZIEGLER, M.D.,	258–283
The Gap Copper Mines, by R. J. HOUSTON,	283–299
Old Mills and County Ordinaries, by SAMUEL EVANS, Esq.,	299–313; 313–323

(iv)

	PAGE.
The Ephrata Paper Mill, by J. F. SACHSE, Esq.,	323–345
Old Welsh Graveyard, by B. F. OWEN, Esq.,	361–376
The Ross Memorial,	376
" " " Programme,	377
" " Presentation Address,	378
" " Acceptance "	378–380
MISS NEVIN'S Poem,	380–389
Address of HON. M. BROSIUS,	389–408

ILLUSTRATIONS.

FULL-PAGE ENGRAVINGS.

	PAGE.
Fac-simile Title of First Bible Printed in America,	323
Rittenhouse Paper Mill Water Marks,	326
Ephrata Paper Mill Water Marks,	335
Zionitic Brotherhood Water Marks,	337
Plan of Old Welsh Graveyard,	367
George Ross,	375
Ross Memorial Tablet,	387
Ross Mansion,	394
Ross Coat of Arms,	408

ENGRAVINGS IN TEXT.

A Stiegel 10-Plate Stove,	47
Stiegel Mansion,	50
Stiegel Office in Manheim,	51
Stiegel Glassware,	52
Stiegel Lutheran Church, 1770,	56
Stiegel Lutheran Church, 1891,	57
Stiegel School House, 1778,	61
Brickerville Church,	62
Elizabeth Stiegel's Tomb,	64
Old Receipt,	73
Wilcox Paper Mill Water Mark,	324
Sauer Bible Water Mark,	334

PAPERS READ

BEFORE THE

LANCASTER COUNTY HISTORICAL SOCIETY,

ON JUNE 5, 1896.

THE NAMES OF THE TOWNSHIPS,
BY JOS. H. DUBBS, D. D.

THE CHICKIES FURNACE,
BY HORACE L. HALDEMAN.

REMINISCENCES OF CONESTOGA TOWNSHIP,
BY CASPER HILLER.

THE CHRISTIANA RIOT,
BY THOMAS WHITSON, ESQ.

LANCASTER, PA.
REPRINTED FROM THE NEW ERA.

The Names of the Townships,
    By Jos. H. Dubbs, D. D..................... 3
The Chickies Furnaces,
    By Horace L. Haldeman 14
Reminiscences of Conestoga Township,
    By Casper Hiller.......... 24
The Hero of the Christiana Riot,
    By Thomas Whitson, Esq................... 27

HOW THEY WERE NAMED

NOMENCLATURE OF OUR TOWNSHIPS.

The township is the unit of Teutonic society. As such it is more ancient than the county, the kingdom, or the empire. In its earliest form it was established by a group of families, holding together for mutual protection and cultivating the soil in accordance with a common system. Among the Germans, as described by the Roman author Tacitus, it existed long before the establishment of settled government. The Romans named it *vicus*, or village community; but the Germans themselves termed it *mark*, because it was surrounded by a mark, or boundary, which was originally a strip of land on which no one was allowed to settle. The earliest laws were determined by the township meeting, and ages passed before a central government appeared which claimed to do more than to settle difficulties between adjacent townships. When the Angles and Saxons migrated to Britain they bore with them their Teutonic ideas of local government; and by whatever name it may have been known— whether mark, vicus, wapentake, hundred, township or parish—this was this fundamental organization that constituted the foundation of the State. By the introduction of the feudal system, it is true, social conditions were greatly obscured; but the people, at any rate, continued to believe that the township had a right to protest against any injustice on the part of the general government; and the township meeting became the foundation of civil liberty.

In America the historical process was somewhat different. The earliest settlements were, indeed, in many instances compelled by the exigencies of their situation to adopt some form of local government before the boundaries of the colonies and counties had been fully determined; but more generally it was the colonial government that established the counties, at the same time granting to the district Courts authority to organize the townships.

In the foundation of our own county of Lancaster these two processes may be said to have been in some sense united. There were a few early settlements which had been named by the pioneers, and several of them had been recognized as townships by the county of Chester, which claimed jurisdiction over all this region; but when the county of Lancaster was established by the colonial legislature, it was one of the first acts of the Court to divide its territory into townships and to give them names. Though it is not our purpose to relate the history of the townships, nor even to enumerate them, it may be well to recall a few of the recorded particulars of this interesting event.

Lancaster county was founded by Act of Assembly on May 10, 1729; and is said to have been named by its first chief magistrate, John Wright, after his native county of Lancaster, in England. He was a man of great ability and personal worth, and our county has no reason to be ashamed of its sponsor. According to the original Act the new county was to include all of Chester lying west of the Octoraro creek and "north and west of a line of marked trees extending from the north branch of the Octoraro to the Schuylkill river." It was no doubt a great relief to the people of Chester county to be freed from the responsibility of caring for the vast, untrodden wilderness that stretched indefinitely towards the west; and whatever may be said of their peace principles, they do not seem to have at any time objected to the stretching of a barrier of Scotch Irishmen and Germans between them and the red men of the forest.

As it was impossible to conceive of a county without townships, the newly-appointed magistrates called a meeting to determine names and boundaries. This meeting was held at John Postlethwait's tavern in Conestoga township, on the 9th of June, 1729. Its report was confirmed by the Magistrates' Court which met at the same place, August 5, 1729.

Lancaster county as then organized extended from the Susquehanna and

Octoraro to the Blue Mountains and the Schuylkill river. It included twenty townships, of which four have since been separated. Peshtauk (or Paxton) and Derry are now in Dauphin, Lebanon is in Lebanon county, and Tulpehocken is divided between Lebanon and Berks. The original townships included in the present territory of Lancaster county were Donegal, Warwick, Cocalico, Hempfield, Manheim, Cæruarvon, Conestoga, Lampeter, Leacock, Lancaster, Earl, Martic, Salisbury, Sadsbury and Dromore. "The Manor" was recognized as a reserved possession of the proprietors, and was therefore not immediately organized as a township. Cocalico is not mentioned in the earliest list, but there is evidence to prove that it was organized in the same year.

It is sometimes said that there is nothing in a name; but the man who originated that saying was no historian. Every name has a meaning, and it may generally teach us something concerning the people by whom it was first uttered. In the present paper we do not propose to consider the origin of the names of the forty-one townships into which Lancaster county is now divided—not to speak of the city of Lancaster and thirteen boroughs—but merely to show by a familiar process how the social history of the county, and the racial character of its earliest settlers, may be determined by the names of its original townships. It will be found that, like the rings of a tree, these names mark the passing of successive periods, and by carefully removing them we may at last discover traces of the original sapling.

A single glance is enough to show that the names of our townships consist of several distinct classes; and by discovering which of these have been longest in use, we are naturally led to what may be termed the substratum of our history. We have, therefore,

1. The Indian Names.

Conestoga is, no doubt, our earliest township. Though greatly shorn of its original dimensions, its name, in one of its many forms, goes back to a period long anterior to the earliest European settlement; and as the chosen designation of a tribe and of a stream it very properly records the fact that the Indians first occupied the land. "Conestogo" is said to signify "the great magic land," which we understand to indicate that the region was even then recognized as possessing extraordinary fertility. It was a name which was readily adopted by the European pioneers, and was by them applied to an extensive region. Long after the organization of Lancaster county, German emigrants are said, in records preserved in the fatherland, to have "sailed to Conestogo."

Tulpehocken is another Indian name that was loosely applied to the great northern region as far as the Blue Mountains. It is said to mean "the land of the turtles," and if we are to judge by the experiences of the early settlers it was not a land of turtle-doves but of genuine "snappers."

Peshtank (now Paxton) in Dauphin county is derived from a word which means "stagnant water"—possibly referring to a stretch of the Susquehanna where the water did not flow swiftly. Cocalico (Koch-hale-kung) means "the serpents' den," and according to the "Chronicon Ephratense" the stream was named after a place not far from Ephrata where serpents abounded.

There are several comparatively recent townships—such as Pequea and Conoy—whose names are remotely of Indian origin, but the above are all that are included in the original list.

2. The English Names.

The earliest officials of our county were almost without exception natives of England, and we are, therefore, not surprised to find that a considerable number of our earliest townships were named after places in the mother country. In some instances they chose the names of cities or counties; in others they were satisfied to commemorate obscure parishes. The contrast thus presented is sometimes remarkable. Salisbury and Sadsbury are close neighbors, but the first commemorates a city whose name appears on almost every page of English history, while the original of the second is so obscure that its name is not even mentioned in the British postoffice list. The comparison appears to suggest a little playful irony, which may be unintentional; as though the pioneers of Sadsbury, whether in Chester or Lancaster county, had intentionally chosen an obscure village as a foil to the historic splendor of Salisbury. Martic township was originally named Martock, from a town of some importance in the county of Somerset, in the west of England, which may have been one of the last places beheld by the settlers before they started on their adventurous voyage to the new world. Hempfield is said to be so named "because much hemp was raised there"; but this may possibly be an afterthought. The name is certainly that of a parish in England. Lancaster township, like the county, is named after the city and county of Lancaster, in England. The name goes back to the time when the Roman legions founded camps in England, and signifies Long Camp. Warwick is said to have been named by Richard Carter after his native county of Warwick. The name was well chosen; for it will be remembered that Warwick is the central county of England, situated where the two great Roman roads crossed. In a somewhat similar way our township of Warwick was situated as nearly as possible at the centre of the county as originally constituted, at the crossing of the western and northern trails. Richard Carter certainly manifested good taste in choosing the name of Warwick for this important township.

Among the more recent place-names of our county there are several whose origin it is not easy to determine. "Bart," as the name of a township, is said by local historians to be an abbreviation of baronet, the title of Governor Sir Wm. Keith; but such an interpretation is hardly credible, and the subject deserves more careful investigation. Tradition must not in such cases be taken too seriously. Elizabeth township is, for instance, declared to have derived its name from a furnace which had been "named in honor of Queen Elizabeth." That the township derived its name from the furnace we do not doubt, but the tradition that the furnace was named in honor of "the virgin queen," one hundred and fifty years after her death, is, to say the least, somewhat romantic.

3. **The Irish Names.**

At the settlement of Lancaster county

the Scotch-Irish— more properly termed "Ulster Scots"—occupied the post of danger in the northwest. They were a bold and vigorous race, which permanently influenced the history of the State and Nation. Naturally enough they named the settlements after the places in the old country, which they most affectionately remembered. Donegal, for instance, was known to every one as a great maritime county of Ireland, from which, for reasons which we cannot now relate, the greater number of our early immigrants had gone forth. Adjoining it is the county of Londonderry, more generally known as Derry. These names came to occupy a prominent place in the early annals of our county. The township of Donegal has been divided and subdivided, and Derry now belongs to Dauphin county; but both names remain to commemorate the heroic people from whom they are derived.

In this connection it may be proper to note that the earliest township to be separated from Donegal was appropriately named Rapho. The town of Raphoe in Ireland is the ecclesiastical centre of the county of Donegal. The Roman Catholic bishop of Raphoe is practically bishop of Donegal; and the Episcopal bishop of Raphoe is also bishop of Derry. It will be seen, therefore, that these names were not given to our townships by mere chance, but rather in accordance with a settled purpose to reproduce as nearly as possible the geographical conditions of the ancient home beyond the sea.

In other parts of the county there are townships whose names are evidently derived from places in the north of Ireland. Coleraine township was organized as early as 1738, and was named after Coleraine in Ireland, a seaport town in the county of Londonderry. Leacock is said by our local historians to have been called after a place in Ireland; but the exact spot we have been unable to identify. Drumore—more properly written Dromore—is a town of some importance in the county of Down. It will be remembered that the great theologian Jeremy Taylor was, in the seventeenth century, bishop of Dromore.

4. The Welsh Names.

The Welsh settlers of Lancaster county were intelligent and influential. They were early in the field and took a prominent part in public affairs. In some instances, we presume, the Welshmen whose names appear on our early records actually resided in Chester county, or possibly in Montgomery, but held lands in this region which they gradually sold as they became more valuable. Those who actually settled here were most numerous in the eastern and northeastern townships where they left many traces of their occupancy.

Following the example of other nationalities, the Welsh applied familiar names to the places where they dwelt. This was more frequently done in other counties than in our own; but at least three of our original townships bear Welsh names. These are Cærnarvon, Brecknock and Lampeter. Cærnarvon, in Wales—now generally written Carnarvon—is one of the most important counties in the principality, and the town of the same name is large and flourishing. Brecknock, or Brecon, is also the name of a county and town in South Wales. Lampeter seems to have given our local antiquarians some trouble; but there was actually no occasion for it. About fifty years ago some person, with a vivid imagination, wrote a local novel which he called "The Man with Two Heads." In this extraordinary book the author boldly asserted that Lampeter township was at first called "Lamepeter," in honor of a certain "Lame Peter," who once kept tavern there. The suggestion is so absurd as hardly to deserve serious refutation. There may have been a "lame Peter" in Lampeter; but for all that, it remains true that the name of the township is derived from Lampeter, in Wales, which is a place of some importance and the seat of an Episcopal Theological Seminary. In the Welsh language the name signifies "Peter's Church."

There is a suggestion of Welsh origin in such a name as " Little Britain "; but as this belongs to a somewhat later period we must leave it unconsidered. More important for our present purpose it is to cast a glance at the names which remind us of another nationality which has contributed the largest quota to our population, and has most deeply impressed its characteristics on our community.

5. The German Names.

At the time of the naming of the townships the German population of the county was small. There were, indeed, a few settlements—locally known by such names as "Graaf's Thal" and "Weberland," but the people were of retiring disposition, and were not acquainted with the language of their rulers. It is not surprising, we think, that the number of German place-names is not large; it is rather a ground for astonishment that such names are found in the earliest records of our county.

Manheim is the name of one of our original townships. The name calls to mind the Palatinate city of that name whose misfortunes must have been still fresh in the memory of our earliest German immigrants. It will be remembered that the German city of Manheim was destroyed during the invasion of 1689. On that occasion the French invaders cast the very stones of which the city was built into the river Neckar; but wherever they went the exiled Palatines bore the memory of the ill-fated city in their hearts. It would be interesting to know which of the German immigrants was the first to suggest the name in connection with one of our original townships. Certainly it was not Baron Stiegel who founded the present borough of Manheim, and is said to have named it after his birthplace; for the township of Manheim was named long before the eccentric baron crossed the ocean.

Another township which may claim a place in the German series is Earl, which was named in honor of Hans Graaf (or Graf), a German pioneer whose surname is an equivalent for the English "Earl." To us it may seem to have been a left-handed compliment to translate a name before attempting to render it illustrious; but this was the usual fashion in colonial days. It would have been in better taste, we think, to have left the name unaltered; and we do not doubt that if this had been done "Graaf" would by this time have sounded as euphonious as "Earl;" but it is pleasant to recognize the fact that, even at this early date, there was a disposition to do honor to a German pioneer.

At a later period other townships were honored with names that suggest reminiscences of the Fatherland. Strasburg, for instance, is said to have been named by Matthias Schleiermacher (Slaymaker) in honor of the beautiful city which "France had seized but Germany has won." It is, however, certain that, to use the words of Bancroft, "the Germans have not claimed the position to which they are honorably entitled;" and in the history of our county this fact is fully exemplified. Ancient customs are giving place to new forms of culture. In the city of Lancaster we no longer recognize our environs by such names as "Bettelstadt" and "Wolfebuckel," and in a few more generations the German language will probably have disappeared, except as a subject of literary study. We hope, however, that the peculiar Anglo-German character of our county will never be changed, and that to the latest generation our people may be characterized by German truth and honesty.

6. The Scriptural Names.

In our local nomenclature the religious character of the people is plainly apparent. In our earliest list of townships, it is true, the only name which is plainly of Scriptural origin is Lebanon—a township which has become the nucleus of an adjacent county. Lebanon, we remember, is a Hebrew word, signifying "white," or "snowy," and may have been properly applied to the range of mountains to which this township originally extended. Not long after its organization it was divided and for the separated portion the name of "Bethel" was chosen. Bethel signifies "the house of God," and the name itself was an acknowledgment of earnest, Christian faith. Within our present limits we have "Ephrata"—a beautiful scriptural name, signifying "fertility." As the chosen designation of a religious society it was known soon after the organization of the county, but it was not until 1833 that it became the name of a township. Other portions of our county are not without religious suggestions. It is a subject of congratulation that "Paradise" and "Eden" are near at hand, and that "Providence" is always with us.

In discussing our early nomenclature

we have but traced the outlines of the subject. If time permitted it would be easy to show that every place-name is a milestone in our history. Coming down to more recent times, we should have to show that even those townships which have been pleased to be known by the names of great men have not chosen their appellations at random. The townships which are thus designated are "Penn," "Fulton" and "Clay." Could any names more completely illustrate the historic origin, the intellectual development and the political preferences of our county?

In studying our theme we have been interested by the fact that every national element in our population, with perhaps a single exception, has left its traces upon our nomenclature. Our townships have no names suggestive of the French traders —the Chartieres, Bizaillons and LeTorts —who were once so prominent in our local history. These people came and went, leaving no impression on our subsequent annals. We have, indeed, many families with French surnames, but we believe most of these to be descended from French Huguenots, who had sought refuge in Germany and had become pretty thoroughly Germanized before they crossed the ocean.

A French origin might, indeed, be suggested for the name of one of our townships and towns, though we are not aware that this has ever been done. Mount Joy is a name which appears to be thoroughly English, and in its present form is suggestive of perfect happiness. It may, however, be remembered that "Mont-Joie" was the ancient battle cry of the French nation; and that many an army rushed into the conflict shouting: "*Mont-Joie et Saint Denis.*" If a French pioneer had been given an opportunity of naming his dwelling place in America, he might readily have called it "Mont-Joie," and it would not have taken long to reduce it to its present form. This, however, is a mere suggestion, which is not seriously presented.

The township is, indeed, declared on excellent authority to have been named in honor of General Robert Stewart, Viscount Mount Joy, of the county of Londonderry, in Ireland.

The history of Lancaster county is an

extensive field, which hitherto has not been extensively cultivated. It suggests many themes that deserve minute consideration. To the earnest student it offers many encouragements; but the successful accomplishment of our task demands faithful and unremitting labor.

HISTORICAL PAPER.

THE FIRST FURNACE USING COAL.

Prior to 1840 no pig iron was successfully produced in this county, or, in fact, in any other portion of the world, except with charcoal as a fuel. Attempts had been made to use charcoal and anthracite mixed, and the latter alone, but they were failures. With the discovery of hot blast, the conditions changed and it was then found that anthracite coal alone could be successfully used in the production of pig iron. As the timber to produce charcoal was not plentiful in Lancaster county, the change to anthracite created quite a small "boom," for those days, in our county, especially as there were many local deposits of brown hematite, or limonite, ores that it were thought could be used to considerable advantage. The fever became contagious, each one seeming anxious to be an "iron master," in which name there seemed to be something particularly attractive, and many paid dearly for the honor!

So far as the records in my possession show the furnaces to use anthracite coal in Lancaster county were:

Shawnee furnace, at Columbia, built in 1844–45 by Robert and James Calvin. Archibald Wright and nephew erected a second furnace here in 1854.

Henry Clay furnace, on the Pennsylvania railroad and canal, between Chickies and Columbia, was built in 1845, by Peter Haldeman, of Columbia.

Chikiswalungo furnace, later changed to Chickies, at the mouth of Chickies creek, was built by Henry Haldeman, who resided just below Bainbridge, for his sons, Professor S. S. Haldeman and Dr. Edwin Haldeman.

Marietta furnaces (two) were erected by Mr. Shoenberger and Henry Musselman, one in 1848, the other in 1849. Later the firm became Musselman & Watts. The latter, Henry M. Watts, was a son-in-law of Mr. Shoenberger.

Rough and Ready furnace, later changed to Cordelia, which is situated on

Shawnese Run, about two and one-half miles northwest of Columbia, was built in 1848 by Cross & Waddell.

Conestoga furnace, in Lancaster, was built as a charcoal furnace in 1846 by Robert and James Calvin and George Ford, a Lancaster lawyer. Later the furnace was changed to use anthracite coal.

Safe Harbor furnace, near the mouth of Conestoga creek, was built by Reese, Abbott & Co., "a few years after 1846."

Sarah Ann furnace, on the north side of Big Chickies creek, was erected in 1839 by Jacob Gamber. It was later owned by Governor Daniel R. Porter, who changed it to anthracite.

Donegal furnace, on the Pennsylvania canal, between Chickies and Marietta furnaces, was built in 1848, by James Myers, of Columbia; Dr. George N. Eckert and Daniel Stein.

St. Charles furnace, at Columbia, was built in 1852 by Clement B. Grubb, of Lancaster.

Eagle furnace, which adjoins the Chickies property, was built in 1854, by S. F. Eagle, Peter Haldeman and Joseph Cottrell. This furnace was purchased by the owners of the Chickies furnace, when its name was changed to Chickies No. 2.

Musselman furnace, later changed to Vesta, was the last blast furnace erected in our county. It was built by Musselman & Watts, the owners of the Marietta furnaces, in 1868.

Owing to the various changes in the modern conditions of producing pig iron all except three of the above thirteen blast furnaces have either been abandoned, or torn down or sold for "scrap iron. Of these three the two at Chickies are now in operation.

The first in Lancaster county to use anthracite fuel were the Shawnee, at Columbia; Henry Clay, above Columbia, and Chikiswalungo, in the order named.

The eight furnaces along the Pennsylvania canal, between Columbia and Marietta, were built there owing to facilities that waterway gave them for transportation; all their coal being received and iron shipped by canal. The ores at first came from the surrounding local mines and were hauled to the furnaces in wagons.

In 1828 Henry Haldeman purchased the Chickies property from the estate of

Christian Hershey, deceased. There was then standing on the property a small saw mill on the grounds of the present mansion. Shortly after purchasing the property he erected the present larger saw mill at the mouth of Chickies creek. This mill was run for him by Samuel Zink. In 1836 Henry Haldeman took his son, Prof. S. S. Haldeman, in partnership in the lumber business. In 1842 Henry Haldeman retired from the partnership, transferring his remaining interest to his second son, Dr. Edwin Haldeman, then a practicing physician. The firm then consisted of Prof. S. S. Haldeman and Dr. Edwin Haldeman under the firm name of E. Haldeman & Co.

Prior to Henry Haldeman's purchase of this property, there was a fulling mill on the same, the remains of the dam for which can yet be seen under one of the present turnpike bridges. There was also a ferry across the mouth of the creek used by travellers before the river turnpike road was built, there being no bridge at that time. The Columbia and Marietta turnpike was incorporated January 21, 1814, but the road was not constructed until 1826-30, at the time the State built the canal along the river shore. "This turnpike followed the canal level from Columbia to Chickies Rock, where it ascended and curved around a large rock down to the face of Chickies Rock, thence along the canal level. This was one of the finest drives in the county. The Pennsylvania Railroad Company having purchased the road bed, the turnpike was changed to its present location over Chickies hill."

Samuel Evans, in his History of Lancaster county, writes: "The Marietta Railroad Company was incorporated in 1832 to build a road from Marietta to a point on the Columbia and Philadelphia Railroad, about six miles east of Columbia. When the Legislature re-chartered the United States Bank, that institution paid a bonus to the State of some thousands of dollars. Henry Haldeman, who had much influence, opposed the re-chartering of this bank, and to overcome his opposition the bonus was taken and appropriated towards the construction of the above railway through his Chickies property. Surveys were made and the line of road located about twenty feet above the bed of the present Pennsylvania Railroad. A portion of the road bod was graded for about two hundred feet in the rear of the large mansion house at Chickies, but nothing more was done. The grading is still shown in the yard of same at this time."

In 1833 Henry Haldeman built as a residence for his son, Professor S. S. Haldeman, the large mansion now standing at the base of Chickies Rock. Professor Haldeman was the architect, making and originating all the detailed drawings and specifications, which are in a good state of preservation to-day.

In 1845 Henry Haldeman built the Chickiswalungo furnace. This furnace and all his other property at Chickies he gave to his sons, Samuel and Edwin, on July 4, 1845.

The furnace first went in blast January 15, 1846. It was originally but thirty-two feet high and eight feet across boshes, but was modernized from time to time, but the original stack remained until 1886, when the old plant was, practically, dismantled and a new one erected, including machinery, boilers and hot blast stoves. From the time the furnace was built up to July, 1893, a period of over forty-seven years, the furnace was never out of blast for more than six months at any one time. During the depression in the iron business in 1893, it went out of blast, but is now in operation.

In 1852 Paris Haldeman, a younger brother, was admitted in the firm of E. Haldeman & Co. In 1869 Prof. Haldeman retired from the business and the heirs of Edward B. Grubb, of Burlington, N. J., entered, they having purchased the Eagle furnace adjoining the Chickies property. This co-partnership continued after the death of Dr. Edwin Haldeman in 1872, until the Chickies Iron Company was formed in 1876. In 1888 the firm of Haldeman, Grubb & Co. was formed, consisting of Paris Haldeman, C. Ross Grubb and Horace L. Haldeman. Paris Haldeman retired from active business in 1891, leaving the members of the firm as at present, C. Ross Grubb and Horace L. Haldeman.

The principal ores used at the Chickies furnaces were obtained from the Grubb and Haldeman's ore mines at Silver Springs, some six miles from the furnaces, and from Cornwall, Lebanon county. Of late years Cornwall ore has been used to produce a Bessemer pig iron.

The several ore properties at Chestnut Hill, which adjoin each other, are, when taken as a whole, one of the largest hematite ore deposits in this State. Ore was first discovered there on the Greider farm, between 1825 and 1832, by Simeon Guilford, the distinguished engineer, who died at Lebanon last year, at the advanced of ninety-three years, and mining has been carried on since the first discovery up to the present day. Most of the furnaces in and around Columbia and Chickies depend on these mines for their principal supply of ore.

There has been some controversy as to the orthography of Chickies and, as frequently is the case, those knowing the least about the subject have the most to say. It is a well-known fact, recognized by those competent to give an opinion, that the spelling of words is by no means a safe guide to pronunciation. In an address to the Spelling Reform Association, delivered by the late Professor S. S. Haldeman, in 1877, he aptly said: "Our spelling is so lawless that we take unscientific rules for our guide and instead of following the great law that speech is older than spelling, we make it newer; and if the spelling depends upon some hidden fact a word may be sacrificed to a fetish or bit of paper with writing upon it. People who learn only spelling and neglect the laws of speech are continually trying to reconstruct words from spelling, the significance of which they do not understand."

In early days, when little attention was given to the matter, there were a number of ways in which the name was spelled, the most common being *Chicques* and *Chiques*, generally with the *qu*. The name is derived from the Chikiswalungo creek, meaning "the place of crabs," which was then also spelled *Chiquesalungo*. The *qu* came from the French surveyors, employed by the French Indian traders, who, in making their maps, used the *qu* to give the *k* sound, pronounced by the Indians as if spelled *Chikis*. This was quite natural and possibly correct from a Frenchman's point of view, as much so as the spelling of any French geographical name, but if we follow that language we would have to change America and the United States into *Amerique* and *Etats Unis*.

In 1846, when the blast furnace was built, it was necessary to give it a name, as well as the brand of pig iron to be produced. Care was taken to investigate the subject by Professor Haldeman, who, at that time and prior, was recognized as an authority on languages and phonology, including Indian dialects of which he had written as early as 1844. After much investigation the name adopted was *Chikiswalungo Furnace*, as is also shown by the furnace account books for the firm, of which Professor Haldeman was the senior member.

This name was used until June, 1858, when owing to the inconvenience of its length it was shortened to *Chickies*, as at present, by Professor Haldeman's advice and consent. In a communication to a local newspaper, of December 8, 1877, referring to another correspondent's communication, he writes: "The original form *Chikiswalungo* was so cumbersome that it broke in two, giving us names for the two towns *Chickies* and *Salungo*...... The original is too inconvenient for post-office and map purposes and the philanthropy which imposed a name like *Philadelphia* is to be doubted. *Naples* and *Paris* are preferable to the old names *Neapolis* and *Lutetia Parisiorum*, and, in fact, abbreviation is one of the laws of language......The post-office department uses *Chickies*, the Pennsylvania railroad *Chiques* (apt to be called *Cheeks*), but of late I often write *Chikis*."

In a letter of Dr. E. Haldeman, of December 27, 1856, he twice uses *Chikis* in referring to the turnpike and creek and this latter spelling was used by Prof. S. S. Haldeman in the later years of his life for the headings of his communications. He also gave the latter as correct to Prof. Persifer Frazer, Jr., geologist in charge of the survey of Adams, York, Lancaster and Chester counties, for the Second State Geological Survey of Pennsylvania, 1876–8, for which the reports were published in 1879. Prof. Frazer wrote him that as the record was to appear in a State document, which would go down to posterity and there seemed to be some question on the subject, he applied to Prof. Haldeman as the only authority he recognized on the matter; the latter gave *Chikis* as correct, and so it appears in these, as well as other publications.

Whilst we would not attempt to dispute Prof. Haldeman's decision, it would have created much confusion, from a business standpoint, to change the name of the post-office, railway station, telegraph and express offices, names of the furnaces, brand of iron and the Company making the same, after having been in use for a quarter of a century, from *Chickies* to *Chikis*, especially as the difference was so slight. No one now pretends that *Chiques* is or ever was correct, except possibly those who do so either from nonsensical sentimental reasons, considering the *qu* more elegant, or else through ignorance.

J. I. Mombert, D. D., in his "History of Lancaster County," published in 1869, in reference to Indian localities, on page 386, gives the "modern name" of this creek as *Chiquesalungo* and the "Indian name" as *Chickeswalungo*, meaning "the place of crawfish."

The scenery around Chickies is varied and picturesque. One of the most beauful views in this, or any other county, can be seen from the top of Chickies Rock, with the Susquehanna winding around at its base, dividing the red and white rose counties of Lancaster and York. A short distance back from the rock can be seen the Chikiswalungo and Donegal valleys, with their fine buildings and farms under the highest state of cultivation, in fact the cream of the greatest agricultural county in the United States. James Buchanan once remarked that this view reminded him of the best agricultural portions of England, and we have frequently heard the remark from strangers, "This is God's own country."

There are some interesting Indian legends connected with Chickies Rock and I feel that it would be well for our society to collect and record such matters for future generations, before they are forgotten or corrupted. The most unique as to the rock is given in a poem, written some years since by Walter Kieffer, entitled:

CHIKISWALUNGO.

Land of Penn! where lies a glen
  Fairly filled with mystic story,
Artist's brush nor poet's pen
  Could e'er paint its wondrous glory;

Chikis-wa-lungo! where Wanunga,
　Bravest of the Indian legion,
Told the romance of each war dance,
　Told of vict'ries in the region.

High o'er all there hangs a pall,
　Seeming lonely, sad, forbidding;
Look again from out the glen,
　See the trees with vigor budding,
Jutting outward, leaning forward
　From the rocks that hang above you,
On that spot, full many a plot
　Closed with vow like this, "I love you!"

And forever rolls the river,
　Full two hundred feet below;
Susquehanna, shout Hosanna,
　As thy waters onward flow!
Surely God, upon the green sod
　On the banks that form thy fetters,
Set his impress of divineness
　In most rare and radiant letters.

Here Wanunga on Salunga,
　Wooed the maiden, Wanhuita,
Told the story of his glory,
　How he slew his rival, Sita;
Never maiden was so laden
　With perplexing doubt and fear,
In her bosom dwelt a passion
　For a pale face lingering near.

Then the pale face, with a rare grace,
　Sought the maiden in her bower,
Never dreaming, danger teeming,
　Till Wanunga held the power;
Hark! a rustle, then a tussle,
　All is silent as the grave,
Then Wanunga, from Salunga,
　Leaps with maiden 'neath the wave.

And the river rolls forever,
　Never giving up its dead,
But tradition (superstition)
　Says there sounds a solemn tread,
As the pale face, with such rare grace,
　Walks upon the giddy summit,
Watching ever for his treasure,
　Torn from him like fiery comet.

And yet the pale face will forget
　The story here depicted,
And the tale of love, on the rocks above,
　Are still not interdicted;
For many a pledge, on that rocky ledge,
　Ascends to heavenly portals,
And the vows there made are thought more staid,
　Than the common vows of mortals.

If the attempt is made to collect these Indian legends, I would suggest that it be done intelligently, otherwise it will become a farce, as was the case with a correspondent, a few years since, in one of our local newspapers, who, referring to his address before a high school, and the advisability of interesting the school children in such matters, wrote:

"Swatara was named after an Indian hunter, who could speak some English, who shot a deer across the stream and ejaculated 'sweet arrow.'

"I have only time in this paper to give one of those from which the name and spelling of our beautiful stream was taken, Chiquesalungo. Several centuries ago a tribe of Indians was encamped on the banks of this lovely stream which is now the rich and fertile valley of Rapho township. Just east of Mt. Joy, near Cedar Hill seminary, is a beautiful dell, surrounded by large trees and dense shade, where lovers often meet. One evening in the long ago an Indian maiden and her lover met here in early September [How the month was fixed the Lord only knows]. The night was balmy and fair. As they sat on a rude log, discoursing about sweet love, they almost got enchanted with the beauty that surrounded them. The harvest moon, now near its full, was rising slowly in the east and shed a radiance of unearthly beauty on the scene. The sharp cadences of the katydid, the ripple of the meandering stream as it passed along the dell, all assisted to make the scene one of unequaled loveliness. They proposed to each other to take a walk along the stream, and as they walked and talked, happy in the charms of each other's company, and as love takes no note of time or distance, it was near the bewitching hour of midnight as they ascended a hill. From its top it seemed like Beulah Land, away across the valley, as it lay bathed in moonlight. The scene was truly enchanting, and they talked about its beauty and their happy wigwam homes, and, looking beyond the hills, they fancied they could see their happy hunting grounds, where they would be forever happy. These souls,

'Proud science never taught to stray,
Far as the solar walk or milky way.'

"And as they were thus walking and musing in each other's arms, (?) they fell over a terrible precipice (Chiques Rock) and met a romantic death. But before they died she was able to say to him 'Chiqua' and he answered 'Salunga.' They were buried on the banks of the beautiful stream that bears their name, and the low moaning of its waters the broad Susquehanna is ever singing a sweet requiem to their memory and their monument is the romantic Chiquesalungo."

My only object in consuming your time by repeating such useless slush is to illustrate the point to which I desire to call your attention, that is, the importance of recording these legends with, at least, an ordinary degree of intelligence. Think of one, who feels competent to address a high school, recording in print such material, and leading the unsuspecting youth to believe that Swatara was ever pronounced by any intelligent being as "Sweet Arrow;" there is no "sweet" in the pronunciation. And then to walk those poor lovers some six miles from near Mount Joy to Chickies Rock and when they tumble over it [mind the night was "fair" so they could see] to have the maiden say—"The place of" and the young buck reply "Crabs," which is what "Chikiswalungo" means.

May our growing generation, hungry for knowledge, be protected from such history (?) and I trust our society will assist in so doing.

CONESTOGA.

REMINISCENCES OF AN OLD TOWNSHIP

When we think of the treatment the Palatinates (from whom most of us have descended) received from their oppressors in their native land, when their homes were destroyed and they were compelled to flee for their lives to such parts of the world as afforded them scanty asylums, we are apt to picture to ourselves a poverty-stricken people. Rupp, in his history, gives the names of over twenty thousand immigrants, many of whom found their way into Lancaster county, and they could not have been so very poor, as their fine farms and substantial buildings of one hundred and fifty or more years ago attest. Of the substantial buildings dating back a century and a-half we have yet five remaining in our township. They are large, two-storied stone structures, so firmly built they will be good for another hundred years. When we compare their living with the present style we might think them poor. Take from us the luxuries to which we have become accustomed and we would consider ourselves poor indeed.

They had no coffee, no tea, no muslin, or calico, nor hundreds of other things which we think we must have. But they had plenty of fish—shad, herring, catfish, rock bass, perch, suckers, mullets, etc. In the forests were found deer, turkeys, squirrels, etc., in abundance. In a very short time they raised their own beef and pork, and the breadstuff was never wanting. They sowed flax, the rain rotted it, and they broke, scutched, hatcheled, spun and wove it in their own houses. The wool was worked into cloth, mostly in the linsey-woolsey style, and then the tailor came around and made suits for the men and boys that were considered good for a year. The women made the bedding and their own clothing.

Our forefathers were not poor. They were a contented and happy people.

Seventy-five years ago (about the limit of my recollection) innovations came in fast. We then had true coffee; on Sundays we had tea—muslin and calico and carpets came in. My first baby clothes were calico. I think it cost fifty cents a yard.

Mills of necessity were the first manufacturing places. Probably the oldest was at the mouth of the Little Conestoga creek; backwater from the building of the Slackwater navigation in 1827 ruined this. The next was the Shenk mill, on the Pequea, on the road between Conestoga and Marticville. This was replaced (after a fire) by a new building. Sawmills were connected with all the old mills. Hard wood furnished all the building material.

Among our old industries was a gun barrel factory. It was owned by Michael Reyner, and stood along the run now the boundary line between Conestoga and Pequea townships. My grandmother Resh, nee Hess, who died many years ago, aged eighty-four years, knew all about the old bore mill. She called the owner "Bore Michael." She said that at one time things did not work right and Michael said things were "ferhext" (bewitched), and he said: "Ich will der hexa a-mol dunner vetter geve." So he got a dead hog, laid it on the fire and put the full blast of the bellows on it and raised a stink that disturbed the whole neighborhood.

It must have been effectual, as "Michael" made gun barrels afterwards. Unfortunately, I failed to get dates, but it must have ceased work shortly after the Revolutionary War. Seventy-five years ago there was not a trace of the building left—only a ditch overgrown with trees and bushes that was the water race that furnished the power. We had an oil factory—the building was torn down within fifty years. Ponderous stone rollers and large presses remained in it to the last. Flax seed was principally used for oil, but castor oil was also made; a half barrel of castor beans remained to the end. When the mill ceased operation history sayeth not.

The stocking weavery operated by John Yentzer ceased working about 1815. It had been in operation many years.

Whisky distilling was introduced early. I can point out ten sites where whisky was made in the past. Probably the oldest was on the Sterneman farm (now J. M. Warfel). It has been out of operation over one hundred years. We have no distillery now.

About the year 1800 weaving began to die out. As late as 1830 we had three weaver shops, using from two to six looms. The general introduction about that time of cotton goods put an end to flax-raising and to the looms. We have not a loom in the township now.

Our only tannery is operated by the great-grandson (A. Myer) of the originator. It is probably 130 years old.

WILLIAM PARKER,

THE HERO OF THE CHRISTIANA RIOT.

To understand the full significance of the Christiana riot, so insignificant in itself, it is necessary to have a thorough knowledge of where we were and whither we were drifting as a nation at the time. An English statesman sojourning in France some years before the great upheaval of 1793 wrote, "I discover here all the symptoms of revolution that I have ever met with in history;" at the same time a weak, conservative, purblind, vacillating, well-intentioned King sat upon his throne and saw nothing of all that. If any intelligent stranger had been sojourning in America in the year 1851, possessed with ordinary powers of penetration, able to see with his eyes and not with his prejudices, he might have said, "I see in the United States a young and growing nation, peopled with the best blood of the Caucasian race, self-deceived, however, by their marvelous growth, standing at the crater of a volcano, trying to keep back the lava by rolling another rock down its throat."

Both immediately before and after the formation of the constitution the representative men of the country, south as well as north, regarded slavery as an evil greatly to be abhorred. General Gates, the hero of Saratoga, had liberated his slaves; Washington, as all people know, did the same; Jefferson had uniformly borne his testimony against it, and manumission societies were formed in the years 1789 and 1791, respectively, in the States of Maryland and Virginia. Among the members of the Maryland society were Samuel Chase, a signer of the Declaration of Independence, and Luther Martin, one of the framers of the Constitution; in Delaware the movement was favored by such men as Hon. James A. Bayard, grandfather of the present Minister to England, and Cæsar A. Rodney, afterwards Attorney General. In the north the first anti-slavery society formed, that of Pennsylvania, was presided over by Benjamin Franklin and then by Benjamin Rush. The New York Manumission Society had for its first president John Jay, and for its second, Alexander Hamilton. Further examples might be given, but this is enough to prove that the leading, enterprising, patriotic men of the country did not regard slavery at that time as a blessing, nor even as something to be looked upon with indifference.

These men must either have had a very poor conception of the kind of government they had been forming and the character of the work they were engaged in, or else their children afterwards woefully misconstrued them. For, in process of time, the discovery was made under the more rapacious lead of the cotton States that such societies were at war with the constitution, with good citizenship, and that it was treasonable and seditious to even petition Congress for the abolition of slavery in the District of Columbia. Relatively speaking, about the same time, the discovery was also made by a young man heretofore unknown to fame, publishing a small sheet from a garret loft in Boston, "That the Constitution of the United States was a covenant with death and an agreement with hell." These two, not to say remarkable, at least most diametrically opposite, interpretations of the fundamental principles of our National Union ought to have convinced the most obtuse mind that the "irrepressible conflict" was at hand.

The truth is, the more clear-sighted and candid leaders of the one or the other side did see it, but the great mass of people were too eagerly engaged in making money, too anxious to avoid any unpleasant relations, and too busy developing the great resources of the Nation to worry themselves about the ethics of the question.

There is neither time nor necessity to review the long legislative history in the great struggle, only this brief prelude is necessary to get a faint idea of the moral forces of the issue. Of all the acts of Congress in the entire drama, none had been so strenuously insisted upon by the South for the moral effect it would have in forcing a proper recognition of the rights of the master to this peculiar species of property as the fugitive slave law of 1850. None, on the other hand, had come so directly in open conflict with the conscience of the North. By the provisions of the Act, every citizen was at once made a slave catcher. If he refused to obey the Marshal in assisting to return a fugitive he was guilty of a misdemeanor and subject to fine and imprisonment. The person claimed as a slave could be arrested upon the warrant of the United States Commissioner, sworn out by any person claiming him as his slave; he was denied the right of trial by jury, the Commissioner could deliver him to the alleged master at his own discretion, and the slave was not allowed to testify in his own behalf.

Such was the law that Daniel Webster said he was willing to vote for "with all its provisions to the fullest extent," because "neither in the forum of conscience or in the face of the constitution are we justified in disregarding it." Such was the law which caused Thaddeus Stevens to exclaim from the other side of the Capitol: "Can the free North stand this? Can Pennsylvania stand it? Great God! can New England endure it?" It was a close question on which side of Mason and Dixon's line the rebellion would first appear.

Such was the condition of things on the eleventh of September, 1851, about one year after the passage of the Act, when Edward Gorsuch, a Maryland slave holder, and his son, Dickinson Gorsuch, Joshua M. Gorsuch, his nephew, Dr. Thomas Price, and two other men from Maryland, with the United States Marshal, H. H. Kline, arrived with warrants regularly issued by the United States Commissioner at Philadelphia, about daylight, at the residence of William Parker, a colored man and an escaped fugitive, about a mile and a-half from the village of Christiana, this county.

The community was settled principally by Quakers and Scotch-Irish Presbyterians, but it would be a mistake, however, to suppose that the anti-slavery sentiment of Southern Lancaster county was so strong at that time as to have prevented the peaceable enforcement of the fugitive slave law in ordinary cases. Public opinion there might properly be divided into three classes, as was probably the case throughout the most of the North. First, the more ultra abolitionist or anti-slavery people, who made no concealment of the fact that they never intended to obey the law. Second, the professional slave hunters and nigger haters, who obsequiously followed the leaders of the South and obeyed their slightest impulse. Third, the great conservative and far more numerous class, who doubtless felt a pang at the hard service imposed upon them by the law, and who ostensibly and for political reasons would profess to support it, but who would secretly aid the fugitive in his flight. To this latter class Castner Hanway, the sometimes recognized hero of the riot, belonged. He doubtless sympathized on that morning with the negroes and desired them to win the battle, if one should commence, which they did. But he would much preferred to have had the Marshal and his posse, or rather Gorsuch and his posse, accept his advice and leave without a struggle, as Kline would have done, (he being pronounced by all parties as the most consummate coward ever seen in battle). This being done, he doubtless would have consulted with the negroes and aided them to escape. But that he ever gave the insolent answers to the Marshal or resisted his authority, as Kline, the champion liar as well as coward, testified on the trial, was not correct. Hanway himself never claimed that he did, and Parker's only regret, as he read Kline's testimony or had it read to him after his escape to Canada, was that he had not killed him on the spot. That Hanway was the first of the white neighbors on the ground was not because he started first, but because Elijah Lewis, when on his way to the place, stopped at his (Hanway's) residence, the brick mill in the valley, now abandoned, and asked him to go along. Hanway, instead of accompanying him on foot, mounted his horse and arrived some few minutes before Lewis on the scene of action. Instinct, stronger than reason, doubtless told the negroes that he was not their enemy, and hoped that he might be turned to account as a friend. But he was there by no prearrangement with them, nor had they regarded him as a special counsellor. Neither was he a member of the Society of Friends as has been so frequently asserted. He simply lived there in a Friends' community; was indicted for treason with Lewis and Joseph C. Scarlet, both of whom were members of the Society, and thus historians have naturally fallen into that error: one recent writer in the Philadelphia *Times* calling it the riot led by three non-resistant Quakers. Elijah Lewis, as already stated, arrived some minutes later than Hanway, and when commanded by the Marshal to assist in the arresting of the fugitives, is reported to have said: "That my conscience will not allow me to do." Joseph C. Scarlet, the other white man who enjoyed the distinction of being indicted for treason and of being shipped to Philadelphia in a cattle car with a lot of negroes to answer the charge, was not on the ground at all. His treason consisted in notifying the blacks of their danger and admonishing them to prepare for it. He seemed to be one who actually did have some intimation in advance of what was likely to happen. He was a man of mighty strength and brawn, and had he been upon the ground, and had occasion, he doubtless would have proved a very good man for slave hunters to keep away from, notwithstanding his Quaker principles.

With this brief mention of these actors in the drama, let me say a word about the real hero of the tragedy. His name was William Parker, the man in whose house the fugitives were concealed, some four in number, for whom the Marshal had warrants. Parker, born himself a slave in Maryland, had made his escape in his early manhood some years before to Pennsylvania, and had settled in southern Lancaster county. Whether he had drifted into that section through that mysterious and invisible agency, the underground railroad, I am not able to say; at all events, he there lived and worked for several years among the farmers, never deeming it necessary to advance on to another station. He at once impressed himself not only upon his own race, but upon the whites with whom he came in contact as well, as a man of wonderful force of character. I remember seeing him but once, and that was as far back almost as memory goes; but his personality is distinctly impressed upon my mind. He was at my father's house the day of the riot, after it was over, but I did not see him on that occasion, nor did my father, as he was away from home. He was a dark mulatto of medium height, wonderful muscle, and possessed of resolution, courage and action. The neighborhood was rife with stories of his physical feats. He could walk leisurely up to an ordinary post fence, leap over it without touching it with his hands, work hard all day, and travel from ten to fifteen miles during the night to organize his people into a society for their protection against the numerous kidnappers who were constantly committing depredations through the community, or rescue one of their number that had been captured, flog the villain who was carrying him away, and return to his labor in the morning with a bullet in his leg, apparently unfatigued and keep his secret well to himself. He was by common consent recognized by his race in the neighborhood as their leader. They depended upon him with abiding confidence to keep them from being taken back to slavery. They regarded him as their leader, their protector, their Moses, and their lawgiver all at once. The white people of the neighborhood knew that he possessed these qualities, that he was the Toussaint L' Ouverture of his people; that he could have commanded an army had he been educated, and he challenged the universal respect of all of them who did not have occasion to fear him.

He of all the men of his despised race along the border in that slave hunting era could have led the riot. Without him there would have been no riot. The rest would have fled upon receipt of the news that their masters were coming, or would have surrendered and gone back with them to slavery. When he was approached by the United States Marshal with his warrants on that eventful morning, his revolvers and his armed assistants, clothed with all the panoply of authority, this colored Spartan stood at the threshold of his humble home and bid him defiance. And in this, be it remembered, lies the real significance of the Christiana riot. In all the slave hunting era, during all the period of mob violence attending the anti-slavery struggle up to that time, there had been no open resistance to the authority of the government. This man advanced out in his yard and struck the United States down in open battle in the person of Edward Gorsuch. It was this that caused the matter to be published in every paper in the land, to be noticed even in England, and made the entire slave power tremble from the Potomac to the Rio Grande. It was not because Gorsuch was killed, or that his son and nephew were badly wounded, that the community was scoured for weeks by bandits disguised as United States Marshals, or that the United States Marines were sent to a quiet, peaceful neighborhood to terrorize it; but because one brave man, preferring death to slavery, said, "I don't care for you or the United States; there will be no slaves taken back from here while I am alive."

It is easy for a white man sitting in the Executive Mansion of a great State, with a powerful public sentiment behind him, to say on a question largely sentimental, "There will be no flags returned while I am governor;" but it required nerve of the stronger quality to utter Parker's words in the face of his powerful and venerated enemy. Gen. Taylor said at Buena Vista to a lot of half-Spanish Mexican drones, "Gen. Taylor never surrenders," and the people made him President. General Sheridan arrived at Winchester in time to say to his brave educated Saxon American army, "Face the other way, boys, you are going the wrong direction," and by his inspiring presence changed defeat to victory, and poetry has made him immortal. General Parker, this representative of a despised race, held his little band of ignorant followers together by the imperial command, "The first man that offers to surrender I will shoot." It was his will and his alone that laid Gorsuch still in death, whom he always spoke of as "a fine soldier and a brave man." And by the aid of that God who notices even the sparrow's fall and sometimes condescends to uphold and strengthen the good right arm of him who strives for the liberties of himself, his wife and children, he made his way through every obstacle to Canada.

And now, when the Lancaster County Historical Society visits this most tragic spot of all within our borders; when they propose to erect some small monument to mark the spot where occurred this first battle of the American conflict; while we all stand reverently at the memories of Grant, of Sherman and of Sheridan, of Reynolds, of Hancock and of Meade, men from whose well-decked brows I would not take a single flower, let us not forget to make one small niche in our tablet of heroes for this Afro-American, William Parker.

PAPERS READ

BEFORE THE

LANCASTER COUNTY HISTORICAL SOCIETY,

ON SEPT. 4, 1896.

THE ACADIANS IN LANCASTER COUNTY,

BY S. M. SENER, ESQ.

BARON HENRY WILLIAM STIEGEL,

BY J. H. SIELING, M. D.

LANCASTER, PA.
REPRINTED FROM THE NEW ERA.
1896.

The Acadians in Lancaster County,
　　BY S. M. SENER, ESQ., ... 35

Baron Henry William Stiegel,
　　BY J. H. SIELING, M. D., . 　　　　　44

THE ACADIANS IN LANCASTER COUNTY.

There is no history in which can be chronologically traced the struggles and changes within that small region known as Acadia, the confines of which were expressly named by Henry IV. of France in his letters patent of November 3, 1603, over the country, territory and coasts from the 40th degree to the 46th degree. Acadia, from its earliest settlement by De Monts, had for a century been repeatedly taken by the English and lost or restored by them. By the treaty of Utrecht, May 22, 1713, France finally surrendered to Great Britain "all Acadia." This vague description left an undefined territory and a disputed frontier.

In reference to the etymology of the word Acadia, it has been written in different ways: La Cadie, La Cady, Accadie, Accadia, Arcadie, Arcadia, and Quoddy. The etymology of the word is not certain. It is certainly not from the Greek "Arcadia," a part of Peloponnesus in Hellas, which for a long time was used to designate an imaginary pastoral country. Benjamin Sulte, the distinguished Canadian archæologist, and Senator Poirier believe it is of Scandinavian origin. Beaumont Small, in his "Chronicles of Canada," says: The aboriginal Micmacs, of Nova Scotia, being of a practical turn of mind, were in the habit of bestowing on places the names of the useful articles found in them, and affixed to such terms the word A-ca-die, denoting abundance of the particular objects to which the names referred. The early French settlers supposed this common termination to be the name of the country. Dawson is of the same opinion. Parkman adopts an entirely different etymology. At page 220 of his "Pioneers of France in the New World" he says in a note: "This name is not found in any earlier public document. It was afterwards restricted to the peninsula of Nova Scotia, but the dispute concerning the limits of Acadia was a proximate cause of the war of 1755. This word is said to be derived from the

Indian word aqquoddiauke, or aquoddie, meaning a fish called a 'pollock.' The Bay of Passamaquoddy, 'great pollock water,' derives its name from the same origin." He also cites Potter in the "Historical Magazine;" F. Kidder, in "Eastern Maine and Nova Scotia in the Revolution," and "Blackwood's Magazine," vol. xvii., p. 332. However, this may be, it is certainly an indigenous word, as it is found many times in the composite names Tracadie, Shubenacadie, Chicabenadie, Benacadie, Shunacadie, etc.

By the capitulation of Port Royal the Acadians were permitted to sell their lands and remove from English territory or remain as British subjects. Queen Anne, by letter of June 22, 1713, confirming the agreement. The authorities in England as early as 1720, however, decided that they ought to be removed, and a proclamation was issued requiring them within four months to take an unqualified oath of allegiance or suffer the loss of their property and be driven from the colony. They remonstrated, but finally taking the oath of fidelity were allowed to remain. Some writers assert that they were granted the fullest and freest exercise of their religion, while others deny this. The priests could not say Mass under pain of banishment, as in 1724 it was ordered that "no more Mass should be said up the river and that the Masshouse should be abolished " This state of affairs continued for some years, until in 1755, when it was resolved to apply the penal laws against Catholics to the Catholics or Acadians in Nova Scotia. The oath required to be taken by them was that of royal supremacy, involving an abjuration of the Catholic religion.

A peremptory decree was issued that the Acadians were to be banished, and that 7,000 of them were to be seized; 500 to be sent to North Carolina; 1,000 to Virginia; 2,000 to Maryland; 300 to Philadelphia; 200 to New York; 300 to Connecticut, and 200 to Boston. The colonies thus selected were not notified that people were thus to be thrown upon them, and no provision was made for their support there.

Troops were collected at various points with numbers of schooners and sloops to transport them. The Acadians were on September 5, 1755, assembled and disarmed, only five hundred escaping to the woods. Their cattle were slaughtered, their houses and churches set on fire, and the Acadian coast was one vast conflagration. The unfortunate people were marched upon the ships and the voyage began. One party turned on their captors, and seizing the vessel ran her into St. John's river, where they escaped. The rest reached their several destinations.

Georgia had expressly provided in her charter that no Roman Catholics should be allowed to settle there, and when Governor Reynolds found 400 Acadians in his limits he decided that they could not remain. With courage and perseverance they made their painful way to New York and Massachusetts. The 1,500 sent to South Carolina were apportioned among the parishes there, but many found their way to France. A few remained there, while some sought Louisiana. Those that found their way to Long Island were distributed in the most remote parts of the colony. Those sent to Virginia found a home, finally, in France. Those sent to Maryland seem in a great measure to have been left to do for themselves. Some of them got back again to Acadia; others went to the West Indies; others, finding themselves in new environments, started to work to begin the world afresh. In Baltimore stood a half finished house which was begun in 1740 by an Edward Fotterall, from Ireland. In this deserted dwelling a number of the Acadians established themselves. Mr. Piet, the well-known Catholic publisher of Baltimore, traces his descent from these exiles.

Arrive in Pennsylvania.

On November 18, 1775, a vessel ascended the Delaware river bearing several hundred of these persecuted people, many of them being sickly and feeble, and on November 19 and 20 two more vessels ascended the same river, bearing, all told, 454 Acadians. The ships which brought them were the Hannah, Three Friends and the Swan. At once idle fears were excited lest they should join the Irish and German Catholics and destroy the colo

The operations of the French in Western Pennsylvania at that time kept the people in constant terror, and when the Acadian or French Neutral Catholics were brought to Philadelphia it was thought hazardous to the peace and safety of the people.

Governor Morris wrote to Governor Shirley, of New York: "The people here, as there is no military force of any kind, are very uneasy at the thought of having a number of enemies scattered in the very bowels of the country who may go off from time to time with intelligence and join their countrymen, now employed against us, or foment some intestine commotion in conjunction with the Irish and and German Catholics in this and neighboring Provinces." A recruiting company of a New York regiment was in Philadelphia at the time, and Governor Morris kept the company from returning to New York, and asked the advice of the Governors of the Provinces what to do with the Acadians. Chief Justice Belcher, of Nova Scotia, sent to Governor Morris to the effect that he thought they should have been transported direct to France, and this only added to the fears of the Governor and people of Pennsylvania.

Though the people were thus affrighted, yet the Quakers had pity on the exiles and treated them with respect and benevolence. The Acadians located in Philadelphia were quartered in a row of small huts on Pine street, which were long known as the "Neutral Huts." The small-pox broke out among them there and depleted their number very much. Finally the Provincial Assembly was called upon to provide for the distress among the people about whose coming into the province they had not been consulted. A few of those quartered in Philadelphia were arrested as being badly-intentioned persons, but they were subsequently released. The philanthropist Anthony Benezet did much for their relief, and Father Harding, whose name was always coupled by Pennsylvanians with that of Benezet as a man of unbounded charity to the poor, gave these exiles not only relief, but the consolations which he as a minister of God could impart. According to Thompson

Westcott, more than half of these people died within a short time after their arrival in Philadelphia.

In Lancaster County.

In the early part of 1756 a number of these exiles were brought into Lancaster county through the passage of an Act of the Provincial Assembly. On February 20, 1756, a bill entitled "An Act for dispersing the inhabitants of Nova Scotia imported into this Province into the several counties of Philadelphia, Bucks, Chester and Lancaster, and the townships thereof, and making provision for the same" was introduced. It passed second reading on March 3d and third reading on March 5th, the Governor signing it the same day. It was afterwards sealed with the great seal and entered in the Office of Rolls in Laws Book No. 3, p. 320, and in this connection the writer begs leave to express his thanks to ex-Secretary of the Commonwealth W. F. Harrity, for a copy of the Act in full, which he courteously had copied for the writer two years since. The act is not found entire in any of the volumes of the "Laws of Pennsylvania" and is in manuscript in the folio in the State Department at Harrisburg.

An examination of the act shows that by it there were appointed the following gentlemen to order and appoint the disposition of the Acadians: For Philadelphia county, Wm. Griffitts, Jacob Duche and Thomas Say; for Bucks county, Griffitts Owen, Samuel Brown and Abraham De Normandie; for Chester county, Nathaniel Pennock, Nathaniel Grubb and John Hannum; for Lancaster county, Calvin Cooper, James Webb and Samuel LeFevre.

The act required them within twenty days after its passage to order and appoint the Acadians as to them appeared most equitable so as to ease the Province of the heavy charge of supporting them. The overseers of the poor of the several townships of Lancaster were to receive the Acadians allotted to them and provide for them, not more than one family, however, to be allotted to any one township. The overseers were directed to keep just and true accounts of all charges and expenses accrued, which accounts were to be transmitted to the gentlemen named in the act. Those of the Acadians who had been bred to farming were to be placed upon farms rented for them at a reasonable rate, and some small assistance was to be given them toward settlement thereof. The commissioners were to procure stock and utensils for them, provided the supplies allotted to each family did not exceed ten pounds. All expenses were to be paid out of the money given to the King's use by an Act of Assembly. Just how many Acadians came to Lancaster county under this act, their names, where located and expenses incident thereto cannot be stated, as there are no records of the same extant. That a number were located in this county, however, is evident from the fact that in January, 1757, a bill was passed whereby certain of their children in this county should be bound out and the aged, maimed and sick provided for; the children to be taught to read and write the English language. The males were to be bound out until twenty-one and the females until eighteen. A number of those who had been located in this county finally found their way back to Philadelphia, where they were found in distress in 1758. We doubt not there may be some of the descendants of the Acadians, or French Neutrals, resident in this county. Marie Le Roy in her narrative states that in 1757 there were, among others who had been captives in the hands of the Indians, "a Anne Marie Villars, a French girl, an Acadian, who had a brother and sister residing near Lancaster." An early record of burials at St. Mary's church, this city, contains an entry under date of December 15, 1798, of the burial of Jean Algliso, born an Acadian. The marriage records of St. Joseph's church, Philadelphia, contain a number of entries of marriages relating to Acadians, among them being such names as Landry, Le Blanc, de la Beaume, David, Boudrat, Blanchat.

On the London lands, of which there were 47,800 acres in this county and Berks, an Acadian, named Brazier, had squatted on that portion allotted to a man named Slaymaker. A peculiar fact may be mentioned in connection with this, that a township of this county, which was laid out about the time of the

Acadian dispersion into Lancaster county, is named Bart. Reese, in an early edition of his cyclopædia, states that Bart is the name of a sailing port in Nova Scotia. Is it probable that the naming of this township could have been brought about by any coincidence of names suggested by any one of Acadian birth in memory of the old Acadian home?

Of the seven thousand Acadians thus "scattered like leaves by the ruthless winds of autumn," from Massachusetts to Georgia, among those who hated their religion, detested their country, derided their manners and mocked their language, "few comparatively remained to swell the numbers of the Catholic body in the United States. Landed on distant shores, those who had once known wealth and plenty were scouted at as vagrants, reduced to beggary," and the last official record that concerns them in Pennsylvania has all the sadness of an epitaph; it is the petition of an undertaker, addressed in 1766 to the Legislature, and sets forth "that John Hill, of Philadelphia, joiner, has been employed from time to time to provide coffins for the French Neutrals who have died in and about the city; that his accounts were allowed and paid until lately and that sixteen coffins are unpaid for, and he, therefore, prays for relief in the premises."

Longfellow, in his "Evangeline, a Tale of Arcadie," says:

Still stands the forest primeval but far away from its shadow,
Side by side, in their nameless graves
* * * * are sleeping.
Under the humble nolls of the little Catholic churchyard.
In the heart of the city, they lie, unknown and unnoticed.
Daily the tides of life go ebbing and flowing beside them.
Thousands of throbbing hearts, where theirs are at rest and forever,
Thousands of aching brains, where theirs no longer are busy.
Thousands of toiling hands, where theirs have ceased from her labors,
Thousands of weary feet, where theirs have completed their journey!"

BARON HENRY WILLIAM STIEGEL.

> "He was one who stood alone,
> While the men he agonized for
> Hurled the contumelious stone.
>
> "We in silent awe return,
> To glean up his scattered ashes
> Into History's golden urn."

Preface.

It is difficult to bring the life of such an extraordinary man as Baron Stiegel, who was born at least a hundred years in advance of his time, before an audience in such a manner as not to weary the most enthusiastic local historian at a single sitting.

So large and voluminous is the traditionary history of this one individual's doings that it would cover many pages if dealt with minutely. This man was both over and under estimated by a people who had not the ability to judge and were in consequence awe-stricken by his magnificent equipage as well as his extreme poverty.

It has been the purpose of the author, in writing this short biographical sketch, to set the character of this great man vividly before his hearers at this time and trust to a convenient season for an opportunity to compile the great mass of facts and fancies (for every foot of ground from Manheim through Elizabeth furnace and Schaefferstown to Charming forge is historic) at hand which have been gathered from various sources into a little volume embellished with illustrations by the aid of the camera obscura for the gratification of those who have heard in part what would be a veritable romance taken from actual life without a single draught on imagination.

Early Life.

Baron Henrich Wilhelm Stiegel was born in Germany, presumably near Mannheim, in Baden, evidently of a noble and wealthy parentage, in A. D. 1730. At the age of twenty he became dissatisfied with the slowness of the good old home and mother country and he determined to gather up his portion of this earth's goods, which amounted to £40,000, and venture forth into the New World to prove the many stories scattered broadcast over the Old concerning the golden opportunities in the New, and by so doing soon outstrip his European friends and especially his brothers, with whom he couldn't agree because of his eccentricities, in wealth and honor and fame.

The title of "Baron" is disputed by some historians because he never used it in signing legal documents, simply Henry Wm. Stiegel. We do know that he permitted the Baron to be used on certain of his stoves and in signing his name to the constitution of the old Brickerville Lutheran Church, September 10th, 1769, which he wrote as chairman of the committee, and is a masterly instrument still in force, having governed those people these 127 years and brought them safely through the destructive litigation just closed. To this document he signed Henrich Von Stiegel. Dr. Jos. Dubbs, historian of Franklin and Marshall College, who some years ago had this subject under investigation, didn't find the name recorded at all in Mannheim, but found that about this time a young Baron answering the description of Stiegel left Mannheim for the New World by the name of Stengel, presumably a clerical error, or the Baron purposely changed his name for some reason. It is positively known that he went on business trips to England but never extended his journey up the Rhine to his "Vater landt." The writer has only last year had two eminent clergymen "Stadt pfarrer" Hitzig and Greiner look over the records of Mannheim with the above result. In our little Manheim lives a man who goes by the name of Spickloser, who was registered in Germany by a tipsy clerk for Spikolitzer.

Again the manner of living denoted royalty. It is said that he always wore his Baronial costume whenever he went abroad.

On the 31st day of August, 1750, the gallant ship Nancy, Thomas Cauton, master, sailed from Cowes with 270 passengers on board, landed in Philadelphia, and in the list of names we find "Henrich Wilhelm Stiegel." During the first two years he traveled about seeking a suitable location, which resulted in the selection of Philadelphia, and Elizabeth, daughter of Jacob Huber, ironmaster at Brickerville, Lancaster county, as a helpmate November 7, 1752. He built a house in Philadelphia, in which he lived till 1765.

In 1757 the Baron purchased his father-in-law's furnace property in Elizabeth township, which was one of the largest and oldest furnaces in the United States. Hans Jacob Huber, who erected the furnace, had the following inscription cut on a large stone and placed in the stack:

"Johann Huber der erste Deutsche mann Der das eisen werk follfuren Kann."

The old furnace was torn down and a new one erected on or near the same spot and named after the Baron's wife "Elizabeth." The township was named after the furnace and not Queen Elizabeth. Early in the next year (February 3d, 1758) the Baron's faithful wife died in confinement, leaving him with two little children—Barbara, born November 5, 1756, and Elizabeth. She died at her father's house, and was laid to rest in the family burial plot in the Lutheran graveyard at Brickerville. The furnace was new and in first-class order and the Baron determined to engage in the manufacture of stoves. After the death of his much-loved wife he expressed his inclination to mourn even on one of the many varieties of stove plates which bears this inscription : " H. Whlm Stiegel Und compagni for Elizabeth." The first stoves were jamb-stoves with this inscription :

"Baron Stiegel ist der mann
Der die Ofen Giesen Kann."

A STIEGEL TEN-PLATE STOVE.

These stoves were walled into the jamb of the kitchen fireplace with the back projecting into the adjoining room. Mr. Wm. Taylor, owner and proprietor of Charming forge, is one of the many living witnesses to the truth of this statement.

These stoves were without pipe or oven. Improvements soon followed and the excellent ten-plate wood stoves resulted. People came from all parts of the country to see these great stoves. At this time the Baron was the most enterprising and speculative ironmaster in Pennsylvania.

In 1760 Elizabeth Furnace was in a highly prosperous condition; the busy hum gladdened the hearts of the many laborers and the community and filled the proud Baron's pockets with filthy pelf.

There were about seventy-five men in his employ; and twenty-five tenant houses stood in close proximity to the furnace. A number of them are still standing and from present indications they will withstand the decay of many ages yet to come.

During the fall and winter season many men were employed in cutting wood in the eternal hills nearby, which was converted into charcoal used in smelting the ore. The furnace lands at this time covered about 900 acres, much of it timber, which is being cut down about every seventeen years to this day. A very spacious house, substantially built of sandstone, stands firmly near the site of the furnace which the Baron occupied during his visits to the furnace, which occurred once a month. The imposing appearance of this house caused the simplicity of the surrounding neighbors to call it a mansion, which it still bears very modestly. A number of servants were always kept at the mansion ready to minister to the wants of the Baron and his friends on these periodical visits. This same year the Baron bought a one-half interest in Charming forge, near Womelsdorf, on the Tulpehocken creek, Berks county. The Baron knew that it was not good for man to be alone, especially when prosperity was turned on him in copious showers. He wooed and wedded the noble Elizabeth Holtz, of Philadelphia, in the autumn of 1759, after being a widower one and a-half years, who bore him one son, Jacob, in 1760, who settled in Boiling Springs, Va., September 1st, 1783, shortly after his father's death. The little plain wedding ring now in the possession of Mr. John C. Stiegel, of Harrisonburg, Va., bears this inscription on its inner surface: "H. W. Stiegel and Elizabeth Holtzin," the "in" denoting the feminine gender. The ring, the hymn book and the dictionary in four languages were left in the possession of Judge Ege's family for befriending the Baron in his last days. This ring tells the tale and beyond a doubt the Woods in and around Philadelphia all came from the same family tree.

Manheim Founded.

In February, 1762, Charles and Alexander Stedman, merchant and lawyer of Philadelphia, purchased a tract of land containing 729 acres and allowances from Isaac Norris and his wife Sarah. This land had been claimed in 1733 by James Logan, which upon his death reverted to Norris, a son-in-law of Logan.

The Baron had become intimately acquainted with these men during the recent prosperous years and the Stiegel Company was formed, the Baron paying £50 sterling for his one-third interest. This partnership was formed in September, 1762.

Toward the close of the year the Baron, who was highly educated and a fine surveyor, divided the tract into lots, with streets and alleys, for the purpose of erecting a town which he named and laid out after the city from which he came, "Mannheim." On this beautiful spot on the north bank of the Chickies Creek we find the new Manheim of to-day, the finest and most healthful country town in Pennsylvania, fashioned and shaped after the city whose name it bears beyond the dark blue seas. The Baron's idle dreams of one hundred and thirty-four years ago are slowly but surely maturing.

When this town was founded there were only two houses in it and these were little log structures. Stiegel himself was the first to build a house on the ground laid out. Work on this house was commenced early in 1763, but it was not finished till 1765. It was erected on the northeast corner of Market Square and East High

THE STIEGEL MANSION AT MANHEIM.
THE SOUTH WALL IS STILL
STANDING.

street in the form of a large square; each side was forty feet long, made of red brick, which were imported from England and hauled from Philadelphia by the Baron's teams. This in all probability accounts for the long time required in building. The plain neighbors called it a "Mansion" also. This building had two floors. The second floor was divided into three parts by halls; the half of it on the south side was arched and constituted the famous "chapel" which contained a pulpit from which the Baron was wont to teach to his working men and others at times the doctrines of the Lutheran faith in the German language. The other half was divided into two apartments, front and rear. The former had beautiful decorations of tiles with scriptural texts and scenes about the mantles. The same division of rooms by hallways was had down stairs; the great parlor was hung with tapestry on which were painted hunting scenes, life-size, with falcons. Some of this tapestry is still in the hands of Mr. Arndt, the present owner, but the largest part is safely in the Pennsylvania Historical Society's rooms in Philadelphia. The mantles were also adorned

STIEGEL'S OFFICE IN MANHEIM, STILL STANDING.

with beautiful blue tiles and heavy woodwork doors, wainscoating, etc. This was the most handsome parlor in the community, excelled by very few in the city. Back of this room was the dining hall and back of it the kitchens. The house was two-storied and on the roof surmounting the whole was the gigantic cupalo, extending from chimney to chimney, to which the workmen repaired to entertain the Baron with sweet strains of music. Inside the house were found remaining in after years the finest chinaware, telling of the high aspirations of the people who once resided there.

About the time this house was finished the Baron brought his family from Philadelphia, to Elizabeth, this being a larger place than Manheim.

Glass Works.

The success at Elizabeth Furnace made the naturally enterprising Baron still more so. It was quite evident to him that his embryonic town could not grow without the stimulus of some industries. Consequently between the years 1765 and 1768 he erected a glass factory on the

GLASSWARE MANUFACTURED BY STIEGEL, AT MANHEIM. THE TABLE IS A FALLING TOP, ONE OF STIEGEL'S.

northwest corner of Stiegel and Charlotte streets. This factory was so large that a four-horse team could easily turn around in it and come out at the place of entrance. It was built of the same imported brick, ninety feet high, in the shape of a dome. The manufacture of glass was commenced in the latter part of the year 1768. (Early in this year he gave a mortgage on his one-third of all the properties of the company, 14,078 acres of land, for £3,000 to Daniel Benezet). Skilled workmen were brought from Europe to carry on the work. At this time this was the only glass factory in America. In 1769 the factory was run to its fullest capacity, employing thirty-five men. A very interesting agreement with a decorator can be seen in Mr. Danner's relic room. The stipulations are that he shall do first-class work in handpainting and receive £40 yearly, house rent and firewood for said services.

The products of this factory were vases, sugar and finger bowls, salts, flasks, pitchers, tumblers, wine glasses of every imaginable shape; toys and scores of other articles were manufactured in various colors and handpainted. Much of this superior glassware is still in existence, and quite a large part of it is in the hands of relic hunters. This ware has a characteristic ring that puts all imitations and impostors to shame.

August 4, 1769, the Stedmans sold their interest in the 769 acres upon which the town of Manheim stands to Isaac Cox, who on February 1, 1770, sold the same to the Baron for £107 and ten shillings. This gave him the sole ownership of Manheim.

The Baron very soon after this moved his family from Elizabeth Furnace to the stately mansion already described, which he had completed five years before. At this time, 1769 and 1770, the Baron was considered one of the wealthiest and most influential men in Pennsylvania. He had invested all of the £40,000 which he had brought with him from the old country in tracts of land in many parts of the State under the title of the Stiegel Company. He had 200 to 300 men employed; Elizabeth Furnace was in a flourishing condition. Stoves were sent out to all parts of the inhabited country. The other furnaces and forges in which Stiegel had an interest, as well as the glass factory, were run to their greatest capacity; the glassware was carried into the markets of Boston, Philadelphia and New York. Quite a goodly portion, fortunately, was sold about home.

The Baron was accumulating wealth which made him still more ambitious. He lived very extravagantly and invested freely in almost anything to which his attention was called by a friend. He was in the habit of inviting his city and country friends to a banquet at the mansion at Elizabeth, or the chateau at Manheim. In 1769 George Washington was his guest while he lived at Elizabeth. The room in which he slept is pointed out with great pleasure, to this day, by those who occupy the mansion.

The Tower.

During the latter part of 1769, Stiegel built a tower, or castle, on a hill near Schaefferstown, Lebanon county, Pa., five miles north of Elizabeth Furnace. This hill is called to this day "Thurm Berg" (Tower Hill). The tower was fifty feet square at the bottom and ten feet at the top, and seventy-five feet high, built solidly of heavy timber; some of the logs are still preserved in the composition of an old barn in the immediate vicinity. This tower was built for the purpose of entertaining his friends as well as a place of safety. It consisted of several spacious banquet halls in which the Baron banqueted his friends. It is said that every time he visited the castle, or Elizabeth, his coming was announced in thundering tones from the summit of Cannon Hill by the mouth of a signal gun, from which the "Hill" took its name. This hill rises majestically to the height of about 600 feet, on the northeast side of the site of Elizabeth Furnace, and is still known by this name, or "Stick Berg."

Characteristics.

Baron Stiegel visited Europe at intervals on business. It is said that upon one occasion he took the family with him. The account books at Charming Forge, now in the archives of the Pennsylvania Historical Society, show that severa times he drew £1,000, an allowance, for a trip to England. It cannot be ascertained that he ever returned to his native place even on these trips. While he lived in Philadelphia and managed the works in this and adjoining counties it was his custom to start out in his chariot drawn by four spanking horses, of which he was a great fancier. He was always suspicious of his surroundings, fearing that some one might seek his life, consequently he never traveled without postillions ad an pack of hounds running ahead of his horses. The watchman stationed on Cannon Hill, "Stick Berg," made the joyful announcement. At Manheim the workmen gathered in the cupola of the chateau and played sweet strains on their well-accorded instruments, the people flocked to the house and Stiegel entered the town amid the strains of music, shouts of the inhabitants and the barking of dogs.

The Baron's appearance at each place was the signal for a good time all around. The cannon also announced his departure for the city, as well as to the distant charcoal burners and wood choppers it meant pay day. The Baron's workmen looked forward with great anticipation to these seasons. He treated his men exceedingly well, and his presence was their highest joy. For those of his workmen who were musically inclined he bought instruments and hired teachers. He took great interest in their spiritual welfare, gathering them and others into the chapel in his house and preached to them whenever opportunity offered. Some of his bearers came fifteen miles on foot. Stiegel was a great public benefactor. He held a note of £100 against the Lutheran congregation at Schaefferstown. On one of his visits the behavior of those people toward him so pleased him that he gladdened their hearts by drawing from his vest pocket the note and handed it to the officers of the church to be reckoned against them no more. To Zion's people of Manheim he gave the beautiful lot upon which the church now stands for the sum of five shillings, to

EARLY LUTHERAN CHURCH BUILT 1770,
ON LAND DONATED BY STIEGEL,
AT MANHEIM.

make the deed lawful, and the annual rental of "one red rose" in the month of June, forever. The payment of this rose is an occasion of great rejoicing in said church each year, a monument to the noble Baron's memory more lasting than 10,000 towers erected on old "Thurm Berg."

His Downfall.

The Baron lived extravagantly and made a great display of wealth not warranted by his income. The glass factory, which had cost so much, brought in meagre returns ; the market was too far off and the labor very expensive, as only high-classed workmen were employed.

A number of people preyed upon his generosity. It is said that the Steadman's were his evil genii ; their sanguinary proboscis had a depleting effect, but this was only one of the factors that led on to financial ruin and a prison cell. The impending Revolutionary War cloud that

PRESENT CHURCH ON THE SITE AT MANHEIM, DONATED BY STIEGEL.
BUILT 1891.

overshadowed and stagnated every branch of business, added to his many human leeches, proved too much for the once great Baron. On August 4, 1774, he wrote Judge Yeates of his having done all to keep back the Sheriff, having as a last resort pledged his wife's gold watch. Under date of October 14, written at Manheim also, he addresses Honorable Jasper Yeates again, begging for more time to get his goods to market:

To Jasper Yeates, Esq.

Sir—I have been awaiting your answer to my last price. Mr. Singer is come home but none we yet received; let me therefore beg the favor of you to send it hereby and, if possible, prevail on Mr. Singer to sent me his answer to my last. I make no doubt but if he was to come here we could fall on a method that might serve me and at the same time secure him and Mr. Stone.

I remain in expectation of yr hereby
Your most obliged
Hble Servant
HENRY WM. STIEGEL.
MANHEIM, October 14, 1774.

About this time he wrote a remarkable prayer on the fly leaves of his hymn book which bears the same distressed state of mind and soul of the letter which he poured out in fervent supplication before a throne of grace.

Although he made a brave and manly effort to surmount his difficulties, he had to succumb to the inevitable and shortly after the date of the last letter he was incarcerated. Numerous efforts were made to keep him out of prison by the people of Lancaster, Lebanon and Berks counties, but since they were nearly all poor and the creditors inexorable they failed of their purpose.

In this hour of trial and great distress some of those rich Philadelphians whom the Baron so often befriended and entertained so royally at his mansion refused to sacrifice a single dollar to save his credit or his honor. A few, however, spent considerable money in his behalf, but not sufficient to keep him out of prison. The employes were very devoted to their employer and when they learned that he was being cast into prison for debt, wailing and lamentations were substituted for the jollifications and feastings of bygone days. The once energetic community must sink back into nothingness and obscurity for the want of stimulation. The smoke ceased to curl along the valleys and over the hills from the furnace and forge and glass factory, and the busy hum was hushed and a foreboding silence indicated that life was extinct.

On the 15th day of December the Baron sent out a circular letter to each of his creditors, of which the following is a copy:

PHILADELPHIA, Dec. 15, 1774.

Please take notice that I have applied to the Honorable, the House of Assembly, for a law to relieve my person from imprisonment. If you have any objections please to appear on Thursday next, at 3 o'clock in the afternoon at the gaol in this city before the committee of grievances.

Your humble servant,
"HENRY WM. STIEGEL."
To John Brubacher.

On Christmas eve, December 24, 1774, Baron Stiegel stepped out of prison a free man. He had in all probability never received such an appreciable Christmas gift as this special Act of Assembly. His friends advanced him money and shortly after his release he started Elizabeth furnace once more. All the Baron's interests everywhere were in the hands of some one else and he was obliged to remove from Manheim to Elizabeth. There was no more extravagant living on the Baron's part. His costly outfit had been sold and he didn't try to replace it. His only hope was that the faithful furnace would help him pay every dollar of his indebtedness. The war broke out, to the utter dismay and discomfiture of the well-minded Baron, for many of those debtors who withheld his money were among the loyalists and their property was confiscated. Stiegel himself was for a time charged with loyalism, which proved to be on the side of the colonies from first to last in their great struggle for liberty and independence. A letter written to Judge Yeates, January 24, 1776 (now in the possession of Mr. George Steinman), explains the distressing situation. Very soon thereafter large orders for cannon, shot and shell for the patriotic army relieved the oppressed condition. The furnaces were few in America, and these were taxed to their fullest capacity for the production of munitions of war. Stiegel made known to the authorities that more power could be had by conducting the water from "Seg Loch" (Saw Hole) around the base of Cannon Hill to Furnace Run. The authorities sent him a large number of Hessian prisoners, captured at Trenton (it is said 200), to dig the desired canal, which was over a mile in length. Although the water long since ceased to flow through this ditch it is still plainly visible; in some places the solid rocks have been severed to the depth of ten feet. This digging took place in the winter and spring of 1777. Many of the Hessians remained in this country and became good citizens, very notably George and John Biemesderfer. The former settled near Pennville, Lancaster county, the latter in Lebanon county, from whom nearly all that excellent stock of Biemesderfers sprang. The Baron was obliged to procure food for the laborers. He bought two steers and some wheat from Andreas Wissler, living near Clay, and not being able to pay for them he pledged his fine turtle shell cased gold watch and failed to redeem it. About forty years ago it had come down to Mr. Aaron Wissler, foundryman at Brunnerville, this county. He took it to Mr. Zahm, jeweler, and traded it for a fine up-to-date watch. Mr. Zahm cast it into the smelting pot. This watch had "H. Wm. Stiegel" and a rose engraved on the inside of the lid.

Toward the close of 1778 the government orders ceased, and the creditors once more began pressing the Baron for money. He had made money on the government orders but not enough to meet all his obligations. He struggled manfully against the tidal wave, but ruin and disaster came in its wake and the great, manly Stiegel was overwhelmed. His great yearning and all-absorbing thought was how he might satisfy all his creditors.

SCHOOL HOUSE WHERE STIEGEL TAUGHT
SCHOOL IN 1778, STILL STANDING.

At the close of this year, 1778, we find him penniless, nothing left save his education. He removed his small belongings to the Lutheran parsonage at Brickerville, where he taught school and surveyed land and preached. This combined effort gave him a scanty living at the age of forty-eight, in the prime of life. Some of those who formerly were employed by the Baron and for whose musical education he had paid, now paid him a small sum per week to teach their children, and many who had listened to his sermons years before now paid out of sympathy. In 1780 he was privileged to occupy the Castle, in Schaefferstown. From the Castle, in which he remained but a short time, he moved into a little one and a-half story tenement house, which is still standing, in which he taught school. He carried his little belongings to or near Charming Forge, in 1781, teaching school at Womelsdorf and later quite close to the Forge, probably in his dwelling house. He was employed for a time as bookkeeper at the Forge. In 1782 his bosom companion went to Philadelphia on a visit, to her

BRICKERVILLE CHURCH WHERE STIEGEL'S FIRST WIFE IS BURIED, AND IT IS BELIEVED, HE ALSO.

relatives and friends, took sick and died, and the Baron never saw her again.

This blow, added to his many misfortunes, caused him to slowly pine away and in the following year, 1783, he died, at the age of fifty-three, in the very prime of life, in the mansion at Charming Forge, and was presumably buried on the family plot in the Lutheran graveyard at Brickerville.

Children.

Barbara, born November 5, 1756, married Mr. Ashton, of Virginia. No issue.
Elizabeth, born February, 1758, married Wm. Old, Pennsylvania.
Jacob, born of second wife, 1760. Moved to Virginia. Married Rachel Holman. Had only one son, Jacob.

The Stiegel Descendants.

The children of Elizabeth Stiegel, wife of William Old, were :
1. William, married Elizabeth Nagel.
2. Joseph, married Rebecca Ege, daughter of Judge Ege, of Charming Forge; both died at Schuylkill Forge. No issue.
3. James Old, born 16th day of October, 1773; died 10th day of May, 1777, and lies buried beside his grandmother in the Brickerville churchyard.
4. Jacob, born December 25th, 1777; died unmarried at St. Croix, West Indies, September 20th, 1802.

William Old, jr., of the third generation, married Elizabeth Nagel as above stated and had the following children:
1. Louisa, born March 9th, 1799; married Thomas Mills.
2. Caroline, born February 7th, 1801; married Henry Morris, of Philadelphia.
3. Morgan, born August, 1803; died at Richmond, Indiana; left issue.
4. Elizabeth, born 1805; married Dr. Hamilton Witman, of Reading. Among the descendants of this union are Mrs. Elizabeth M. Luther, of Pottsville; her son, R. C. Luther, is chief engineer of the Phila. & Reading R. R.
5. Rebecca, born September 7th, 1808, at Ephrata; married Dr. Louis Horning, of Montgomery County. The result of this union was one daughter, Martha M., still living. Dr. Horning died in 1837, and his widow subsequently married Jerome K. Boyer, of Harrisburg, in 1841. This

union resulted in four children, George G., Jerome K., Annie L. and Alvah H. All of these children are now living except Jerome K., who died in 1860. Mr. Boyer died in 1880. Mrs. Boyer died on May 21st, 1896.

Jacob Stiegel, son of the Baron, had only one son, Jacob, who married Catherine Brecht (or Bright), daughter of Michael Bright, of Reading, Pa., who had eight children:

1. Rachel, who married David Dixon, had ten children.

ELIZABETH STIEGEL'S TOMBSTONE.

This Stone is a Hard Brownstone, in an excellent state of preservation, 5 feet 8 inches long, 2 feet 2 inches wide and 6 inches thick, resting on two upright stones, one at either, end of the width and thickness of the slab.

To the right of Mrs. Stiegel's tomb is that of James Old, a grandchild, which can be read with the aid of a lens.

2. Elizabeth, married W. A. Quick, had one child, Nannie C., living at Boiling Springs, Va.

3. Louisa, married M. B. Stover, had four children.

4. Michael, died at the age of twelve years.

5. A. William Henry, died in Texas.

6. David, married Sarah Libert, had five children; among them were John C. and Elizabeth Stiegel Henkel.

7. Charles, married Sarah Coffman, had five children; married a second time to Sarah Craig, by whom he had five children also.

8. Sarah, married F. Koiner, ten children.

Inscription.

Here rests Elizabeth whose lifeless body is committed to the earth until Jehovah calls her to another life. God has already freed the soul in the love and wounds of Jesus, from the fetters and thralldom of sin. This is the tribute which posterity pays her memory.

Elizabeth, daughter of Jacob Huber, departed this life at the home of her father. She was born 27th March, 1734, and was married the 7th November, 1752, to Heinrich Wilhelm Stiegel; died February 3d, 1758.

A Singular Coincidence.

Elizabeth Furnace, started in 1757, was finally shut down in 1857, after running exactly one hundred years.

The church building which he helped to erect in the town of which he is the founder, was razed the same year, 1857.

PAPERS READ

BEFORE THE

LANCASTER COUNTY HISTORICAL SOCIETY,

ON OCT. 2, 1896.

ANN HENRY; LANCASTER COUNTY'S WOMAN TREASURER,
BY GEORGE STEINMAN, ESQ.

THE OLDEST DAILY PAPER OF LANCASTER COUNTY,
BY F. R. DIFFENDERFFER.

INDIAN TRIBES OF LANCASTER COUNTY,
BY F. R. DIFFENDERFFER.

ADDRESS,
BY HON. W. U. HENSEL.

CONSTITUTION.

———

LANCASTER, PA.
REPRINTED FROM THE NEW ERA.
1896.

Ann Henry: Lancaster County's Woman Treasurer,
    By George Steinman, Esq.   69

The Oldest Daily Paper in Lancaster County,
    By F. R. Diffenderffer, ... 72

Indian Tribes of Lancaster County,
    By F. R. Diffenderffer, ... 85

Address,
    By Hon. W. U. Hensel, ... 89

Constitution, ... 92

ANN HENRY: LANCASTER COUNTY'S WOMAN TREASURER.

Ann Henry, the treasurer of Lancaster county and wife of the Hon. William Henry, was the daughter of Abraham and Ursula Wood. According to the family records she was born in Bucks county, but the records of the Moravian Church, of Lancaster, show her to have been born in Burlington, N. J., January 21, 1734.

Her grandfather, John Wood, was a son of George Wood, of the Darby Quakers. John Wood married October 12, 1703, Jane, daughter of John and Barbary Bevin. John Bevin came from an ancient family, was a man of large means and lineally descended from Edward III. of England, the Beauforts and Somerset family, of England, and the Cymri Kings.

William Henry was the son of John and Elizabeth Henry. He was born in Chester county, May 19, 1729. His parents came from Ireland and were married in this country. They both died on the same day and are buried at the Old Octoraro meeting house, Chester county.

William Henry, in the fifteenth year of his age, was sent to Lancaster to learn the trade of a gunsmith with Matthew Roeser. He made Lancaster his home and soon became the head of a large establishment for the manufacture of guns. His residence and store stood at the corner of Moravian alley and Market Place. Moravian alley entered West King street at the west end of what is now known as the old Market House, which was not then built, and where it now stands was Market Place.

William Henry lived with his sister, Mary Bickham, a widow, who kept house for him. An amusing family tradition is told of his courtship. Mrs. Bickham invited Miss Wood and another friend to spend the day with her. Part of the time was spent in the garden. Standing in the hall through which the ladies had to pass was a broom, which Henry placed on the floor, and watched the coming of the ladies. His sister stepped over it, her friend pushed it aside with her foot, but Miss Wood picked it up and put it in its place. After the ladies left, Henry told his sister, "Miss Wood loved order, and would make a good wife. I shall strive to win her."

Mrs. Henry was of domestic habits and devoted to her family. She was competent to look after her husband's affairs when the various positions he filled during the Revolution called him from home.

When the British occupied Philadelphia the Henry house was an important place. He had living with him David Rittenhouse, John Hart and Tom Paine. The latter, on account of his drunken habits and "agnostic" views, was very much disliked by Mrs. Henry.

During Henry's absence from Lancaster his house was open to his friends, who were always welcomed by Mrs. Henry. A paragraph in a letter from a member of the Assembly describes her as having an attractive face which in conversation brightened and she entertained with much grace and dignity.

Among the many positions filled by Henry were Armourer to Braddock and Forbes expedition; Justice of the Peace, 1758, 1770 and 1777; Member of the Assembly, 1776; Armourer of Pennsylvania, 1777; Assistant Commissioner General,

1778 ; Member of Congress, 1784-1786 and one of the founders of the Juliana library, of Lancaster, and at the time of his death treasurer of the county.

During his last illness his wife gave up everything to nurse him and prepared his business affairs. He died December 15, 1786. At the time of his death the State owed him a large amount, and the difference in value of Federal and State money and specie made it very difficult to adjust the accounts. His wife was then continued by the Governor as Treasurer, and remained so for several years, and, with the help of her sons, filled the office with credit. She had thirteen children. The best known of them were William Henry, who was Associate Justice of the Courts of Northampton county from 1788 to 1814 ; John Joseph Henry, Judge of the Courts of Lancaster county, and Benjamin West Henry, who was an artist of some merit and died young. Six of the children died in infancy.

Ann Heury died March 8, 1798. She and her husband were prominent members of the Moravian Church, and both are buried in the old Moravian burying ground of this city.

THE OLDEST DAILY PAPER IN LANCASTER COUNTY.

It will be generally conceded, I think, by those who have given the matter any attention or who are acquainted with the facts, that there is no city of equal size in the country more given to newspaper reading than Lancaster. It is to-day supporting five daily newspapers. There is hardly a family in the city, however humble, that does not take a daily newspaper, and many persons take two and three.

But how many of the present readers of the daily newspapers know anything about the early publications? How many in this audience know when the first daily was issued in this city and what was its name? If there is a single one who believes he can answer these questions it is not 16 to 1 but 1,000 to 1 that he will say the paper was the *Inland Daily* and the date of first publication, 1853.

Until a few days ago I would have said the same thing, because I read that paper from day to day, and knew its editor, Harvey L. Goodall. To-day I confess that I have been as much in the dark about the first daily paper published in this city as those here who have never heard of the *Inland Daily*. There have been lists of the publications issued in this city and county published in our county histories, but the compilers of these were unacquainted with all the facts.

There came into my possession a few days ago a small piece of old-time, hand-made paper, brown with age, containing only half a dozen lines of pen writing in the hand so well known to all who have been accustomed to handle the manuscripts of the men who lived and wrote a hundred years ago.

The writer is indebted to Julius F. Sachse, Esq., of Philadelphia, Editor of the *American Journal of Photography*, for the use of the above note.

This is what is written on this time-stained piece of paper which I hold in my hand:

SIR—I am requested by John Bartholomew, who has subscribed for your daily Paper, that for six weeks past they have came irregular and frequently not more than four a week. Yesterday there was three iuclos'd in one packet & at other times two. He flatters himself that you must not be acquainted with the Negligence, or it would be immediately corrected.

BENJAMIN BARTHOLOMEW.
Near the Warren (Tavern), Lancaster Turnpike. Decr. 18, 1811.
MR. E. BRONSON, Lancaster.

That is the whole story. It is a brief one, but it is satisfactory and convincing. Nothing could be more so. It bears evidences of truthfulness in every line, word and punctuation mark. The paper and the style of hand-writing are corroborating proofs. It was no weekly. It says "your daily newspaper." Only one thing is lacking, the name of this pioneer of the daily press of this city. What was its name and who was Mr. E. Bronson? Shall we ever know? In all human probability no one is living to-day who knew the man or saw his paper.

And yet it is possible that somewhere there is a record that will answer both questions. Just as this old letter was preserved for nearly a century to tell its story to us to-day, so, perhaps, there is hidden away in some neglected box some other document that can give us the information we wish to have. I have not had time to examine the list of taxables in this city for 1811. That might tell us something about Mr. Bronson. Some old deed or other paper may be recorded in the county offices. That was the period when most of our local newspapers were short lived. There were several papers established about that time, the newspaper chroniclers tell us, but they cannot give us their names. This was one of them, and as its contemporaries also died without leaving a tombstone and an epitaph, I do not know where to turn for further information concerning Mr. Bronson and his early daily newspaper.

But this tell-tale little piece of brown paper comes to us bringing with it a reminder to us all as members of this Society. There are very few families who have lived in this county three or four generations who have not in some obscure and neglected corner, in box, or chest or elsewhere, a store of old papers that have been handed down for a century or more. It may be they have not been looked at for a hundred years. Their present owners do not know what they are nor what they mean. Who can tell what golden nuggets may lie hidden among them? There may be many that have a story to tell just as this little note has, and perhaps a still more important one. Every member of this society ought to appoint himself a committee of one to take up the work of searching out these hidden deposits and overhauling them, and in this way contribute his mite to the work that lies before our society.

Turning from the story of this early daily newspaper, published in this city eighty-five years ago, I freely express the belief that there will be no more interesting chapter in our local history than that which shall fully go into the details of the newspaper history of Lancaster county. There cannot be a more fruitful or interesting field. Has any one here any idea of the number of newspapers and other publications that have been born in this city, lived their short or long share of existence and then died as more than 50 per cent. of all newspapers do, unknown and for the most part unremembered? I question whether any one who has not looked up the subject has any idea of what a center of literary activity this city has been during the past hundred years. There are several lists of the newspapers established in this place to be found in our local histories. I have taken all they named and added such others as I could procure and I found the sum total to be 126. Think of it, 126 newspapers, magazines and periodicals of all kinds that have seen the light in this good city of Lancaster!

But that is not all. There were papers started of which neither the names nor those of their proprietors have survived the tooth of time. I have not the least doubt that, if I had a complete roster of all the publications that had their birth in this city alone, it would reach a total of 140, or even more. In addition, it should be said that the outlying towns of this county have also been very prolific in this matter. I have no doubt that, from first to last, there have been published in this county more than 200 periodicals of different kinds during the present century. This may seem almost incredible, but the known facts warrant the conclusion.

I have prepared a list by years of the papers that have seen the light in this city, from the first one of which we have any record until the present time. It is an interesting record, but how much more so would it be if it could be made complete. It is largely made up of the lists to be found in Mombert's and Everts & Peck's histories, and I make no claim to anything, save about thirty-five new names, which I have added.

The first newspaper published in this

county was called the *Lancaster Gazette*. It had its birth in 1752 and was a fortnightly publication, printed in alternate columns of German and English, by Miller & Holland. It went out of existence the following year.

No one was found courageous enough to start a new paper until the well-known printer, Francis Bailey, did it in 1775. There was evidently no paper published in this city for some years prior to the Revolution. This seems certain from the fact that in 1772 the Burgesses of the town ordered some of their proceedings published in the *Gazette and Journal*, of Philadelphia. Had there been a home paper this would not have been done. Francis Bailey published the *Die Pennsylvanische Zeitung* in 1775. One account gives 1778, as the date. In the same year a paper called the *News* was started.

In 1787 the *Neue Unparthenische Lancaster Zeitung und Anzeigs Nachrichten* saw the light; Steimer, Albrecht and Lahn were the publishers. It was printed mostly in German. In 1797 the name was changed to *Der Deutche Porcupein* and in 1800 to *Americanishe Staatsbote*.

Fortunately, I am able to accompany the notice of this last named paper with the prospectus issued by the proprietors prior to beginning its publication. As you see, it is almost as bright and fresh as when it was printed, 109 years ago. It seems there were two other German newspapers published in Pennsylvania at that time. As a matter of interest and also as a matter of permanent record, I have translated the prospectus and insert it here.

LANCASTER, June 5, 1787.

TO THE GERMAN PUBLIC.
FRIENDS AND COUNTRYMEN.

A German newspaper, the third to be published in Pennsylvania, would seem to be somewhat superfluous, and the publishers of the two others might complain especially, and not without reason, because of the trifling price, as thereby they would suffer harm. We believe, notwithstanding that argument, that we percieve no difficulty and dare to lay our proposition for a third newspaper before the esteemed public. Lancastèr, where we have set up our printing press, lies not only more in the middle of the country, by which a quite considerable sum of money for postage will be saved, but it also has a peculiar advantage in that it is almost entirely German and surrounded by German settlers, and even now has been selected as the site of a German high school. Shall we not, therefore, hope to receive numerous readers for our new newspaper? The opportunity is not wanting, nor the good will to make it pleasant and instructive to our countrymen. We receive the English inland newspapers and consider this noteworthy therefore to set it before our fellow-citizens at the outset. We also carry on an extensive correspondence with Germany, and hope to be able to report European news, especially German news, as soon and as early as any other newspaper. We also expect inland news from trustworthy sources, and with pleasure will receive and make known such news. Any short and instructive treatises which will be of use to the reader above all the countryman, both for pleasure and for profit, will be acceptable to us. Men who are well known for their ability have already, beforehand, promised us many contributions of this kind.

Our terms are as follows: Every week a whole sheet will be printed upon good paper, with neat and altogether new letters.

We promise this for $1 per annum, half

of which must be paid at the time of subscribing and the other half at the end of the first six months.

The price of a single copy will be three cents.

Every one can see our terms are uncommonly low and that in our undertaking we are considering the public more than ourselves. We commend ourselves and our newspaper to our German citizens and remain their obedient servants.

STEIMER, ALBRIGHT & LAHN.

The *Journal* had its birth in 1794 and under various editors and owners was published until 1839, when it was merged into the *Intelligencer*, which had been established in 1799. The consolidated paper bore the name of *Intelligencer and Journal*, and which, under the name of the *Lancaster Intelligencer*, is still published, and is, therefore, the oldest newspaper in the city or county.

Since 1800 the newspapers published here have been numerous. Hardly a year has passed since that time that has not seen the birth of one or more. I have prepared a list of them chronologically arranged. It is as complete as I have been able to make it, with the brief time at my disposal.

1752. *The Lancaster Gazette.*
1775. Paper published by Francis Bailey. Another account gives 1778 as the time and the name *Die Pennsylvanische Zeitung.*
1778. *The News.*
1787. *The Neue Unparthenische Lancaster Zeitung und Anzeigs Nachrichten.* Name changed in 1797 to *Der Deutche Porcupein*, and in 1800 to *Amencanische Staatsbote.*
1794. *The Journal*—merged with *The Intelligencer* in 1839.
1799. *The Intelligencer. Der Wahre Amerikaner.*

1800. *Americanische Staatsbote.* (See 1787).
1803. *The Hive.*
1808. *Der Volksfreund. The Gleaner.*
1810. *The Conditional Democrat.*
1811. Daily, name unknown; published by E. Bronson.
1816. *The Lancaster Patriot.*
1817. *The Lancaster Gazette and Farmers' Register.*
1819. *The Free Press.*
1820. *Lancaster Journal.*
1821. *The American Sentinel.*
1822. (About). *Die Stimme des Volks.*
1825. *Political Sentinel and Literary Gazette.*
1826. *Lancaster Eagle. Standard of Liberty.*
1827. *Lancaster Reporter.*
1828. *Der Lancaster Wahre Amerikaner. Anti-Masonic Herald.*
1829. *Boquet, or Ladies' Library Portfolio Keepsake. Anti-Masonic Opponent.*
1830. *Lancaster Examiner. Lancaster Beobachter.*
1831. *Lancaster Republican. Standard of Liberty,* and *Lancaster County Democrat and Public Advertiser.*
1833. *The Inciter.*
1834. *The Lancaster Register. Lancaster Union.*
1835. *The Lancaster Miscellany.*
1839. *The Old Guard,* (or 1840). *The Age. Semi-Weekly Gazette.*
1840. *The Buckeye. Wahre Demokrat.*
1842. *Semi-Weekly Gazette.*
1843. *The Saturday Express;* changed in 1853 to *Saturday Evening Express.*
1844. *The Mill Boy. The Workingman's Press. Lancaster Democrat. The Moral Reformer,* afterwards *The American Reformer.*
1845. *The Lancaster County Farmer.*
1846. *American Republican. The Tribune and Advertiser.*
1848. *Rough and Ready. The Grape Shot.*

1848. *The Farmer and Literary Gazette.
The Lancasterian. The Lancaster
Inquirer.*
1849. *The Guardian.* Perhaps also this
year the *German Democrat*, afterwards called the *Harrisburg and
Lancaster Democrat.*
1851. *The Farm Journal. The Independent Whig. The National Whig.*
1853. *The Public Register. The Inland
Daily Times.* (Morning).
1854. *Public Register and American Citizen. The Inland Weekly.*
1855. *Conestoga Chief. Pennsylvania
School Journal. Mechanics' Councillor. The Scott Bugle. The Daily
Free Press,* (Liquor organ.)
1856. *The Daily Express. The Pathfinder.*
1858. *Lancaster Union. The Temperance
Advocate.*
1859. *The Church Advocate. The Morning Herald.* (Daily).
1860. *The Educational Record. The Constitution.*
1862. *The Daily Inquirer.*
1864. *Daily Intelligencer.*
1866. *The Keystone Good Templar. The
Monthly Circular.*
1867. *The Sunday-School Gem.*
1868. *The Voice of Truth. Father Abraham.*
1869. *The Lancaster Farmer. Mechanics'
Advocate. Christlicher Kundschafter. The Bar.*
1871. *Die Laterne.* (Weekly).
1872. *Daily Examiner. Der Christlicher,*
and in 1882 as *The Torch of Truth,*
or *Fackle der Warheit.*
1873. *The Laterne.* (Daily).
1874. (About.) *Der Waffenlose Waechter.*
1875. *Monthly Intelligencer.*
1876. *The Morning Review.*
1877. THE NEW ERA (Daily). THE NEW
ERA (Weekly). *The Owl.*
1878. *The Footlight.*

1879. *The Coin Journal. Knights of Pythias Magazine.*
1881. *The Record.*
1882. *The School Journal. The College Student. Lancaster Freie Presse. Weekly Ledger and Market Directory.*
1883. *The Law Review.*
1884. *Sontag's Journal. Tempus Fuget.*
1886. *The Modern Crematist.*
1888. *The Home. Grand Army News.*
1889. *Life.*
1890. *The Morning News* (Daily). *The F. and M. Weekly. Homœopathic Envoy. Christian Culture.*
1891. *Lancaster Tobacco Journal. Evangelical Worker.*
1892. *The School Forum. The Labor Leader.*
1895. *The Pennsylvania Malt and Liquor Journal.*

Of the foregoing, eleven were daily papers; of these five survive until the present moment. Six have dropped out. There are at this time twenty-one separate publications issued from the Lancaster press. In the county, outside the city, there are twenty-seven, making forty-seven for the entire county.

One other interesting fact deserves to be noticed. Lancaster county, as every one here present knows, is the richest agricultural county in the United States. The value of its agricultural products in a single year has reached the great sum of $7,657,790. During the past half century three purely agricultural publications have been started for their instruction and entertainment of our agricultural population: the *Lancaster County Farmer*, in 1845; the *Farm Journal*, in 1851, and the *Lancaster Farmer*, in 1869. All were first-class publications. To-day not one of them is here. All died the death. Does not this seem something of a reflection upon the farmers of our county.

But I wish to direct attention to another point. Lancaster was almost exclusively a German community in the last century, just as it has largely been in the present one. Read over the names of the men who have published papers in this city. Miller—and he was the first of all—Albrecht, Lahn, Steimer, the Grimler Bros., Benjamin and Henry, Huss, Breiner, Ehrenfreid, Albright, Baer, Kling, Wagner, Shrier, Seigfreid, Baab, Frank, Myers, Harbaugh, and many more. These were all Germans, or of German-American descent. Many of their papers were printed wholly or partly in the German language. And yet the charge has again and again been made that they were opposed to education and to progress. A grosser libel was never uttered against our people. This German town of Lancaster stands next to Philadelphia and Pittsburg among Pennsylvania cities in this particular. It leads cities that have twice as many inhabitants as it has.

Talk about the culture and intelligence of New England! We believe we may safely challenge any city of 40,000 inhabitants in any of the New England States, or for that matter anywhere in the entire Union, to show such a record as I have briefly presented to your notice. If there is such a city we would be most glad to hear from her. That is the record we have made and it is one every man in this room may be proud of, whatever his ancestry.

But I have digressed from my subject, which was to bring to your notice this early daily newspaper, which, so far as I am aware, is the first time mention has ever publicly been made of it.

I cannot help observing right here that there is a kindred field in which unfading laurels are to be won by the man who has the courage and the ability to enter upon the task—the preparation of a bibliography of Lancaster printed books. Our German printers and writers turned out books by the score. Who will consecrate himself to the work. I see before me the man of all men best qualified for the work. Will not Dr. Dubbs some day enter upon the task?

INDIAN TRIBES OF LANCASTER COUNTY.

The names and the history of the Indian tribes who have dwelt within the boundaries of Lancaster county during the historic period present a most prolific field for conjecture, doubt and confusion. I have within a week examined many pages of records and the result has been only to convince me that our Indian history is not in good shape. I do not think I can add anything to the general stock of information, but I will try to unravel the twisted skein a little.

In our local history we find the names of the following tribes: Susquehannocks, Piquaws, the Shawnese, the Conestogos, the Nanticokes, the Ganawese, the Conoise or Conoys, Mingoes, Minquays and the Delawares. Here we have ten tribes as resident in this county between 1650 and 1750. We had the names but we did not have the Indians, as I will attempt to show.

The Susquehannocks were the most numerous tribe that lived here. In 1608, according to Capt. John Smith's narrative, he found them all along the Susquehanna River for 100 miles northward from Chesapeake Bay. They were tall, athletic and courageous. He describes their appearance both with pen and pencil. At one time they could put 600 warriors in the field from their stockaded fort at Turkey Hill, in Manor township. They were unable to adapt themselves to civilization, and were swept out of existence.

The Conestogos are best known to us by name. They were Susquehannocks, and were called Conestogos when they settled along the Conestoga. They were given that name by the whites. At other times they were called Mingoes and Minquays and Hickories, five names for one tribe.

Redmond Conyngham has written a pamphlet about the Piquaws. He says tradition has it that 200 years before the whites came there were no Indians in Lancaster county. If tradition says that then I don't believe tradition. This name was given to these Indians because they resided on the Pequea creek. They were Shawnese who went from Ohio to Alabama, thence to Georgia, where the Catawbas and Cherokees got after them and drove them North, after which they asked Penn to let them live here. He consented, the Susquehannocks becoming their sureties. They were next to the Susquehannocks in numbers. They lived on the Pequea thirty-four years. They had a town of 500 souls about two miles from Christiana. Other of their towns were in Sadsbury township and on Shawnee run, at Columbia, where they went and remained until the whites became too numerous. They were a roving, gypsy tribe. In 1737 only 130 were left in the county. They departed secretly and went beyond the Alleghenies.

The Ganawese came into the county in 1698 from the Potomac region by permission of Penn, and located at Conejohala, where the borough of Washington now stands, and built a town there. A few years after they removed to the mouth of the Conoy creek. In 1748 they removed to Shamokin. They were known as Ganawese, Conoys, Conoise and even as Nanticokes.

Other accounts say the Nanticokes came over from Berks county and settled in Cocalico township, where they were numerous and had a town. It is said the Nanticokes and the Ganawese spoke the same tongue. I have already partially identified the Nanticokes with the Conoys and Ganawese. How they could come both from the Potomac and from Berks county I cannot tell. There seems to be hopeless confusion here. Heckwelder says the Ganawese and Conoys were the same.

The Delawares, who settled in this county in considerable numbers, previously lived along the Brandywine, in Chester county, crossed over into this county, where they remained only a short time. Despite Cooper and the "Deerslayer," they had a bad reputation here.

There were four or five large Indian villages in the county and many smaller ones. The dialects spoken were different even in near localities. As already said, the Ganawese and Nanticokes had allied languages.

Pennsylvania seems to have been an asylumn for many tribes of Indians.

Every tribe in the county was brought under the yoke of the Five Nations. The Susquehannocks, aided by troops from Maryland, fought a bloody battle near Turkey Hill in 1676 with the Northern Confederacy and defeated them, but later became a vassal tribe, as did all the rest, to the Five Nations.

In 1680 the Cayugas and Senecas almost exterminated them. The last remnant of them, known as the Conestogos, were slain in 1763 by the Paxtang boys, six at Conestogo Town and the remaining fourteen within a few yards of this spot.

All these Indians, I believe, belonged to the Algonquin family.

I think it can be established that our numerous Indian tribes can be traced to these five tribes:

1. Susquehannocks, (called later Cone-

stogos, Mingoes, Minquays and Hickory Indians.)

2. Ganawese, sometimes known as Conoys, Conoise and Nanticokes.

3. Shawnese, often also called Piquaws.

4. Delawares.

5. Nanticokes, if it is conceded these Indians have not been sometimes confounded with the Ganawese.

In all four tribes, or five at most, instead of ten.

In all the conferences held by the Provincial Agents with the Indians in this locality between 1721 and 1750, only four tribes of local Indians are mentioned, the Conestogos, the Shawnese, the Ganawese and the Delawares. It is a most reasonable inference that the Piquaws, Conoys and the Hickories were only settlements of the above who took their names from the localities where they had their villages.

In all probability the number of Indians in this county at no period exceeded 3,000 or 4,000.

ADDRESS BY HON. W. U. HENSEL

Mr. Hensel then addressed the meeting briefly on the general purposes of the Society and the best methods of promoting them. He thought it should be steadily kept in mind that the objects of the Society were permanent improvement and instruction, as well as entertainment, from meeting to meeting. The meetings should be made popular, but, at the same time, they should keep in mind the ultimate purpose of the Society, namely, the preparation and publication of a reliable history of Lancaster county. The amount of historical matter which might be procured was surprising. Every locality was rich in it and the number of persons throughout the county who might be made serviceable to the Society was very great. Many of these are modest people and some of them live in remote localities. Some special effort should be made to reach them. In the first place, the meetings, he thought, might be held at a more attractive place, and a room should be secured for the permanent depository of books, manuscripts, papers, &c., that might be left with the Society. We should have all the histories of Lancaster county ever published, and he was prepared to present the Society with Ellis & Evans', Mombert's and Harris' Biographical History. Rupp's should be secured, together with all the maps ever published of the county and general works containing Lancaster county historical matter. There were many old deeds and papers which persons would present to the Society if they knew they would be preserved, as well as old china, furniture and other articles illustrating our history. In illustration of this, Mr. Hensel said that he would present to the Society, on behalf of Mr. Jacob Hildebrand, some old Penn deeds, patents and a very beautifully illuminated manuscript, which, upon examination by Dr. Dubbs, turned out to be a very florid recommendation of a skilled gardener who came to this country in 1750 from Sweden.

Mr. Hensel further suggested that permanent committees be appointed on different branches of the Society's various lines of work, and it was agreed that the president should appoint three members each on special committees as follows: Archæology, topography, nomenclature, local records, bibliography, periodicals, biography, education, church history, scientific research, political history, and forestry statistics.

Mr. Hensel also called attention to the danger of the remote sections of the county, like Brecknock and Adamstown, Peach Bottom and Fulton, the Lower Octoraro and Conewago region, being neglected unless persons living there were interested in the work. There was a great deal of tradition in the county, picturesque incidents, eccentric characters, old houses and historical homesteads, the country seats of prominent people, the old industrial interests of the county, the abandoned mills and broken water powers, which needed the hand of an accurate historian with some imagination to give them their proper setting.

If we are to have a history, it must be constructed on historical and literary principles, and everybody and everything be given their proper proportion without regard to commercial features or to the willingness of people to subscribe to it or to pay for a place in it. The department of bibliography ought to comprise a collection of every book ever written by a Lancaster county author or published in the county. The number of these would be found to be unexpectedly large. The interest of the teachers and pupils of public schools ought to be enlisted in such a way as to have a representative of the society in every school district. The number who attend its meetings should be hundreds instead of scores, and it is worth while to consider whether a special popular meeting might not be held quarterly, perhaps not always in Lancaster city, but at such places as Donegal, Lititz, Ephrata, Christiana and other points which are abundantly rich in historical matter.

THE CONSTITUTION.

I.—NAME.

The society shall be called the Lancaster County Historical Society.

II.

Its objects shall be the discovery, collection, preservation and publication of the history, historical records and data of and relating to Lancaster city and county, the collection and preservation of books, newspapers, maps, genealogies, portraits, paintings, relics, engravings, manuscripts, letters, journals and any and all materials which may establish or illustrate such history, the growth and progress of population, wealth, education, agriculture, arts, manufactures and commerce in this city and county.

III.

The society shall consist of resident, corresponding and life members; resident members must be at the time of their election actual residents of the county. For membership persons may be proposed by any member in writing to the Executive Committee and, upon its recommendation, such persons may be elected by a majority vote of those present at the next monthly or annual meeting.

IV.—THE MEMBERS.

Resident members shall pay an admission fee of two dollars at the time of their enrollment and an annual fee of one dollar, payable January 1st of each year. Arrearages for three years will cause the delinquents to be dropped from the rolls. The fee of life membership shall be $50, such members to be exempt from all dues and entitled to receive free of charge one copy of each of the publications of the society.

V.—THE OFFICERS.

The officers of the society shall consist of a president, two vice-presidents, recording secretary, corresponding secretary, treasurer and librarian. Their duties shall be such as usually pertain to officers of like title.

VI.—THE EXECUTIVE COMMITTEE.

There shall be an Executive Committee of seventeen, composed of the officers and ten members of the society, to be chosen at the annual meeting. The duties of the Executive Committee shall include all those duties that commonly belong to the Board of Managers and Trustees of such associations. It shall also arrange and digest the historical material collected from month to month, and present the results of its labors to the society at its monthly and annual meetings, besides making all the necessary arrangements to insure the interests and usefulness of said meetings.

VII.—ELECTIONS.

The regular elections of officers and of the Executive Committee shall be by ballot at the annual meeting, and their term shall be for one year.

VIII.—VACANCIES.

Any vacancies occurring in the Board of Officers or Executive Committee during the year shall be filled by election at the next monthly meeting after the vacancy occurs.

IX.—MEETINGS.

The Executive Committee shall meet at least once a month, at such time and place as it may determine. The society shall meet monthly at 2 p. m., on the first Friday of each and every month; and in annual session at 2 p. m. on the first Friday after New Year. Special meetings may be called by the president at the request of nine members.

X.—QUORUM.

Five members shall constitute a quorum of the Executive Committee, and nine a quorum of the society to transact business at the monthly or annual meeting.

XI.—AMENDMENTS.

These rules may be amended by a two-thirds vote of the members present at the monthly meeting next subsequent to that at which the amendment is proposed.

PAPERS READ

BEFORE THE

LANCASTER COUNTY HISTORICAL SOCIETY,

ON NOV. 6, 1896.

REMINISCENCES OF STRASBURG.
BY JACOB HILDEBRAND, ESQ.
IRISH OCCUPATION OF LANCASTER LAND.
BY R. M. REILLY, ESQ.
WAS THERE EVER A SERIOUS IDEA OF LOCATING THE CAPITAL OF THE COUNTRY ON THE SUSQUEHANNA.
BY HON. W. U. HENSEL.
CORONER'S VEDICT IN THE CHRISTIANA RIOT CASE.
BY HON. W. U. HENSEL.
A WILLIAM PENN DEED.
BY HON. W. U. HENSEL.
REUBEN CHAMBERS.
BY R. J. HOUSTON.
SAMUEL BOWMAN AND THE VILLAGE HE FOUNDED.
BY A. G. SEYFERT.
COMMITTEES.

LANCASTER, PA.
REPRINTED FROM THE NEW ERA.
1896.

Reminiscences of Strasburg,
 By JACOB HILDEBRAND, ESQ., ...   97
Irish Occupation of Lancaster Land,
 By R. M. REILLY, ESQ., ... 109
Was there ever a Serious Idea of locating the Capital of the
 Country on the Susquehanna,
 By HON. W. U. HENSEL, ... 111
Coroner's Verdict in the Christiana Riot Case,
 By HON. W. U. HENSEL 114
A William Penn Deed,
 By HON. W. U. HENSEL, ... 117
Reuben Chambers,
 By R. J. HOUSTON, ... 119
Samuel Bowman and the Village he Founded,
 By A. G. SEYFERT, ... 133
Committees, ... 141

REMINISCENCES OF STRASBURG.

The first settlements were made in 1709 by the Swiss Mennonites on the banks of Pequea creek. The name Strasburg was no doubt brought with them from their native country, but in the organization of Lancaster county in 1729 and the division into townships there seemed to be a prejudice against the German Mennonites, and the name Strasburg was entirely ignored, and what is now known as Strasburg and Paradise townships was included within the boundaries of Leacock township, although at that time patent deeds had been granted to the first settlers for over 20,000 acres of land, and in the deeds is mentioned Strasburg, Chester county. I have never been able to find any legal or Court records showing when the boundaries of Strasburg township were defined. It was only by common honesty and in justice to the first settlers that the name has been continued.

The first patent deeds are dated June 30th, A. D. 1711. The number of patent deeds for the whole township is forty-six, and they contain over 14,000 acres. The names of the original patentees are Martin Kendig, John Funk, Jacob Miller, Able Strettle, Isaac LeFever, Hans Howery, Daniel Ferree, Samuel Taylor, Jacob Groff, John Taylor, Thomas Smith, Henry Kendig, John Bowman, John Rush, John Herr, John Eckman, Isaac Whitelock, George Smith, Henry Stoner, Jacob Kendrick, John Mosser, Jacob Eshleman, John Miller, John Breckbill, Benjamin Groff, James Scott, David Witmer, John Hubley, J. and M. Fouts, Francis Bowman, Conrad Hoak, John Neff, Samuel Peoples, Samuel Hathorn and Annie Neff.

The first house of any pretensions to be a roomy and comfortable dwelling was built by Martin Kendig in the year 1717, out of walnut logs and with a straw or thatched roof. It was located about 200 yards south from the Strasburg borough line, and was occupied as the farm house until 1841, when Davis Gyger erected a fine large two-story brick house near the same place.

In the year 1816 Strasburg borough was incorporated, to contain 400 acres. In 1843 the township was divided and the eastern end of what was formerly Strasburg township is now known as Paradise.

Some Old Mills.

From the most authentic records the first mill erected in Lancaster county was on Pequea creek, about one mile northwest from the borough, along the Strasburg and Millport turnpike, and known for many years as "John Musselman's." It was built by Martin Kendig about the year 1720, on the northwestern part of his one thousand acre tract, and he sold five hundred and thirty acres, together with the water right and grist mill, to Emanuel Herr. The deed is dated the eleventh day of November, A. D. 1725, and recorded at Lancaster in Book W. W., page 305, etc. The mill is now in possession of Kendig & Pugh and has been converted into a roller mill. Previous to the building of this mill the people had to go to Wilmington, Delaware, for their flour and it took three days to go and return.

About one mile southeast from the borough, along the "Mine Hill" road, is quite an old mill built in the early part of the last century by Jacob Eshleman on the north branch of Little Beaver Creek. The head of this stream is the famous "Kelsey Springs." Some old records say the first French burrs introduced into the county were in this mill, and it was at that time called "Eshleman's Big Mill," but now it is known as the "Little Red Mill." In fact, the mill never was red, but a very large doubledecker barn standing near the mill was painted red.

On September 25, 1728, a patent was granted to John Herr for eleven hundred acres of land and on this tract, in the extreme northeast corner of the township, he erected a two-story stone mill on the Pequea, about the year 1740. The original mill is yet standing, but was converted into a distillery about the beginning of the present century, at which time a new mill was erected about fifty yards further down the stream. That part of the original tract, containing about fifty acres, upon which the mill stands is yet owned by one of his descendants.

In the year 1759 Joseph Haines sold to John Herr a tract of land and saw mill located on the Pequea about midway between Strasburg and Lampeter, and in 1769 John Herr sold to Abraham Herr the saw and grist mill. This mill is on part of a tract of land patented to Jacob Miller, containing one thousand acres. The deed is dated June 30, 1711.

In the year 1733 James Scott settled on a tract of land about two miles south from the borough, on the south side of "Bunker Hill," on the road to New Providence, and erected on Little Beaver Creek the first fulling mill of which we have any record, and on June 12, 1767, he sold the fulling mill tract, containing about one hundred, acres to Jacob Neff. He and his descendants carried on the fulling mill business for many years. A later Jacob Neff was a very conspicuous citizen of this section of the county. He was prominent before the war as a Democratic politician, one of the faithful adherents of the late Col. Reah Frazer. His homestead was notable for striking architectural quaintness, and an immense chestnut tree which stands at the old gateway is a landmark the country around. His two sons, Aldus, a promising member of the Lancaster Bar, and Jefferson, who was of a decided mechanical turn of mind— both went into the Union army, and died early in that struggle.

About this time John Neff built a mill about one-half mile east from the fulling tract on the south branch of Little Beaver, and after some years he was succeeded by his son, John Neff, who became a Mormon, and in the year 1844 he left his large farm and mill property in charge of Samuel P. Bower, Esq., and moved to Nauvoo, Illinois, a town founded by the Mormons in 1840. With the migration of this people toward the Far West, Mr. Neff and his family accompanied them. While he embraced the tenets of the church, he never practiced polygamy. One of the sons of his wife by a former marriage, Mr. A. Milton Musser, became one of the apostles of the Mormon Church, and is to-day a pillar in that organization.

Mines and Railroads.

The iron ore mining interests of Strasburg township are not very extensive. The Eby mines, located about two miles south of the borough, were first opened in the early part of the present century They were worked for about twenty years and then abandoned; reopened in 1862 and operated by the Phœnix Iron Company until 1870, when they were again closed. The ore is of a very good quality, but expensive to mine.

In 1879 Peacock & Thomas opened and operated a mine on the farm of Daniel

Helm, about one mile north from New Providence. The ore is of a very superior quality; it was hauled to New Providence by wagons and shipped on the Lancaster and Quarryville railroad.

There were two other mines operated for a short time near Refton, but on account of the dull times they have been closed.

In the year 1832 a charter was obtained for the railroad from Strasburg to connect with the Pennsylvania railroad at Leaman Place. Work was soon after commenced, and the road was graded from Swan Hotel to within about one hundred yards of Leaman Place, but owing to the lack of funds was not completed until 1852. The Lancaster and Quarryville railroad passes through the southwestern part of the township at Refton, and was opened for travel on May 11th, 1875.

Churches.

In the year 1740 John Herr, a Mennonite preacher, who was a grandson of Hans Herr, built a dwelling house on his farm about one-half mile southwest from the borough on the farm now owned by John Keener, in which the upper story was arranged for holding public worship. In this house and others the society held regular worship until 1804, when the society built the stone meeting house, 40 by 60 feet, near the west end of the borough, where regular service has been held to the present time. It was enlarged in 1877, and again enlarged and much improved in the year 1887.

In 1894 about five acres of ground adjoining the old graveyard were purchased and a beautiful cemetery laid out.

The first Mennonite preachers for the Strasburg district were Ulrich Breckbill and the above-named John Herr, who was afterwards appointed Bishop. He served in that office till his death. About the year 1812 Peter Eby was appointed and in 1840 Christian Herr; in 1848, Joseph Hershey; in 1856, Benjamin Herr and in 1878 Isaac Eby. Amos Herr was ordained a minister in 1850. He was the first Mennonite preacher in the county who conducted religious service in the English language. After nearly fifty years in the ministry he survives, much honored and respected, having wrought great good in his life.

The above-named Bishop John Herr was the grandfather of John Herr, the founder of the Reformed Mennonite Society. Early in the year 1812 the first meeting was held and this Society organized at his house, about one-half mile north of the borough. At this meeting John Herr was unanimously chosen as pastor and Bishop. In the latter part of the same year their first meeting house was built on the west side of the Strasburg and Millport turnpike, and it is known as "Longenecker's Meeting House." The Society now has a neat brick meeting house on North Jackson street, in the borough. The founder of the Society died in May, 1850.

What was known as "the old Dutch Church," located about two miles southeast of the borough, was a small log building, about twenty feet square, erected by the German Reformed and Lutherans, and used as a union church until 1796, when the German Reformed Society built a stone church, with a gallery, about one-fourth of a mile north of New Providence. The old structure was removed in 1868 and a new brick building erected in its place, and in 1894 it was remodeled and greatly improved. The word German has been dropped from its title and is now known as the Reformed Church, with Rev. J. M. Souders as the pastor. Its recent centennial was an event of much historic interest.

The Lutherans continued to use "the old Dutch Church" until the beginning of the present century, when they built the large two-story brick church, with gallery and large pipe organ, on East Main street, in the borough, on a lot of ground which was a gift from Edward Dougherty, by deed dated February 7th, 1760, "In trust for the use of the Lutheran congregation for burial and church purposes."

The first church building in the borough of which we have any positive record was built in 1807 by the Methodists at the south end of Decatur street. The building is now known as Temperance Hall. In the year 1839 they built a two-story brick church on West Main street, and remodeled the same in 1868. In 1893 the old building was entirely removed and a very substantial brick church and chapel erected and dedicated January 1st, 1894. Centennial services were held in January 1896. The present pastor is Rev. Gladstone Holm.

The Presbyterians were organized into a society in 1832. They immediately commenced the building of a church on the southwest corner of Decatur and Franklin streets, and on Christmas day, 1833, the church was dedicated. In 1892 Mrs. Wm. Spencer erected a neat brick chapel to the west end of the church. About the same time the whole church was remodeled and greatly improved. The society now has a very nice brick church and chapel, and their present pastor is Rev. David F. Giles.

Educational and Literary.

In the year 1808 the first regular school house in Strasburg borough, a small one-story brick, was erected on the east side of North Jackson street. It was built by private contributions, and a few years afterwards an association was incorporated.

In the year 1812 Mrs. Haynes commenced and taught a private school for girls in a small one-story log house which stood just east of the present M. E. Church in the borough. The house was afterwards sold to the church and occupied by the sexton. One of the requirements of Mrs. Haynes was that each pupil should furnish her own chair. The branches taught were spelling, reading, writing, arithmetic and sewing. Some of the pupils daily rode on horseback four or five miles to attend this school.

The Strasburg Academy was founded in 1839 by the Rev. David McCarter as principal. This school was largely attended by young men from all parts of the United States, and was very prosperous for about twenty years.

About the year 1845 Miss Ann McCullough founded and taught a select school for young ladies. This school was very well patronized for a number of years.

In 1870 the School Directors of the borough erected a large and imposing two-story brick building on Franklin street. This building is arranged to accommodate all the children in the borough and is divided into Primary, Secondary, Grammar and High Schools, with Superintendent and Principal, who has charge of the whole school.

The township now has ten schools, with good teachers, and school supplies and buildings that will compare very favorably with any district in the country.

Strasburg claims the honor of being the birth place of the Hon. Thomas H. Burrowes—on the 16th day of November, 1805—to whom the people of Pennsylvania are greatly indebted for our common school system. Through his influence in January, 1831, George Hoffman, Geo. Diffenbach, Alexander H. Hood, James

McPhail, Benjamin Herr and others held a meeting in the little brick school house on Jackson street, which was the first effort to found a system of public schools. The first petition was presented and signed at that meeting and it was afterwards sent to Mr. Burrowes, who was then a member of the Legislature. Some who attended that meeting never lost sight of the measure until our free school system was formally established in 1835. One who was present at the meeeting is yet living.

In January, 1837, application was made for the use of a church or school house for Charles C. Burleigh to lecture on the subject of negro slavery, but the request was refused. Shortly afterwards, through the influence of George Hoffman and A. H. Hood, permission was granted to use the little Brick School House on Jackson street. On the evening of the lecture Daniel Gibbons and his son, Joseph, of Bird-in-Hand, brought Mr. Burleigh to Strasburg. There was so much feeling upon the subject that after the lecture we found that the linch pins were removed from the wheels of the carriage, and it was considered prudent to have an escort for Messrs. Burleigh and Gibbons from town. The committee consisted of Joseph Bowman, Alex. H. Hood, Joseph Gonder, Jr., Samuel Spiehlman, Benjamin Herr, George Hoffman and Jacob Hildebrand.

A few days after this, through the influence of the late Col. Joel Lightner, the school house in the rear of the M. E. Church in Soudersburg was procured, and to Mr. Burleigh was granted the privilege of lecturing therein. During the lecture eggs were thrown at the speaker. Fortunately, he escaped the missiles, but the secretary of the meeting was hit with one. The person who threw the eggs was himself hardly responsible, and when captured he gave the names of the parties who furnished the bad whisky he drank and also the eggs.

In December, 1850, Martin M. Rohrer published the first newspaper in Strasburg, called *The Strasburg Bee*. He continued it for several years, and was succeeded by Dr. George S. Whitehill. Dr. Whitehill was a scholarly man and was quite deaf. He was a great student and admirer of Shakespeare, and a very close and congenial friend of the late George W. Hensel, of Quarryville, with whose family he spent much of his time. He was a most excellent penman and bookkeeper, and finally met with a tragic death on the railroad at Erie, Pa. The *Bee* was published afterwards by W. T. McPhail, Esq., until 1855, when Samuel B. Markley became the proprietor for about one year, when the paper was discontinued. In 1858 William J. Kauffman published the Strasburg *Herald* and continued it until 1861. The office was then closed as a newspaper, but the material was purchased and continued in use as a job office by Jacob Hildebrand until 1870. That year a stock company was organized with George B. Eager as editor. He published the *Free Press* until 1879, after which J. W. Sando became the editor and publisher until 1881, when it was again discontinued.

In 1883 Frank P. Eberman purchased and renewed the office with new type and steam press and published the *Free Press* for five years. He then concluded to try farming and let the printing office take care of itself, but in March, 1890, Frank P. Hart became the publisher for about one year. Since that time no paper has been published, but an excellent job office is now carried on by John G. Homsher, Esq.

The First National Bank of Strasburg was organized in 1863, with John F. Herr as president and Edward M. Eberman cashier. The capital stock now is eighty thousand dollars, with A. R. Black, president and George W. Hensel, cashier.

During the past year a water company has been incorporated to supply the borough with spring water by gravity from the Mine Hills.

In 1857 Martin and John S. Rohrer carried on distilling in the borough and were feeding from three hundred and fifty to four hundred hogs. Disease broke out amongst them and from five to forty would die in a day. Martin concluded that the hogs were bewitched and sent for Dr. Mylin, who was considered a great witch doctor. Mr. Mylin came, burned tar, witches, &c., in a large iron pot for several days, but he did not succeed in getting them all burned, for the hogs continued to die until there were only a few left. One old farmer, a near neighbor and a great believer in "spooks" and witches, became so much interested in seeing the witches burned that he neglected to go to his dinner, but remained on the ground until some of his family persuaded him to return home and get something to eat.

In the year 1837 Wm. Echternach, Maux Fidel Gertizen and Jacob Brackbill left Strasburg on horseback and when at Paradise, about one mile west of Leaman Place, they agreed to run a race down the Lancaster turnpike and that the last one to arrive at Leaman Place would have to stand the treat. They started on the run, but Mr. Brackbill for some reason was detained on the way. Echternach and Gertizen went on at a pretty fast gait. At the bridge crossing of the Pennsylvania railroad, near Leaman Place, the turnpike and bridge formed something like the letter S. At this bridge horses and men plunged over the side of the bridge and fell about twenty feet to the bed of the railroad. Both horses and Gertizen were killed, and Echternach was very badly injured, so that he never fully recovered.

In 1840 Benjamin Barr was building a large double decker barn on his farm about midway between Martinsville and Refton and at the raising by some mishap the scaffolding gave way and a number of the men and timber fell a great distance. Jonas Long and a man named Eckman were instantly killed and others very severely injured.

IRISH OCCUPATION OF LANCASTER LAND.

"'Why did so many prominent Irish railroad contractors settle in Lancaster?' is a question frequently asked. A generation ago this would have been a more pertinent inquiry. Thirty years ago Lancaster contained many of the most noted railroad contractors of the country, and all were sons of Erin who came to this land with no fortune save with stout hearts and willing hands, with no advantages save those which they carved out for themselves from adverse circumstances. The fine old stock is fast passing away, and while yet their memory remains it may not be amiss to consider the causes which operated to bring them to a city which contained few, if any, Celtic traditions.

"These men first became noticeable in Lancaster's citizenship at the time of the building of the old 'State Road' from Philadelphia to Columbia, which was begun in 1831. All along the line of this pioneer railroad Irishmen held important construction contracts for grading and bridge building. When the time came for them to enjoy the fruits of their toil it was but natural that they should be attracted to this goodly city as permanent residents. Rev. Bernard Keenan, the kindly old pastor of St. Mary's Church, who rounded out fifty years of spiritual service in Lancaster, and whose death twenty years ago was mourned as a public loss, was also an important factor in drawing hither these Irish pioneers. His missionary labor at that time extended as far east as Downingtown, and we may eel assured that he was not blind to the advantages, spiritual and temporal, which would accrue to his needy flock by the accession of these intrepid railroad builders.

"And when they set foot on Lancaster soil they attested the permanence of their stay by at once becoming large purchasers of farm properties lying in or near the city limits. It is a noteworthy fact, remembered by many yet living, that Lancaster was at one time nearly encircled by farms owned by these pioneer Irishmen and their descendants. This will be evident when mention is made of the following group of farm owners: Richard McGrann, Michael Malone, Hugh Fitzpatrick, Patrick Kelly, Bernard Flynn, Patrick Brady, Bernard McGrann, John Kelly, John Dougherty, Patrick McEvoy, Phares Cassidy, Andrew Reilly, John McGrann, John R. McGovern, Michael Kelly and Michael Barry.

"The ownership of land has always been the laudable ambition of the best Irish immigrants. The impossibility of possession in fee simple of their native acres induced these Lancaster Irishmen to look with special favor upon the possessions of the fair lands that surrounded Lancaster city. They formed an important and substantial element in the citizenship of the county, and their influence was felt in all that concerned the moral and material interests of the home of their adoption."

Was there ever a Serious Idea of Locating the Capital of the Country on the Susquehanna?

"On the 7th of March, 1789, Jasper Yeates, who was a prominent jurist of Pennsylvania, resident in Lancaster, sen to the Federal Congress, on behalf of the corporation of Lancaster a lengthy communication setting forth reasons why Lancaster should be selected as the permanent place of residence for the Federal Congress. The original of this paper is in the possession of D. McN. Stauffer, of New York, and it was published in the Lancaster *Intelligencer* December 29, 1886, as part of an address by Mr. Hensel before the Lancaster Board of Trade. The argument upon the selection of a site for the Federal capital began in the Federal House on September 3, 1789, and was, according to McMaster, "one of the longest and most acrimonious the members had yet engaged in." Every one of the fifty-nine had something to say ; and, though the eastern members were indisposed to consider the subject, being driven to it, they caucused with the representatives from the Middle States, and concluded that the capital, keeping close to the centre of population, wealth and territory, and with easy connections with the Atlantic and Ohio river, should be located at least somewhere on the east bank of the Susquehanna. When Lee challenged the advocates of this plan to name a place meeting these requirements, it was then the claims of our own Columbia were presented. Says the historian: "Hartley took him at his word and answered him. Wright's Ferry was such a town. It stood upon the east bank some thirty-five miles from sea water. As for the Susquehanna, so great was the volume of its waters that ships could at any time of year sail up it to the waters of Otsego lake. Three fine rivers ran into it from the north, the west and the south. The Tioga was navigable for a great distance, and was connected by an easy portage with the Genessee, which emptied into Lake Ontario. The Juniata nearly connected with the Kiskiminetas, and that with the Ohio. A short land-carriage joined the head of the west branch with the Allegheny, which gave easy connections with the frontier towns of Kentucky. As to the town, it was no mean place. But ten miles separated Wright's Ferry from the greatest city of America. The climate was salubrious. The soil and the river yielded plentifully. If the honorable gentleman was disposed to give attention to a dish of fish he could find none finer than could be drawn from the waters of the Susquehanna. 'Then, why not,' said Lee, 'go at once to Yorktown?' Why fix on the banks of a swift river when it is possible to occupy the shores of Codorus creek?'

"He was assured by Goodhue that the Susquehanna was much to be preferred. There was the centre of territory. The centre of population, it was true, lay to the northward. But the eastern members were ready from a spirit of conciliation to let that pass. They well knew that the centre of population would not change for ages, and that when it did the movement would be to the eastward, not to the south; to the manufacturing, not to the agricultural States."

The passionate southerners protested, and there was much mind measuring of the relative distances of points north and outh, east and west to Wright's Ferry.

Peach Bottom was even named as a compromise. The proposition to appoint a commission to select a spot on the banks of the Susquehanna prevailed by 28 to 21 after days of ill-natured debate. The Senate amended the bill and made the location one mile from Philadelphia. The House sullenly concurred and adjourned. It was nearly a year later that the vote was reconsidered and the capital site fixed on the Potomac.

AN INTERESTING PAPER.

On behalf of Mr. Ambrose Pownall, of Sadsbury township, W. U. Hensel presented to the Society two pages from the magistrate's record of the late Joseph D. Pownall, J. P., of Sadsbury township, upon which was recorded the Coroner's inquest upon the body of Edward Gorsuch, the Maryland slaveholder, who was killed in what passed into history as "The Christiana Riot," an account of which was the subject of an interesting paper some months ago read before the Society by Thomas Whitson, Esq. The following is a transcription of this inquest:

LANCASTER COUNTY, ss.:

"An inquisition indented taken at Sadsbury township, in the county of Lancaster, the 11th day of September, A. D. 1851, before me, Joseph D. Pownall, Esq., for the county of Lancaster, upon the view of the body of a man then and there lying dead, supposed to be Edward Gorsuch, of Baltimore county, Maryland, upon the affirmations of George Whitson, John Rowland, E. Osborne Dare, Hiram Kinnard, Samuel Miller, Lewis Cooper, George Firth, William Knott, John Hillis, William H. Millhouse, Joseph Richwine and Miller Knott, good and lawful men of the county aforesaid, who, being duly affirmed and charged to enquire on the part of the Commonwealth when, where and how the said deceased came to his death, do say upon their affirmations that on the morning of the 11th inst. the neighborhood was thrown into an excitement by the above deceased and five or six persons in company with him, making an attack upon a family of colored persons living in said township near the brick mill, about four o'clock in the morning, for the purpose of arresting some fugitive slaves, as they alleged many of the colored people of the neighborhood collected, and there was considerable firing of guns and other firearms by both parties. Upon the arrival of some of the neighbors at the place after the riot had subsided, found the above deceased lying on his back or right side dead. Upon a post-mortem examination made by Drs. Patterson and Martin in our presents, we believe he came to his death by gun shot wounds that he received in the above mentioned riot caused by some person or persons to us unknown.

In witness whereof as well as the aforesaid justice, as the jurors aforesaid, have to this inquisition put their seals on the day and year and at the place first aforementioned."

    JOSEPH D. POWNALL, Esq.

George Whitson (L. S.), John Hillis (L. S.), John Rowland (L. S.), William Knott (L. S.), E. Osborne Dare (L. S.), Samuel Miller (L. S.), Lewis Cooper (L. S.), Joseph Richwine (L. S.), Hiram Kinnard (L. S.), George Firth (L. S.), Wm. H. Millhouse (L. S.), Miller Knott (L. S.)

Some of the names of the jury are strongly suggestive of Quaker origin, and the language of the verdict indicates their sympathy with the anti-slavery cause. In offering the paper, Mr. Hensel emphasized the great historical interest which attached to this event. The occurrence has almost passed out of the common mind, and yet, in its day, this riot threatened to provoke such a conflagration of war as subsequently followed the "John Brown raid." Gorsuch was of a conspicuous family in Maryland, and his brother was an Episcopal minister, who most severely arraigned the civil authorities of Pennsylvania for their supineness in allowing the murderers of his brother to escape. Wm. F. Johnson was at that time Governor of Pennsylvania, having as Speaker of the Senate succeeded ex-officio to Francis R. Shunk, who died in the gubernatorial office. The riot occurred in the midst of that campaign, and it is said that Johnson, who was in Philadelphia at the time, passed westward on the railroad without stopping at Christiana, where the dead body of Gorsuch lay. He was a Whig and was charged with permitting his anti-slavery sympathies to weaken his enforcement of law as an executive; and so strong was the pro-slavery feeling at the time in Pennsylvania that the incident is said to have largely contributed to his defeat by Bigler, the opposing Democratic candidate.

A WILLIAM PENN DEED.

In answer to a referred question as to what is a "William Penn Deed," Mr. Hensel exhibited an original deed from William Penn for three hundred and seventy-five acres of land situated in that portion of the "Chester Valley" which runs through Lancaster county beginning at Quarryville. It is signed with the genuine signature of William Penn himself and is written on stout parchment, with his seal. The full text of the deed is as follows, and the land, therein described rather indefinitely, comprises the tract upon which Ambrose Pownall now resides, east of Nobleville in the township of Sadsbury:

"This Indenture witnesseth yt William Penn of Horminghurst in the county of Sussex, Elgd., for & in consideration of Twelve pounds four shillings to him in hand paid Hath by these presents granted Three Hundred Seventy-five acres of Land Cleare of Indian incom-branches in the Province of Penusylvania (towards the Susquehanna River) to John Kennerley of Shavingta, County, Chester cheese factor his heirs and assignees & him there of enfeoffed every acre to be computed according to the statute of ye thirty-third of King Edward the First to have and to hold to him his heires and assignes for ever together with all & every the Lands Isles Islands Mynes Mineralls (Royall one Excepted) woods fishings hawkings fowlings & all other Royalltyes profits comodityes & hereditaments insoever unto the same —belouging Yielding & paying therefore yearly and every year unto the sd William Penn his heirs and assignes imediatly from and after the expiration of the first five years next after the day of the date hereof the Rent of one shilling for every hundred acres of the sd Three hundred seventy five acres NEVERTHELESS the sd William Penn for himself his heirs & assignes dote agree to & with the said John Kennerley his heirs and assignes yt ye sd Rent of one shilling for every hundred acres of ye sd three hundred seventy five acres is only to becum due & payable imediatly from & after the taking up & seating of ye sd lands & not before & proporeanably for ye sd rate for every Quantity there of yt shall he taken up & seated & not otherwise, & the said William Penn hath Made Thomas Loyd Robert Turner Willm Markeham Arthur Cooke John Goodson Samuel Jenings Samuel Carpenter or any three of them to Deliver Seven thereof accordingly in Witness where of the sd Willm Penn hath here unto sett his hand & seale this Sixtenth Day of ye fifth Month Called July In ye year of our Lord One thousand six hundred Ninety one.

      WM PENN [Seal]
 Signed sealed and delivered in the presence of us
     SUSANNA MORRY
     JEAN X JEND
       her mark
Wm Penn to John Kennerley.

REUBEN CHAMBERS.

The subject of this sketch was adorned from childhood with the neither euphonious nor fashionable name of Reuben—Reuben Chambers. He was born about the beginning of the present century in London Grove township, Chester county, Pa., and resided there until he reached manhood.

He was of Quaker parentage and inherited many of the well-known traits of that sect, who are noted for their high moral character, general intelligence and their desire to investigate things for themselves and not take their opinions from others.

Reuben received a good common school education, and being fond of reading and investigating continued to learn all his life. He had great faith, moreover, in his own ability and would tackle without hesitation every new question or ism or doctrine that sprung up, no matter how weighty or difficult it might be, and after making up his mind about it would defend his conclusions with great zeal. It must be confessed, however, that Reuben had many novel ideas and queer ways of doing things. For example, his mode of securing a wife was quite unique. It was related by himself about as follows: "When I got old enough to think about marriage I got myself a neat memorandum book to carry in my pocket. Whenever I saw a girl that I thought would be suitable I entered her name and residence in this book, and when I had about twenty names I started in to get acquainted with them. In this I did not adopt the usual plan and call on the girls in the evening when their work was done and they were presumably fixed up. I called in the day time when they were at work or should be; many of them I found at the wash tub. I never remained very long and could generally make up my mind in one or two visits whether they would suit me or not. When I decided that any one would not suit I crossed her name off, but in the meantime continued to add new names as at first. I continued this until my book contained about eighty names, and all but one was crossed. I was then ready to marry. So I went to see her and told her I wanted to marry and believed her the most suitable girl for me that I was acquainted with, and that if she was willing to marry me I should be very glad. She said she was willing, so we were married very soon." Mrs. Chambers' maiden name was Christiana Lefever and she was born and raised near Hopewell borough, Chester county, Pa. I think the general notion of the neighbors was that Christiana made him a very faithful wife, notwithstanding her methodical and business-like courtship.

Reuben began life as a school teacher and about 1829 or 1830 came into Lancaster county and started a subscription school (there being then no free school) in a small village on the road from Strasburg to the Gap, about two miles west of the latter place. Reuben baptized the village Bethania, but it was more generally known in the neighborhood as Puddingtown.

I have not been able to find any one who went to Reuben's school at this time, but believe he was fairly successful with it. At the end of the first year, however, the image of the maiden whose name alone stood out unmarked among her seventy-nine crossed off sisters in the little book he carried in his inside vest pocket grew so vivid that Reuben could no longer resist its mute appeals, and having meantime purchased the house in which he taught the school and a few acres of land with it, he went back to Chester county and soon returned with his bride to Bethania.

Reuben's marriage seemed to stir him with higher ambitions and stimulate him to attempt greater achievements than fall to the lot of the humble teacher, and having a taste for printing and as he believed a talent for writing, he allowed his school to close and providing himself with material for a small printing office began to do small jobs of printing.

His ambition now was to edit and publish a great newspaper which should educate and elevate mankind, and he consequently tackled all sorts of isms and doctrines. In religion he became a Free Thinker; in earthly matters a Communist, and in everything else a little different from those he met with. Reuben's Lancaster county neighbors didn't take much stock in new isms or doctrines and hadn't time to chop logic or split hairs with him on subjects they neither knew nor cared about and it was not long until they came to regard him as a pestilent, quarrelsome fanatic; an infidel and a totally impracticable crank, with whom the less they had to do the better.

The charges of infidelity and crankiness were not without foundation, but it cannot be fairly said that he was quarrelsome, though the pertinacity with which he adhered to an argument and the fact that the hotter it became the better it seemed to suit him naturally gave rise to this opinion. Reuben was very fond of discussion and would miss a meal any time to argue a question, though in these discussions he was usually good humored and fair. Many of Reuben's ideas were far ahead of his time and surroundings; for example, on finance he was 100 years ahead of either Greenbackers, Populists, Gold Bugs or Silverities. He held that as labor was the source of all wealth, the money or currency of the country should directly represent the labor and not by the indirect method of reckoning it in dollars and cents. To reduce this theory to actual practice he printed a series of notes reading as follows:

No. 14.   AMERICAN PRODUCT.   10
Letter 1.   Picture of   Hours.
      Car, Tender and Locomotive.

TEN HOURS.   The bearer is entitled to receive on demand Ten Hours Labor of the BETHANIA MANUAL LABOR and MANUFACTURING COMMUNITY, or an equivalent in goods the product of the Community at the Magazine.
Bethania, January 1st, 1837.
           REUBEN CHAMBERS,
                       Director.

These notes were made in all denominations from six minutes to twenty hours and perhaps higher, but that is the highest I ever saw. It will be readily seen that while the world was being converted to Reuben's system of currency he must in order to have it circulate with other money fix a rate for its valuation in dollars and cents. While Reuben strongly regretted this, he admitted its necessity and fixed the rates at five cents per hour, which at that time, 1837, was about the price paid for ordinary farm labor. The notes, therefore, reduced to dollars and cents ran as follows:

6 minute note, ½ cent.
12 minute note, 1 cent.
1 hour note, 5 cents.
10 hour note, 50 cents.
20 hour note, 100 cents.

Many issues of these notes were made. I have in my possession one of 10 hours or 50 cents, printed in 1858, and Mr. J. M. W. Geist, of THE NEW ERA, has one of 12 minutes, dated 1842.

He also set apart a small room in his house as a magazine in which to store the products of the community and got so far as to dig part of a cellar for the contemplated magazine, but it stopped there and never got farther. I might say here that both the Bethania Manual Labor and Manufacturing Community and the magazine were purely imaginary and never had any existence except as above stated. Reuben never learned any trade, but was a natural Jack of all trades. He was a tolerable carpenter, wagon maker, harness maker, tooth puller, painter, plasterer, potter and indeed almost anything that did not require much exertion, for he could not be charged with any extraordinary fondness for hard work. He preferred thinking to working, and in pursuance of this preference soon discovered that a newspaper run on different lines from any then issued was absolutely necessary and that he was the man to furnish it.

So on 6th day, 6th month, 8th, 1832, he issued the first or specimen number, calling it the *Bethania Palladium.*

An extract from the prospectus reads: "The *Palladium* will therefore advocate universal peace, freedom, temperance and the just rights of man. It will encourage husbandry, manufactures and the arts; it will also encourage public schools for the education of the youth and will particularly plead the cause of the poor and oppressed."

And in his leading editorial he says: "When I consider myself that I have never wrought in any printing office one hour except my own, being self-taught in the business and especially having never done anything at printing a newspaper before, I must ask to be excused for any inconsistency or omission on these accounts. His second number was issued 6th day, 7th month, 27th, 1832, seven weeks after the first number, and thereafter during its existence of about two years at uncertain intervals of one to three weeks.

The paper was intensely anti-slavery, anti-Masonic, anti-Jackson, anti-lotteries and anti-horse racing, this last feature getting him into innumerable wrangles which he seemed to thoroughly enjoy, for Reuben was at home in a scolding match.

A great feature of the *Palladium* was its number of departments, though they were not at all uniform in the different numbers. When Reuben saw an article he wanted to publish and had no department that seemed to exactly fit it, he at once made one. For example, I find in one issue the following departments: Education department, Indians' department, anti-slavery department, peace department, temperance department, gamblers' department, political department, farmers' department, news department, advertising department, didactic department, ladies' department, mechanics' department, youths' department.

Reuben had no patience with fun or sport of any kind, even on the part of boys, and in his issue of November 2, 1832, thus curries down some of the village lads who had been enjoying Hallowe'en: "The evening before last was that termed Hallowe'en, which is devoted to night raking by the mischievous, owlish boobies, who pretend that they take a pleasure in pulling up their neighbor's cabbage, over-turning privies and yelping about the hills like a set of crazy fools."

On a later occasion the village tavern keeper, John Rockey, made a fox hunt from his hotel of which Reuben delivered himself as follows: "With feelings of disapprobation I have witnessed the collecting together of a number of my neighbors to-day to have a chase after a Bag Fox with their half bound canine breed of yelpers that look their masters in the face and try to bark after the fox was far enough over the mountain, fully evincing their knowledge of hunting to be about equal to that of their owners." This was copiously embellished with italics and small caps, and he continued : "Is not this altogether a scheme of tavern keepers to entice the young, the thoughtless, the idle, the vain, the unstable, the wavering and light-minded to flock to and rendezvous at these places, drink grog and be gulled out of their clear cash? Is not this low-minded custom a breach of our laws and ought it not to be frowned out of countenance till it be altogether done away?" The tavern keeper promptly sued Reuben for $1.24½ he owed him, and the resulting wrangle furnished editorial matter for the *Palladium* for some time, as well as enabling Reuben to free his mind as to the tavern keeper and some of the other participants in the fox hunt.

The *Palladium* had always been very free in criticising what it called the Lancaster Jockey Club, and especially its treasurer, one Edward Parker, and probably for this reason arrangements were made in September, 1833, for some racing on the top of the Mine Ridge, about a mile from the office of the *Palladium*. Then the cup of Reuben's wrath overflowed and he was compelled to issue a supplement of a half sheet printed on one side to express himself, which he did in a lengthy article entitled, "The Lower Regions, or a Second Sodom," in very large type.

Reuben's charges against the horse race were that they had a number of tables from which whisky and other liquors were sold ; that there were three gaming tables, one of which was kept by

John Bowman, of Strasburg; that there were gamblers there from New Jersey who swindled much money from the poor Irish railroaders (the State road then being built), and that he saw several men and one woman lying in fence corners dead drunk.

Reuben also gave considerable attention to a certain Judge Lightner, who lived in Williamstown, and who he claimed could have prevented the racing and would not.

Reuben not only wrote the editorial and local matter appearing in the *Palladium*, but to a large extent set the type, made up the forms and printed the edition on an old hand press. He was also an author, as I can attest, for I took my first lesson in a blue-covered primer compiled and printed by him, and want to say for him that it was a very good primer, arranged in a scientific manner and quite the equal of some modern books with more pictures. This opinion is not founded on my early researches, but from subsequent examination of the primer. He also took up the Thompsonian System of Medicine and practiced it upon himself and anybody else that would let him (though they were not numerous), and wrote, printed and published quite a large and pretentious work entitled "The Thomsonian System and Practice of Medicine," which he sold for $2, if he ever did sell any.

I have read this medical work to some extent, but the only thing I can now recall in it was its strong recommendation of quill toothpicks in preference to all others, with detailed instructions for making them. He also engaged largely in compounding Thompsonian medicines, for which purpose he purchased from the village boys during the summer months vast quantities of herbs and weeds of every obtainable kind (the Thompsonian preparations being purely vegetable), paying for the same in the labor notes he issued.

He also carried on a pottery for making stovepipe guards, crocks, jars, etc., but they were mainly used for holding the weeds and liquors while he was brewing and compounding the Thompsonian medicines.

The most popular and best remembered of these preparations was known as No. 6, and the triple extract of the strongest cayenne or red pepper couldn't hold a candle to No. 6 for biting and burning properties. It was used extensively for toothache, and was pretty effective, for after you put it in your mouth it took an hour or so to convince you that mouth, teeth and all were not burned away.

Bread of Life, a hot biting candy, was popular with the children.

My first personal acquaintance with Reuben was in the fall of 1850. It seemed that in the spring of that year Reuben had hauled down to a mill in the western part of the village of Christiana, then run by a certain John Boone, an ox cart load of dried sumac berries, leaves and twigs, and left them to be ground. The stuff was packed in coffee and salt sacks and piled up in one corner of the mill. Boone's lease of the mill expired soon after and he did not grind the sumac. He was succeeded in the mill by a Samuel Harley, who would not grind it, and in the fall of the year I, an over-grown boy of eighteen, was appointed to teach the village school at Christiana, and I secured boarding with the miller, Harley. Very many of those coming to the mill would inquire what was in those sacks, and being told it was sumac belonging to Reuben Chambers, would at once cut a slit in the sack to see what it was like. To prevent the stuff from running all over the floor Harley would turn the cut side round against the other sacks and the next inquirer would cut a fresh slit for himself.

Harley, on learning that I was going up to Bethania one Saturday, made me promise to call on Chambers and tell him that he would not grind the sumac and if he did not come down and take it away he would throw it out.

I called on Reuben and delivered the message and he said he would come down in a day or two. He came and of course discovered how his sacks were cut up. He went home and the next day a man came with the oxcart for the sumac and Reuben came with a large roll of flaring hand bills, which he proceeded to put up all over the village and neighborhood, offering $50 reward for information as to the guilty parties and paying his respects to them as follows:

"There was left in the third month (March) last at J. G. Ernst's mill, while said mill was in the occupancy of John Boone, a number of bags of mine, since which some rascally, good-for-nothing biped puppy brute scoundrel (all without commas), one or more such did since then with an instrument to me unknown cut a number of holes in several of them to the great loss and detriment of the owner and greatly against the public peace and the laws of this Commonwealth."

Reuben was never called on for the reward, as I suppose half the adult males of the village and all the boys had at one time or another investigated the sumac.

I removed to Bethania in the spring of 1853, and a year afterwards our family came there to live, so I got quite well acquainted with Reuben. He had long before that given up the newspaper, which had surely lost him considerable money, but he still continued the printing office, doing such job work as came to him.

In printing sale bills he insisted on saying that the sale would be *in* instead of *on* a particular day, and he spelled cook stove kook, with other similar improvements as Reuben termed them, but it led to frequent squabbles with customers who desired him to follow copy. Reuben's rules, however, were ironclad, and no bills left his office without the improvements.

For several years about this time we had a lyceum at the Bethania school house which I think was the strongest in the county. Sylvester Kennedy, father of Horace E. Kennedy, of *The Morning News*, was its president, and Thomas Whitson, father of our lawyer of the same name, Dr. W. H. Boone, Henry Umble, J. Williams Thorne and Major Ellwood Griest, of the *Inquirer*, all practiced debaters, were among the members. Reuben was prominent in this lyceum, but was not a ready or effective speaker and therefore when he wanted to do his best wrote out his speeches and read them.

On one occasion a heavy debate was on hand on the well-worn question of abolishing capital punishment, and Reuben prepared for it by writing out a lengthy speech. When he got up to deliver it the lights did not seem to suit him. He changed positions several times, but it would not work. He then got his high silk hat, which he wore for this occasion, and put it on to shade his eyes, and the irreverent small boy snickered thereat, but even the hat improvement would not answer the purpose. So Reuben got his old style tin lantern which he never went without at night; it was all tin, with slits and holes in the tin to let some light out. He deliberately lighted this lantern and hugging it to his side, and opening its door to let the light shine on his manuscript, started to find his place. By this time the house was in a roar, but Reuben was serene as a sunflower, paid no attention to the uproar and soon as he could be heard started again on his speech. When his time expired he wrangled with the president for charging him for the time spent on the lantern, but the president did not allow his decisions to be disputed and promptly seated Reuben, much to his disgust.

Outside of a real hot scolding match Reuben liked nothing so well as an opportunity to practice his system of medicine and about this time he managed to secure a rare opportunity. The victim was a German man living in the neighborhood of Oregon, this county. How or where Reuben met him I never learned nor can I recall the man's name, but he was troubled with rheumatism and Reuben undertook his cure. So he came down home and at once commenced the erection of a steam chest. This occupied a couple of weeks, during which I saw nothing of him. One afternoon a small girl who lived with them came up to the store and said Reuben wanted me to come down, he wanted to show me something, and the others present, she said, might come too. Several of us went down and she told us to go back into the kitchen. We went and there was Reuben in this box. The top lid was made to fit tightly around his neck, and his face, which was outside the box, was as red as blood and had a most agonizing expression. I supposed he was being choked to death and I dashed at the lid to try to relieve him, but he shouted to me not to touch it; that he was taking a steam bath. I said, "Why, your face shows you are suffering great agony," and he replied, "Thee knows nothing ab ut it; the sensation is just delightful." I presume that he exposed himself improperly after this bath, for I met him the next day and he was quite hoarse. I said, "Reuben, your steam bath seems to have given you a cold." He flew into a towering rage at once and said, "Thee's a liar. It is not a cold at all. Just a little roughness in the throat and the bath had no connection with it whatever." In a few days Reuben appeared upon the street one afternoon. He had a market wagon, in which was loaded this steam chest with the necessary pipes and fixings and upon either side of the wagon were strips of white muslin the whole length of the wagon, and say, eighteen inches wide, on which printed in large letters were these lines:

"There is balm in Gilead
And a physician there—"

a seeming answer to the Biblical question. And thus equipped he started to Oregon to cure his patient. Reuben would never say much about this case afterward, and I never learned whether he steamed the man or not, but one thing is sure, it did not take the man or his friends long to get the measure of Reuben's medical knowledge, for I think that was his only visit to Oregon.

Reuben, while never suspected of any undue intimacy with Amos Clemson, whose house was recognized as the headquarters of the notorious Gap gang, had always been on friendly terms with him and after Clemson's conviction, and in the absence of any near relations took charge of his property. Clemson's place was about two and a-half miles east of Bethania, and while down there picking apples on Tuesday, September 27, 1859, he fell from a tree and injured himself very seriously. He was brought home, but none of his neighbors were informed of his condition, nor would Reuben permit any physician to be called. He was treated by his wife under his own direction, and growing rapidly worse died on Saturday, October 1.

His funeral took place on the following Tuesday, when a short but very sensible address was delivered at the house by his aged mother, a very fine-looking and intellectual old lady. The remains were interred in the burying ground of "Old Sadsbury," a well-known Friends Meeting House, near the Lancaster and Chester county line, in Sadsbury township, this county.

SAMUEL BOWMAN AND THE VILLAGE HE FOUNDED.

On the largest tombstone in the Mennonite graveyard in the rear of the new Mennonite Church, near the village of Bowmansville, is the following inscription:

"In memory of
SAMUEL BOWMAN;
Was born December 1, 1789.
Died, January 19, 1857;
Aged 67 years, 1 month and 18 days.
Here rest the ashes of the founder of the village of Bowmansville, the capital of Brecknock."

Mr. Bowman was born at Bowman's Mill, in Allegheny Valley, Berks county, on the first day of December, 1789. His father was a Swiss Mennonite, whose ancestors had emigrated to America on account of the religious persecution that followed the revocation of the Edict of Nantes by Louis XIV. His mother was Nancy Huber. Of his early years little is known, except what we learn from John B. Good, who knew him more intimately than any one else. He tells us that his mother in early childhood noticed that he was different from the rest of the children and was much concerned about him, not knowing whether his peculiarities indicated mental vigor or imbecility. As soon as he was sent to school, however, it became evident that he had a natural fondness for learning, and he soon made such progress that he far outstripped all his schoolmates. English schools had no existence in those days in the vicinity where Bowman was born and raised. The only language heard in his father's family or for many miles around was Pennsylvania German. He, however, studiously applied himself to the study of English and with the aid of the best dictionaries to be had he made wonderful progress. After he attained all the knowledge he could from the crude country school of his neighborhood, he attended the Churchtown Academy, where he had the opportunity of learning to converse in English. Here he studied surveying, which he afterward so extensively and successfully practiced for many years, and in which he attained much skill and accuracy. His clear head and logical mind were eminently fitted for practical geometry. His love of justice and equity, and his high character for honesty and uprightness of purpose all combined to make him afterwards the most successful surveyor in the northeastern end of the county. In his library were found some of the best classical authors in the English language. From 1815 to 1820 he was during the winter months engaged in teaching school. Surveying, scrivening and ordinary labor took up the rest of his time. As a teacher he acquired a wonderful reputation among his neighbors for the great amount of knowledge he possessed, and was especially famous for his success in keeping good order and governing his school. Some of his pupils are still living, and acquainted as they are with modern school discipline, say, "It was not so in Sam Bowman's school." His life was one of constant and unremitting toil of mind and body. He had a laudable ambition to be esteemed a correct and competent business man, and all who knew him and had any business transactions with him can bear testimony to the ability and honesty with which his affairs were conducted. He was a man of great power and worth, the ideal leader and adviser around whom his neighbors flocked for advice ; the centre of a community which he founded; the father any settlement may be proud of. Like the mighty oak in a great forest, he was the giant among those who gathered around him. I am digressing from my subject, but no sketch of any place is completed unless something is known of the founder. It is true, most admirable biographical sketches of this marvelous man appear in several of our county histories, but his noble, rugged character is deserving of a wider acquaintance, and for that reason I have at some length referred to him. In 1820 Mr. Bowman built a house on the southeast corner where the road leading from Reamstown to the Plow Tavern crossed the State road. The house was arranged for keeping a country store. Here he commenced the mercantile business immediately after the building was finished, and was succeeded by his son-in-law, Jonas Musselman, and he in turn by his son, J. B. Musselman, who does a flourishing business at the old stand to-day. This was the first house of the now thriving village and from whence the name of the place was derived. Martin Bowman erected the second house, Daniel Bowman the third, and John B. Good and Peter B. Good followed with substantial stone buildings. The latter built upon the northwest corner of the cross roads and opened a hotel, the only public house the place ever had. Now the village contains over a hundred houses, many of beautiful, modern design, four churches—two Mennonite, a Lutheran and Reformed, an Evangelical Methodist—and a handsome, substantial two-story school house. In 1840, just twenty years after the first house was erected, a post-office was established at Bowman's store and named Bowmansville. Mr. Bowman was appointed Postmaster, the only office, outside of Justice of the Peace, he would accept, the latter only for the convenience of acknowledging his official papers. The establishing of a post-office and naming it after the founder, with the attachment of ville to it, was a fortunate occurrence, for by it the place received its baptism by the authority of the Department at Washington, or else more than likely the village would be known to-day by the inelegant title of Buckstown.

About a mile southeast of the then hamlet lived an old bachelor, Samuel Good. He was an eccentric old hermit, whose chief delight was in a flock of sheep, but he had a singular hatred for any sheep which was so unfortunate as to have black wool. In other words, he had more contempt for a black sheep than for his satanic majesty. This the villagers knew, and one morning as Good viewed his flock he was amazed to find a black buck among them. He accused certain ones from the town of having perpetrated the joke, and from that morning on he called it Buckstown, or, in Pennsylvania German, Buckstettle. The name stuck to it like wax and is now and then heard yet when one wants to refer to the place in a contemptuous way.

One of the "eyesores" to many of the village people was the Mennonite meeting house that stood on the square for many years. From 1870 to 1880 the village enjoyed quite a building boom and the real estate became too valuable for hitching posts and was sold, the old stone building or meeting house removed and a new one erected by members of the Mennonite Church near Von Neida's mill, about a mile south of the village. In one end of the old church lived for many years an old woman, whose name I have forgotten. She was the sexton of the meeting house and a terror to the boys who played upon the village green. In this quaint old house of worship preached for many years, every fourth Sunday, Jacob Moseman, a learned Prussian Lutheran, who forsook that church and joined the Mennonites, and was undoubtedly the ablest minister that church ever had in the eastern end of the county. The hitching posts and the old shed upon the village green were never sufficient to accommodate all the teams when Moseman's turn came to preach. In 1854 a new Mennonite meeting house was erected several hundred yards south of the village on the edge of a grove of magnificent pines. But three partly decayed trees remain, standing as sentinels of the many giants that stood there half a century ago. The new church has had but few members since its organization forty-five years ago. It was originally supplied by ministers from Montgomery and Bucks counties, but in 1860 Rev. Solomon Ott was ordained and has proclaimed the gospel for thirty-six years in the little church beside the pine grove. On the same road north of the town stood the little stone school house, now the site of the handsome school building of the town. Here Brecknock's fight for the free school system was repeated. What occurred in every other of the little temples of learning, the story of which when told is as interesting as Eggleston's "Hoosier Schoolmaster." From 1820, when Bowman built the first house, up to 1860, a period of forty years, the village made but very little improvement. Bowman's store and dwelling, the hotel, the residence erected by John B. Good on the northeast corner of the cross roads and now occupied by 'Squire Stover, a brick dwelling a little north of Good's house and then occupied by Joseph Musselman, another brick house west of the hotel erected by Jonas Musselman and occupied by his son, Israel, the dwelling, shoemaker shop and tin shop that stood on the edge of the hitching post ground of the Mennonite Church, and occupied by Benjamin Lausch, the village shoemaker, and his son, Reuben, the tinsmith of the hamlet, the farm buildings of Daniel Bowman, another most substantial and large dwelling house then occupied by Jacob Hoover and now by Michael Witmer, and a brick dwelling now owned by G. L. Bowman, of Reading, and occupied by John M. Weaver, were all the houses the village contained when the civil war broke out in 1861. Reuben Lausch, who hammered tin in the second story of his father's house and later in a commodious shop erected near his residence, was a man of far more than ordinary ability. He not only illuminated the homes of the neighborhood with the first coal oil lamps, but his genial, well-informed mind was a source of delight to the young men who gathered in his shop to listen to his interesting talks. In 1861 the war excitement created a stir in the village that was not surpassed by any other in the county. An immense pole was erected and a large flag flung to the breeze. This suggested the idea to some one that the village ought to have a large bell. A tall pole with a frame was put up on the corner of the tin shop, a bell hung in the frame, and for many years the shoemaker or the tinsmith rang the bell morning, noon and night, and also at the death of any one in the entire neighborhood. At the tolling of the bell for some one's funeral it broke; the second was bought but broke when put in place; the third was purchased and put upon a new frame erected in the rear of the old Bowman store stand, where the custom of ringing the meal time hour three times a day to all the inhabitants for miles around is still observed. This quaint observance is part of the daily life of the village, to which everyone has become so used that to do without it would be like omitting an event of the day. No township in the county witnessed such exciting times as Brecknock did during the war. The district was strongly slavery, and contained many outspoken disloyal men who would defiantly at any public gathering yell for the Confederacy. Many of them were densely illiterate and had no more conception of the principle at stake than they had of the French revolution. The inhabitants of the capital of Brecknock, to their lasting honor and credit, were all loyal and stood by the flag that floated from the village flag staff. The Silver Hill rebels, as they were called by the villagers, were a terror to all law-abiding people. Philip Huber, the Berks county chief and organizer of the Knights of the Golden Circle, or Enemies in the Rear, came to Bowmansville and held a public meeting at the hotel then kept by Samuel Eshleman. The Saturday afternoon was a memorable event for the loyal people of the town. Huber, surrounded by several hundred of disloyal, cowardly enemies in the rear, many of whom came across the line from Berks county, was in his glory, and made the most treasonable speech that was ever publicly delivered in Lancaster county. The excitement was intense. This was the same Huber who afterwards was arrested at a public sale and put upon a rail and ridden to Reamstown, followed by all the people at the sale. And later when he marched to Reading at the head of the Heidelberg brigade was run out by the fire engines which he thought were cannons. The first political meeting ever held in the village was a Lincoln meeting in 1860. The speech making took place from the porch of John B. Good's house opposite the hotel. The New Holland band was present and caused an unusual crowd to assemble. Brecknock has reversed herself politically, and to no cause can the result be attributed so much as to the disgusting, treasonable expressions of those who were in open sympathy with the Confederacy, and yet too cowardly to go and assist them. The fight for free schools and war times in Brecknock would make a subject for an interesting volume. As Bowmansville has improved, so has the township, and to-day no more thrifty, honest, conscientious and enterprising people are to be found anywhere in the county than in Brecknock.

COMMITTEES.

The following standing committees were announced in accordance with a resolution offered at the October meeting, and also an additional one on Indians and Indian Relics :

A resolution to print the names of these committees in the Society's next publication was carried.

Committees.

Archæology : Dr. Joseph H. Dubbs, Dr. N. C. Shaeffer, Prof. H. J. Roddy.

Topography : S. M. Sener, D. W. Gerhard, Dr. J. H. Sieling.

Periodicals : R. M. Reilly, Thos. B. Cochran, C. S. Foltz.

Bibliography : A. F. Hostetter, Dr. Jos. H. Dubbs, Chas. A. Heinitsh.

Biography : B. C. Atlee, Alfred C. Bruner, W. N. Appel.

Forestry Statistics : Simon P. Eby, Dr. II. F. Bitner, W. A. Heitshue.

Political History : W. U. Hensel, Thos. Whitson, Chas. I. Landis.

Scientific Research : Miss Anna Lyle, Daniel H. Heitshu, Adam Geist.

Church History: Rev. John W. Hassler, Rev. C. F. Eberman, A. E. Witmer.

Education : Wm. Riddle, M. J. Brecht, Dr. E. O. Lyte.

Nomenclature : Dr. M. W. Raub, Dr. H. E. Muhlenburg, Geo. F. K. Erisman.

Local Records : Edward P. Brinton, John B. Eshleman, Mrs. Lydia D. Zell.

Indians and Indian Relics : Peter C. Hiller, Dr. J. S. Stahr, Henry B. Shuman.

PAPERS READ

BEFORE THE

LANCASTER COUNTY HISTORICAL SOCIETY,

ON DEC. 4, 1896.

WHEN WAS STRASBURGH ERECTED INTO
A TOWNSHIP.
BY SAMUEL EVANS, ESQ.

REMINISCENCES OF PARADISE TOWNSHIP.
BY A. E. WITMER.

AN OLD PETITION FROM CITIZENS OF MARTIC
TOWNSHIP.
BY SAMUEL EVANS, ESQ.

SOME EARLY COUNTY MILLS, ETC., ETC.
BY SAMUEL EVANS, ESQ.

OFFICERS OF THE SOCIETY FOR 1896.

LANCASTER, PA.
REPRINTED FROM THE NEW ERA.
1896.

When was Strasburgh Erected into a Township ?
BY SAMUEL EVANS, ESQ.,....................................146

Reminiscences of Paradise Township,
BY A. E. WITMER,...150

An Old Petition from Citizens of Martic Township,
BY SAMUEL EVANS, ESQ.,....................................160

Some Early County Mills, etc., etc.,
BY SAMUEL EVANS, ESQ.,....................................167

Officers of the Society for 1896...................................176

WHEN WAS STRASBURG ERECTED INTO A TOWNSHIP?

When I came to arrange some stray notes pertaining to the early settlement of the locality embraced within the limits of Strasburg township as it was bounded one hundred and sixty-five years ago, I found a good many snags in my way. Some of the earliest settlers came from Strasburg on the Rhine, and the neighborhood came to be known as "New Strasburge" and was thus designated in 1716 by the Assessors or Surveyors of Chester county. There were no definite bounds to the district and it was not set apart as a township before the erection of Lancaster county, in 1729.

One of the London land patents in this county contained 5,553 acres, and was surveyed in the year 1716. According to Isaac Taylor's draft the southern line is bounded by "New Strasburge" and the landholders close to the line were: Isaac Lefever, who took up 300 acres the 15th of 4 mo., 1713; Daniel Ferree, 600 acres, 4th of 8 mo., 1716; Philip Ferree, 300 acres, 24th of 6 mo., 1716, and Henry Carpenter, 1,000 acres, 7 mo. 27th, 1718.

In these years the Constables returned them in the Conestoga assessment. In the year 1720 the Ferrees and Lefevers were returned in the Pequea assessment, which also included all the settlers along or near the head of Pequea creek. The settlement along the east branch of the Conestogae, now Cœruarvon, was in the Conestogae rate. I find a number of titles of settlers in the year 1717, marked in "New Strasburge." There seems to be no record in Chester county of any township named "Strasburg." When Lancaster county was organized and divided into townships, in the summer of 1729, none was named "Strasburg." But I find its territory and that of Paradise were included within the bounds of Leacock; and after a diligent search among the records in Lancaster, I cannot find the date when Strasburg township was erected, or taken from Leacock. This is a strange omission and has puzzled the local historians and land surveyors of the county. I can only appoximate to the date.

In the year 1730 a road was laid out from Samuel Taylor's mill, in Strasburg township, to North East, in Maryland. This mill was probably on Big Beaver creek, above Wm. Smith's mill, where the Zooks in our day have a fulling mill.

Daniel Ferree and Isaac Lefever took out a patent for 2,000 acres of land in Strasburg township in 1733. In the year 1734 Casper Bowman took out a patent for land, and also Mathias Slaymaker took out a patent for 150 acres in the same township in the year 1735.

I can only approximate the date of "New Strasburge" into a township, which was probably in the early part of the year 1730.

Anecdotes of Reuben Chambers.

Upon one occasion a farmer of Sadsbury township went to Bethania to get Reuben to print some sale bills. The latter wanted to know "who has thee got to cry thy sale," and when informed that no person was engaged, Reuben volunteered to do the job for him.

When the time of sale arrived Reuben was on hand, and he stood up in a feed cutting box which was on the bridge of the barn and began to cry the sale, when a boy named Joseph Cannard knocked a leg of the cutting box to one side and Reuben was thrown down upon the barn bridge. He got into a cart body and continued to sell, when some person, who had evidently been watching for the opportunity, noticed that he had got beyond the centre of gravity, and pulled out the plugs, and the body of the cart tilted and threw Reuben to the ground. These tricks did not seem to disconcert him, for he went on and finished the sale.

Reuben's Remedy for a Kicking Horse.

Reuben had an old bay horse, supposed to be about fifteen years old. Hearing that a neighbor named Benjamin Brackbill had a fractious gray mare, which would invariably kick herself out of the harness when hitched up, Reuben took the old bay horse to Brackbill's and offered to trade for the gray mare. Benjamin said he did not want to sell or trade, because the mare was vicious and "might hurt thee." Reuben replied, "Benjamin, thee need not be afraid of that, she will not hurt me." The trade was duly consummated and Reuben took the gray mare to Bethania and hitched her to a cart and put her into a grass lot, where she was at liberty to kick, which was done. For two or three days and nights this was kept up to the annoyance of the neighbors, who complained of the noise caused by the cart coming in contact with the fences, when active operations were in full sway. After a struggle of two or three days the gray mare surrendered, and thereafter for many years she became one of the best family driving horses in the county. This was heroic treatment, but most effective.

How Reuben Managed an Apprentice.

Reuben Chambers had an incorrigible apprentice boy who gave him a great deal of trouble. In order to bring him into proper submission he confined him in the attic of his dwelling and fed him on bread and water, and occasionally chastised him with a rod. This caused much talk and indignation among his neighbors. I do not remember whether the Court called him down, but I have no doubt the apprentice, after this heroic treatment, became quite docile.

Several Notable Discussions.

In the days of lyceum discussions, two incidents occurred in old Sadsbury which, if written out, would make entertaining reading, and I hope the subjects will be placed in competent hands to be written up for the entertainment of this society.

Thomas Whitson, Sr., and perhaps Lindley Coats, challenged Dr. Timlow and others to discuss the slavery question in a hall at the Gap. Whitson is said to have talked all day and a whole night, which brought the other side to a standstill.

There was a political discussion in the brick school house in Sadsburyville. My impression is that Whitson and Coats were in the debate. The Locofocos and Whigs were getting the worst of it, when the Locofocos sent a message to Hugh Maxwell in Lancaster to send out some of the young orators of his party. He sent John W. Forney, who was a minor. This was the first political speech Forney made.

Miscellaneous Notes.*

May it please the Proprietor.

This bearer, Michael Baughman (being apprehensive that he can agree with ye Indians to remove from Conestogae Manor), desires to purchase the spot where the Old Indian Town Stands with the whole vacancy between ye lines of Henry Bostler, Michael Moyer, James Logan, John Cartlidge and Peter Leman, and to extend towards Susquehanna as

*Copied from Surveyor Isaac Taylor's papers.

far as may be not to incomode the other land, the quantity that may be regularly taken there will be I think about 350 As.

Thy Servant,
December 3, 1739. I. T.

Had this offer been accepted the stain of murdering the Conestoga Indians would not have darkened the fair name of Pennsylvania.

Mr. Baughman resided in Manheim township. The Champneys, of Lancaster, are some of his descendants.

When the Indian villuge was attacked in December, 1763, a number of the Indians were at Smith's Furnace selling baskets, and others on a like errand at Swarr's Mill.

Strasburg Manor.

The proprietors reserved a manor in Strasburg township containing 1,475 acres. The date is not given nor the exact locality.†

Palatines at Pequea.

In a letter of James Logan to Isaac Taylor, dated at Philadelphia, 20th of 5th month, 1711, he says "6 or 7 familys of ye Pallatines are settled at Pequea, and more design to go there next winter."

† Copied from Taylor's papers.

REMINISCENCES OF PARADISE TOWNSHIP.

Before attempting to give an account of the early history and traditions of Paradise, Lancaster county, I desire to state to those especially who were present at the meeting, November 18, at the Stevens House, of the Ferree and Lefevre families, that it will be necessary for me to give a brief resume of some of the historical events which I gave then, as the early records of these families are contemporaneous with the early history of the village and its immediate vicinity, by omitting which would be like Shakespeare with Hamlet left out.

The village was given its name in 1796 by David Witmer, and it has always been a source of regret to the writer, who has suffered with many others from the continual strain of stale jokes and witty speeches the name calls forth whenever mentioned, and more especially do we censure our worthy ancestor for giving it that name when he had so much a better one at command, and should have christened it Tanawa, for reasons which will appear later.

Arrival of Huguenots.

The village dates its first advent of a citizen, other than Indian who roamed the wilds of that part of Pennsylvania, in no less a personage than Madame Ferree (a French Huguenot), of whom you doubtless have heard long before this, and her appearance soon followed her landing in this country, where she came bearing letters to the agent of William

Penn, and who advised her to seek a point in the valley now known as Pequea and also instructed her to see the King of the tribe of Pequea Indians (which was one of the few tribes that had a king) and who was then located in a grove on the banks of Pequea about one-fourth of a mile northeast of where the village now stands, and I think I can do no better than give you a short extract from a speech delivered by Redmond Conyngham in the year 1842 and who was an authority on the Indians and early settlers of Eastern Pennsylvania, which address was delivered before the following lyceums: The Philadelphia Lyceum, Mechanics' Institute, of Lancaster, and the Lyceum and Literary Institutes of Lancaster county, composed most of them of the leading and prominent men of that time—John W. Forney, the founder and editor of the Philadelphia *Press*, being one of the number, and it was in this same grove where this meeting was held and Madame Ferree first met King Tanawa. I quote his speech as follows:

"In the evening of a summer day when the Huguenots reached the verge of a hill commanding a view of the valley of Pequea (it was a woodland scene, a forest inhabited by wild beasts, for no indication of civilized man was near), scattered along the Pequea amidst the dark green hazel, could be discerned the Indian wigwams, the smoke issuing therefrom in its spiral from. No sound was heard but the songs of the birds, and in silence they contemplated the beautiful prospect which nature presented to their view. Suddenly a number of Indians advanced and in broken English said to Madame Ferree: 'Indian no harm white; white good to Indian. Go to Beaver, our chief. Come to Beaver.'"

Tanawa.

Few were the words of the Indian. They went to Beaver's cabin, and Beaver, with the humanity that distinguished the Indian of that period, gave up to the emigrants his wigwam and the next day he introduced them to Tanawa, who lived on the great flats of Pequea. And who was Tanawa? The friend of William Penn, who had not only been present, but had signed the great treaty, and was buried on Lafayette hill, located, as a chart which I here present shows, in the west end of the village and on which stands an Episcopal church, and where his ashes rested in peace until the Literary Society of Paradise, filling the part of resurrectionists, had them disinterred and placed what remained, namely, beads, tomahawk and a number of other Indian relics, including teeth and a part of the skull of the Indian monarch (which the writer here exhibits), in the archives of the Society, and which were purchased years after by a member of his family when the Society disbanded; and before we pass on to the next event in the village's history I wish to state that the grave of that Indian chief was paved with flat stones on which these relics are supposed to have been placed.

There passes down through the village (as shown in the chart) a little brook crossing the old Lancaster and Philadelphia turnpike near the centre of the village, having its source about one-half mile to the south of the same and where was located the home of Isaac Lefevre, who was married to a daughter of Madame Ferree and whose parents had perished in the religious wars which had desolated France. Alone he had come to this country and located and married as stated. Their son, Daniel Lefevre, was the first child born in the valley of Pequea. To verify the fact in connection with this little brook that near this point King Tanawa's remains were put to rest, I again quote from Conyngham, as follows:

"A number of Indian chiefs were on their way to Philadelphia to visit the Great Father (George Washington) from Ohio. Ten miles east from Lancaster, where a little brook crosses the road, they suddenly left the road, to the great surprise of the interpreter and government agent, and being asked by the agent their intention, they informed him many of their tribe had been buried there and their king and chief warrior whose grave they wished to visit." The point designated by them is that distance from Lancaster and must have been the spot where rested Tanawa, the king of the Pequea Indians, and, whose grave they wished to visit, which is quite near to the point as stated.

The Revolutionary Period.

We now come to a later period in the history of the village and there appears no record of its having taken an active part in the War of the Revolution, 1776. Nor have we anything connecting it with the stirring events of that time. But that it was visited by the Father of His Country, George Washington, later, there is the following tradition: Stopping on his way to or from the West, and having dined at the stage hotel, he expressed a desire to see a hemp mill, which was at that time a novelty and in full operation a short distance from where he was stopping, and it was also said he had in view the erection of one on his plantation in Virginia. But, unfortunately, the person operating the machine, desirous of giving his distinguished visitor the full opportunity of inspecting it, removed some of the bracing, a planking of which, coming in contact with the rapidly moving machinery, created quite au excitement for a time, seriously injuring the operator and startling his guest. Again we see displayed the sound judgment and good sense of the founder of this great republic in concluding he had no use for such a machine, as I never could learn of any having been erected on his plantation at Mount Vernon. The two large conical stones which constituted the principal part of the machine can to-day be seen in the bed of the stream during seasons of low water, just below the mill, weighing, I suppose, about five hundred pounds.

We next come to the days of turnpikes and Conestoga wagons, and during that time it filled a very important position, both in its construction and management, as it was the headquarters of the section which comprised Downingtown on the east and Lancaster on the west; and there was located the post-office and store in addition to the hotel. Here was made the change of horses and sorting of the mail, and another tradition as told the writer by the postmaster of that time was that while Mrs. Dixon was postmistress of Lancaster, in the hurry and confusion of getting the mail ready for the stage, in the early hours of the morning, her night cap, which was an indispensable article at that time of wood fires and cold houses, got mixed with the mail, and, much to the chagrin of the postmaster, rolled out with the mail for resorting. It was promptly returned by the next mail going West. There are five buildings now standing in the village which were used as taverns at that time.

The War of 1812.

We now approach the second great event of the nation—the war of 1812. While there were a number of its residents and those of the immediate vicinity who took part in it, the only matter of interest which I can recall as a tradition and which was told the writer by an eye witness, who was then a boy, was the passing through of a company of cavalry and artillery on its way to a point near the Canadian border, commanded by Colonel Ross. The narrator said it was an exceedingly wet day, and, something going amiss with one of the artillery wagons, a local smith was called in, and while the repairs were being made the colonel rode up to the front of the hotel and called for a glass of liquor, and while waiting for it to be brought out he kicked his foot out of the stirrup and elevating it as nearly at an angle of forty-five degrees as possible, permitted the water to run out of his boot, much to the amusement and admiration of the small boys who were present, and showing that the soldier was not then, as in later times, protected from the inclemency of the weather by rubber blanket and mackintosh. This wet day may have laid the foundation for later troubles for the gallant colonel. I see in the records of burials of St. James' Church, Lancaster, one of a Col. George Ross, who served gallantly in the war of 1812 "and died from exposure as stated in these records during the late war, in which he served gallantly, taking part in the battle of New Orleans." The date of his death was June 7, 1816. There is also a will on file in the Register's office of a Col. Ross, in which he desires his remains sent to New Orleans in a cask of rum as a preservation. Embalming was not in vogue at that early day. Whether this was the same Colonel Ross as narrated the writer is unable to state, but should it have been, that wet march through Paradise no doubt helped to lay the foundation for his later ill health. It was with feelings of great sadness that the village learned later that the command under the gallant colonel had met the enemy near the point as stated, and, using the language of the narrator, were "cut to pieces," a few returning with their commander.

Lafayette's Visit.

The next event of interest was the visit of General Lafayette and I will quote from the Lancaster *Intelligencer* of Tuesday morning, August 2, 1825, as follows: "The cavalry having formed as an escort the whole moved on to Paradise from Slaymaker's Hotel in Salisbury, where they halted a few minutes at David Witmer's; and the General, having alighted, was introduced to a crowd of ladies and gentlemen of Paradise, who were waiting his arrival." The marble horse-block can to-day be seen in passing through the village, on which the distinguished visitor alighted from his barouche. And I will state here that the hill known as Lafayette hill, mentioned in the early part of this article, received its name at that time from the fact that it was there a company of cavalry encamped awaiting the arrival of the General to escort him to Lancaster.

Then we arrive at the construction of railroads and when turnpikes and stage coaches were on the wane, and again we find the village taking a forward position in it as a means of transportation. The railroad, as all doubtless know, was built by the State and completed in the year 1834. Steam was not then used, the motive power being horses, and the seventh car which turned a wheel on what is now know as the Pennsylvania railroad came from a siding in that village bearing on its side the legend, "Witmer, Paradise," and so continued until a year or two after the Pennsylvania Company purchased the road from the State. The number of cars had by that time increased to forty, were very much larger, painted a light buff, bearing the same name, and were known along the road as the "Paradise Line." Of course, long prior to this horses had been superseded by steam, the State furnishing the motive power and the individual furnishing the cars and paying a toll for the use of the road.

The village from its early date took a great interest in schools and educational enterprises. There was an excellent school owned and conducted by Mr. Fetter at what is known as Oak Hill, a beautiful residence at the eastern end of the village and now owned as a summer residence by J. Hay Brown, of this city. Next there was a seminary under the management of the Episcopal Church, Rev. Dr. Killikelly being the Rector, and it gathered into its fold pupils from as far west as St. Louis, east as far as Boston, north as far as Northern New York and south as far as the Carolinas. A large academy was also started there and both flourished until the late war closed all institutions of that kind.

Prominent Residents.

The village can boast of having sheltered for a time a number of distinguished individuals, many who afterward became connected with great events elsewhere. It was here that the manuscript of that beautiful song, "The Old Kentucky Home," was sung and commented upon before it had been turned over to the publishers to be given to the world. Mrs. Buchanan, the wife of Rev. Edward Y. Buchanan, brother of the president, and Rector of the Episcopal Church, was a sister to Stephen J. Foster, who was also a musician. She received the manuscript from her brother for her criticism and approval, and the writer remembers hearing several of the musically-inclined villagers practice it with a melodeon acompaniment and, of course, giving it a very favorable criticism. J. Hays Linville, afterwards connected with Captain Edds in building the great St. Louis bridge, and who had become a civil engineer of note, had charge of a school there for a time; also, a sister of the district attorney who tried and convicted John Brown, and the village can also claim as a resident for a time an editor and proprietor of one of Lancaster's evening papers. It can also claim as a citizen Dr. Carl Merz, who, as all know, was a celebrated writer and composer and who left Paradise to take charge of a much more extended field in the West.

The head and manager of that band of wandering minstrels, the McGibeny Family, which have amused and interested the children as well as those of riper years in almost all the large cities, had his home there for a time as an instructor in the academy previously mentioned.

Its Only Newspaper.

There was a paper published there, which I here present, and which had quite a large circulation for a time. It was named the *Paradise Hornet*, and this copy bears the date of May 18, 1822. I make no comment as to its appearance and contents. You must be the judges. There is a file of them, I believe, at the Historical Society rooms, in Philadelphia.

I now close the narration of events and tradition of the village. Of later years its history has been similar to that of many others in the county—old families and names have disappeared and their places have been filled by new people and new enterprises; so that one looks in vain for the old familiar names and places and turns away feeling as Goldsmith so beautifully portrays in his deserted village, a stranger among what were years past familiar scenes, and surrounded by those who are too busy with the events and happenings of to-day to give much heed to those of the past; and perhaps it is best so.

A PETITION FROM MARTIC TOWNSHIP.

To understand more fully the grievances which caused it to be signed and presented, it will be necessary to go back a year or two. In the spring of 1776 the Continental Congress advised each colony and province to take immediate measures to frame a new form of government, one more in accordance with the spirit of liberty and independence. The officers who then controlled the colonies generally sympathized with the Crown, and really had a majority of the citizens at their back. The patriots were in a minority; but what they lacked in numbers they made up in zeal. Cumberland and the counties west of that were controlled by Scotch-Irish Presbyterians, who at this crisis of affairs completely controlled the politics in those counties; and they also at this time obtained a majority of their friends in the Legislature. The Legislature issued a call for the election of deputies to meet in convention to consider the resolves of Congress. Those chosen from this county were:

William A. Atlee, of Lancaster, and the second Judge of the Supreme Court under the Constitution soon to be enacted.

Lodwick Lowman, who was an officer in the Revolutionary war, and member of the Legislature.

Col. Bertram Galbraith, of Donegal, who raised a battalion of militia in 1776, and was in the New Jersey campaign, and was the Lieutenant of the county from that date to 1779; also a member of the Legislature.

Col. Alexander Lowrey, of Donegal, who commanded the second battalion of militia at the Battle of Brandywine, and a member of the Legislature for many years.

Major David Jenkins, of Carnarvon, who also commanded a battalion in the Jersey campaign of 1776.

William Brown, a member of the Legislature, and one of the signers of the petition.

John Smiley, a member of the Legislature.

Major James Cunningham, of Mt. Joy township, who commanded a battalion of the "Flying Camp" at King's Bridge and Long Island, and was with Colonel Lowery's battalion at Brandywine. He was a member of the Supreme Executive Council.

The Deputies met in convention at Carpenter's Hall, Philadelphia, on June 18, 1776, and in a few days passed a resolution requesting the members of Congress from Pennsylvania to vote for an independent government. This was ten days before the Declaration of Independence was declared by Congress. But for the energy and patriotism of that man of iron, Colonel Thomas McKean, the members of Congress from Pennsylvania would not have voted for it. And but for the efforts of that brilliant lawyer and orator, James Wilson, most royally assisted by Judge McKean, the Constitution of the United States in 1787, would not have been adopted by the State of Pennsylvania. I heard an honored ancestor of mine, who admired and entertained these great men, state that her father, who was a member of the Legislature which met in the second-story of the State House, when the Convention was in session on the first floor, which enacted the new frame of Government, told her that James Wilson, Esq., was really the author of the greater part of the Constitution of the United States, and was its ablest defender.

The New England people, and some from other States, sneer at Pennsylvania and the part her people took in the early struggle for independence. Our Commonwealth was probably the first to advise Congress to adopt measures for an independent Government, and was the second State to adopt the Constitution of 1787. Although the patriots in Pennsylvania were in the minority they ruled the politics of the State, and were in the front in every battle.

The Convention at Carpenter's Hall took immediate measures to call a convention to frame a Constitution, which met in Philadelphia on July 15, 1776. Benjamin Franklin was President and George Ross, Lancaster, was Vice President.

The members of the Convention were:
Colonel George Ross.
Colonel Alexander Lowrey.
Colonel Bertram Galbraith.
Colonel Philip Marsteller (of Lebanon township).
Colonel Thomas Porter (of Little Britain township).
Captain Joseph Shearer (of Derry township.)
Colonel John Hubley.
Private Henry Slaymaker (who was one of the Justices of the Common Pleas Court under the ne Constitution).

One of the first acts of this Convention was to appoint delegates to Congress.

The Constitution was completed September 28, 1776. It was not submitted to a vote of the people, but went into immediate effect. These patriots were not taking any chances. They held the reins of government and kept them well in hand until the United States was free and independent.

Under this Constitution the Supreme Court was organized. Thomas McKean was made Chief Justice, William A. Atlee second Judge, and John Evans, of Chester county, third Judge. The Court first met in Lancaster, in the spring of 1777, and tried many Tories and confiscated their lands.

This Constitution had defects of form, which it is not necessary to enumerate in this connection; but there was no uncertainty in its hostility to royalty and all that that word implied.

In the fall of 1777 the Assembly passed measures calling for an election of delegates to meet November 28, 1778, to frame a new Constitution for the State. The people throughout the State were indignant and sent many petitions like the annexed one, containing the names of nine-tenth of the voters in the State. This was too much for the Assembly and they rescinded the resolution, 47 yeas to 7 noes.

The Petition.

MARTICK TOWNSHIP.

To the Honorable the Representatives of the freemen of the State of Pennsylvania this Memorial Humbly Sheweth:

That your Memorialists are of Opinion that frequent Changes in Government have a tendency to weaken it, and to Create Divisions and Contests among the people and ought as much as possible to be avoided.

That, therefore, your taking up and passing a late Resolution for taking ye Sense of the people upon Certain Matters in the Constitution of this Commonwealth before the people have had sufficient Experience of it, has a tendency to produce the above Mentioned bad Effects, Especially as said Resolve appears to have been Grounded mainly upon Supposed Inconvencioncys in the present Constitution and form of Government Suggested by Divers petitions to former Assemblies of this Commonwealth and adopted without any call of the Community—without any Representation from the Executive Branch specifying the Incompetency of the present Constitution for the purposes of Good Government—without any Concurrance of that Honorable Body that we know of—or any Opposition or Embarrassment in the way—Obstrucking the Execution of your Laws that we have heard of. We Cannot help, therefore, being of the Opinion—that in passing Resolve in Question—Especially in the Mannor and Circumstances above Mentioned—you have Exceeded the powers Delegated to you—and treated that Constitution of which you were the appointed Guardians with Great Neglect.

That, however, your Memorialists—if just and weighty reasons would be assigned—might not be against calling a convention. Yet we Cannot look upon the Mannor in which you have appointed the votes to be taken to be fare and unexceptionable—the Question is perplexed by your Doubling it, and however they who are for a Convention may vote on Both Sides—we cannot see the propriety or Consistancy of voting against one—and at the same time Electing the Members who are to Compose it.

And there are great Numbers of your Constituents who have taken a solemn oath to preserve the present Constitution —and who deserve well of this Commonwealth, who are apprehensive will not then be themselves justifiable in putting it into the hands of a Convention in any other way than by the Constitution Itself is directed—and who we are persuaded Cannot bring themselves to a Complyance with the Resolve in Question, in its proposed Mode of Execution.

For these Causes—and before you put Good people of this State to the Great trouble and Expense of a New Convention, Your Memorialists presume that you will take the first Opportunity of revising your Late resolve—and that your Wisdom and Goodness and Your Regard to the Peace and Tranquility of this State will Induce you Either to drop it Intirely or adopt it and Carry it into Execution in a Mannor not Lyable to any Great and Just Exceptions.

John McMillan,
John Dutton,
T. C. Mitchell,
James Patterson,
James Hays,
James Johnson,
William Brown,
Robert Long,
—— Long,
Gregory Farmer,
Alexander Coy,
John Caldwell,
Robert Pendry,
John Robinson,
Geo. McLaughlin,
J. S. Black,
Samuel Kirkpatrick,
John Reagan,
John McMillan,
John Brannan,
James Duncan,
John Pagan,
Archibald Pagan,
James Pagan, Sr.,
Andy Pagan,
Andrew Pagan,
John Brown,
James Brown,
James Pagan, Jr.,
Adam Moore,
James Moore,
William Moore,
Samuel Simpson,
David Gibson,
Peter Simpson,
James Savage,
Joseph McCullagh,
William Kennedy,
James Moore,
Samuel McCollough,
David McCollough,

Peter Pulling,
James Patterson,
Robert Sloan,
John Steen,
Hugh Caldwell,
Hugh Caldwell, Jr.,
Thomas Colby,
Andrew McGinnis,
Thomas Reed,
William Pattison,
Michell Deally,
James Robinson,
James Callahan,
John Crago,
William Whit,
William Floods,
Robert Cunningham,
Matthew Cunningham,
John Cuningham,
Robert Snodgrass,
Samuel Snodgrass,
James Snodgrass,
Joseph Steel,
James Steel,
Henry Alexander,
Robert Caldwell,
Fred. McPhaxon,
Samuel Elliott,
Thomas Wharry, Sr.,
David Lowery,
Thomas Wharry, Jr.,
John McCalster,
John Barr,
Samuel Dickson
          (Miller),
James Pegos,
John Boyd,
Thomas Boyd,
John Bleare,
James Blair,
James Blair, Jr.,

Robert McCollough,	Joseph Aird,
Thomas White,	Samuel Wilson,
John Rogers,	Valentain Gaitner,
William Gorman,	James Alexander,
Patrick Cambell,	William Clark,
James Mitchell,	John Hart,
John Snodgrass,	Samuel Wilson, Sr.,
William Snodgrass,	John McCreary,
Jas. Snodgrass,	Hugh Bigham,
John Adamson,	John Reid,
John Clark,	David McDermeet,
William McAdam,	John Reid,
Robert Snodgrass,	Daniel McDermeet,
Joseph Neell,	Daniel McDermeet, Jr.,
	Thomas Clark.

The names on this petition were all English and probably of Scotch-Irish origin. Many of them were members of the Associate Presbyterian Church on "Muddy Run."

Many of them were in the Revolutionary War, and I notice some who were the ancestors of prominent families who now reside in the west and south.

A FULLING MILL IN 1714.

In 1716 Stephen Atkinson, to whom liberty had been granted about two years before to settle on a neck of land between Edmund Cartlidge and the Conestoga Creek and to build a mill and make a dam, and he having built a good fulling mill a warrant was made out for the neck of land and 10 or 20 acres over the creek next his dam.

In the year 1728 he took 138 acres in the bend of the Conestoga. This mill was located in the bend of the creek, between Reigart's and Graeff's Landing. The mill and dwelling were on the south side of the creek and fell in Lampeter township, when the county was organized. This was the first mill in the county which obtained its water power direct from the Conestoga river. After Mr. Atkinson built his dam, it proved to be a complete barrier against the ascent of shad and other fish to the upper part of that stream. The citizens residing along the water course above the dam came down in the night-time and tore the dam away. The Legislature compelled Mr. Atkinson to construct a passage way in his dam to allow the fish to ascend the stream.

Mr. Atkinson died in 1739, and the mill was run by his son, Matthew Atkinson. Thomas Doyle, of Lancaster, married Elizabeth, daughter of Stephen Atkinson. They were the ancestors of Major John Doyle, a distinguished officer of the Revolutionary war, whose remains are buried in front of St. Mary's Catholic Church on Vine street, in Lancaster city. Captain Thomas Doyle, brother of John, also distinguished himself in the Revolutionary war, and after its close joined General Wayne's "Loyal Legion" in his campaign against the western Indians.

Joshua Minshall, an Irish Quaker, married a daughter of Stephen Atkinson. He moved to the west side of the river at Wright's Ferry, in 1730. He was captured, with others, by adherents of Lord Baltimore, and thrown into prison at Annapolis, Md., February 21, 1733. He adhered to Penn's interests, and was against the pretensions of Lord Baltimore. His son, Thomas Minshall, was a prominent person in York county.

Hon. John Wilkes Kittera, the first member of Congress from Lancaster county under the United States Constitution, who served for ten years, married a great-granddaughter of Stephen Atkinson, and a most distinguished lady she was.

John Snyder, son of Governor Simon Snyder, married a daughter of Mr. and Mrs. Kittera. Miss Mary Snyder, daughter of John Snyder, now resides at Selins Grove, Pa.

Grist and Saw Mill.

William Smith, in the year 1728, took up 152 acres of land along Beaver creek, where the village of New Providence now stands. He built a grist and saw mill in 1729. The mill, with meadow containing four or five acres, was in Strasburg township. The balance of the land ran in a southerly direction and was embraced within the limits of Martic township. In 1731 a public road was laid out from Lancaster to his mill, and in the year 173- a public road was laid out, leading from his mill to navigable water, at the mouth of Rock Run, in Maryland. This was at the head of tide water. The great quantities of flour manufactured at this mill, and others, in the lower end of the county, found their way, in a year or two after the Rock Run road was laid out, over another road which terminated at Charlestown, a seaport town in Cecil county, Md. This being the nearest market along navigable water, it commanded a large portion of the trade from this county for several years, and to the time when a public road was built to Newport on the Christiana creek, in Delaware. Mr. Smith had two sons who became prominent in Colonial times, namely Thomas and William.

Thomas had his father's land patented in his own name in 1736, and in 1740 he purchased a farm adjoining on the west, now owned by the Mylins. In the year 1752 Thomas Smith was elected Sheriff for this county. While he held this office he kept open house in Lancaster, where he entertained his country friends, and in consequence of this liberality he went out of office poorer than when he entered upon its duties.

In 1755 Thomas Smith and his brother, William, purchased several hundred acres of land about three miles and a half northwest from "Smith's Mill," where they built a furnace, which stood upon the farm now owned by the Dillers. And in the same year they built a forge about four miles south of their furnace, along Pequea creek. They gradually purchased farms around their furnace and forge properties, which numbered more than four thousand acres.

In 1756 Thomas and William sold their grist mill and meadow to Michael Groff, and that part of the land which was located in Martic township (New Providence) they sold to Jacob Groff (who owned the Eshleman mill, to which 'Squire Hildebrand refers. Mr. Eshleman married his daughter and they were the ancestors of the late David G. Eshleman, Esq). Christian Groff also purchased some of the Smith land. Three acres of iron ore land were reserved for the use of Martic Furnace, which was located upon land now owned by the Mylins. This seems to be a lost ore mine and is overgrown with trees perhaps of a hundred years growth.

In the year 1761 the Smith brothers purchased a farm along the great road leading from Chester Valley to McCall's Ferry, containing one hundred and twenty-one acres. Twenty-five acres of this land, which lay along a running stream at the Green Tree Tavern, they plotted and laid out into town lots and named the place "Smithburg." The lots were disposed of by lottery. I believe there is but one dwelling upon this town site now and that was erected about twenty years ago by the late Joseph McClure. This is one of the *lost towns* of the county. Thomas Smith failed and was thrown into prison for debt in the year 1769.

William Smith, brother of Thomas, married Dinah Edwards, daughter of John Edwards, who resided near the Blue Ball, in Earl township. He was elected Sheriff of the county in 1758. About this time he moved from Strasburg township to Earl. After the expiration of his term, and about the time of the failure of the Smith Brothers, he was appointed one of the Justices of the Common Pleas Court. After the Constitution of 1790 was adopted he was commissioned a Justice of the Peace for Earl township, an office he held until his death, in 1806. He moved from Blue Ball to Diffenderffer's "New Design," now New Holland, where he erected a stone dwelling and had his office. A few years ago it was owned and occupied by one of his descendants. His great-grandson, George Smith, was postmaster in New Holland for some years, and was removed by President Cleveland in 1885.

The Smiths were members of the Established Church of England, and were great favorites with the ruling class in Philadelphia.

Some Early Sheriffs of the County.

The following extracts taken from a letter in the Shippen papers have a peculiar interest in connection with the Smiths and others.

Edward Shippen to Col. James Burd, November 24, 1779, page 280.

The young man (Captain Worke*) who makes his addresses to Peggy is of a good family. He bears a good character. I thought it advisable, as soon as prudent after the wedding, that the young couple should remove to old Mr. Worke's until they could get a place in the country to their mind. Mr. Yeates told me that he understood that they were to reside in this borough. I replied that I was very sure that the profits of a Sheriff's office would never admit of that, when the fees were more than double to what they are now; not to mention that is the most dangerous office a man can undertake. A Sheriff ought to have the heart of a stone to stand against the cries of women, beseeching him to take their husbands' words and fair promises, and so not to put them into prison; frequently to the great loss of the Sheriff. The Shippen papers do not show that Peggy ever married Captain Joseph Worke.

Tom Smith, the Sheriff (though he lived part of his time in the country), was almost ruined by the office. It is indeed true, he was put in jail some time after he was out of office, but that was

*Son of Capt. Joseph Worke, of Donegal township, elected Sheriff October, 1779. The Workes lived a mile and a half south of Donegal Church.

because he was involved in an iron works. Joseph Pugh, was Sheriff from 1755 to 1757, his successor, was so reduced by that business that he was obliged to remove into a remote part of Virginia with his poor family.

Then came in Jimmy Webb, owned and resided where Knapp's Villa is, was Sheriff from 1767 to 1769, who rented a house in town, where he muts live like a gentleman and make every leading man in the county quite welcome that came to see him. If he had not had a good estate he would have failed.

Frederick Stone, who was Sheriff from 1772 to 1773, succeeded him, who thought himself as good a gentleman as his predecessor; but he, a poor, good-natured, tender-hearted man, soon got into jail, and is at this day an object of pity.

After him Johnny Ferree, who was Colonel in the Revolutionary Army, and Sheriff from 1773 to 1775, of Bettell-hausen, (Strasburg borough,) nine miles off, set up for Sheriff, and carried it by a great majority of votes, and called on me for a recommendation to his Honor, Governor Penn, for a commission, which I refused to give until, among other things, he promised to live very frugally, and settle his accounts with me at every Court and pay me the Governor's fees, or fines, and my fees, etc. He was indulged to live at his own house at Bettel House, coming to town once or twice a week, by which means he was able to do everybody justice and save some money to himself.

It must be remembered the emoluments of the Sheriff's office one hundred and fifty years ago were not what they now are.

An Old Grist Mill.

Samuel Taylor, a Quaker, who was born on Tinicum Island, in the Delaware, built a grist mill, in Strasburg township, upon a small stream in the year 1727. It was probably on Little Beaver Creek, north of Smith's mill, which stood at the cross roads where New Providence now is. On May 8, 1728, Samuel Taylor married Elizabeth, daughter of Justice John Wright, of Wright's Ferry. About 1734 William Taylor sold his mill and farm and purchased several hundred acres from Samuel Blunston where Wrightsville now is. His son, Christopher, was a soldier in the Revolutionary War, and was in the battles of King's Bridge and Long Island. The Barbers and Boudes inter-married into this Taylor family.

Richard Loudon, in 1727, purchased a farm adjoining Taylor's land, in Strasburg township. On June 5, 1728, he married Patience Wright, sister of Mrs. Taylor. When the county seat was permanently located at Lancaster he was appointed Prison Keeper. When some of the Marylanders were imprisoned there Betty Lowe, a sister of one of the prisoners, came to Lancaster and induced Mr. Loudon to accept her services in his family, where she was for several days kindly entertained. A body of armed Marylanders came to Lancaster in the night time, when Miss Lowe admitted them to Mrs. Loudon's dwelling, where, after a severe struggle, they subdued Mr. and Mrs. Loudon, and Betty led the way to a bureau where the jail keys were kept. The Marylanders were all liberated.

Colonel John Loudon, a distinguished officer of the Revolution, was a son of this Quaker Prison Keeper.

Letter From the Surveyor General.[*]

PHILADELPHIA, 24th, 7th, 1714.

LOVING FFRD: Isaac Taylor. The bearer hereof, Christopher Schleagel,

[*] This letter was written by James Steel, the Surveyor General, to Isaac Taylor, the Surveyor of Chester County.

complaining that a certain person hath seated himself near the mill he has lately built at Conestoga, by whose means the Indians that are thereabouts are likely to be very troublesome, if not dangerous, to him, and that the said person, so seated, hath no other right than what the Indians have given him, and also that the land where he is seated ought to be included in the 300 acres that is yet untaken up of the Thousand Acres first granted to him, of which he says there is but 700 as laid out. These are to desire thee to order the person soe seated to remove of the said land without Delay, and use thy endeavors to make the man easy and acomodate him in laying out ye 300 Acres soe far as thou can without offending the Indians.

I am with real love and good will thy assured ffrd. JAMES STEEL.

Turnpike from York to Columbia.

Judge Ephraim Cutler, of Ohio, arrived in York in August, 1809, with a large drove of cattle. In his diary of September 3, 1809, we read: "The Dutch are remarkable for having selected the very best lands. They are sure to root out the Irish. There is an irreconcilable aversion between these people. The Dutch are slow, cold-hearted and economical; the Irish warm and quick in their feelings, generous and vain. How can such materials assimilate? They have nothing alike, and there is no adhesive principle to cement them, and of course they do not mix. I am told there is scarcely a Dutchman among the two hundred men at work on the turnpike, although this road is entirely through Dutch settlements." It is an interesting question to know what became of these early Irish contractors and laborers.

Irish Laborers.

Pennsylvania is indebted to the Irish

race for the successful completion of her turnpikes and public works. In the year 1800 and 1801, when the turnpike between Lancaster and Harrisburg was being constructed, large numbers of Irish laborers employed thereon made Elizabethtown their headquarters. Many of the old citizens of that place and vicinity were Catholics, who worshipped in a church in that place. Some of the contractors made that place their home after the work was completed. In the year 1801, when General Thomas Boude, of Columbia, was a candidate for a second term of Congress, the Irish laborers at Elizabethtown voted solid for the Democratic candidate and defeated Boude by a few votes. The Celt was potent in politics, as will be seen, at a much earlier period than is generally supposed.

OFFICERS FOR 1896.

President:
GEORGE STEINMAN, ...Lancaster.
Vice-Presidents:
SAMUEL EVANS, ESQ., ... Columbia.
JOSEPH C. WALKER, ... Gap.
Recording Secretary:
F. R. DIFFENDERFFER, ...Lancaster.
Corresponding Secretary:
W. W. GRIEST, ...Lancaster.
Librarian:
SAMUEL M. SENER, ESQ., ...Lancaster.
Treasurer:
B. C. ATLEE, ESQ., ...Lancaster.

Executive Committee:
HON. W. U. HENSEL, ...Lancaster.
HORACE L. HALDEMAN, ... Chickies.
ADAM GEIST, ...Blue Ball.
REV. C. B. SHULTZ, ...Lititz.
DR. C. A. HEINITSH, ... Lancaster.
J. W. YOCUM, ESQ., ... Columbia.
RICHARD M. REILLY, ESQ.,.. Lancaster.
PETER C. HILLER, ...Conestoga.
HON. ESAIAS BILLINGFELT, Adamstown.
PROF. H. F. BITNER, ...Millersville.

The officers proper are also members of the Executive Committee by virtue of their office.

PAPERS READ

BEFORE THE

LANCASTER COUNTY HISTORICAL SOCIETY,

ON JAN. 7, 1897.

THE PEOPLE WHO MADE LANCASTER COUNTY.
BY W. M. FRANKLIN, ESQ.

EARLY INDUSTRIES ON THE OCTORARO.
BY DR. J. W. HOUSTON.

SOME HELFFENSTEIN LETTERS.
BY DR. JOS. H. DUBBS.

THE EARLY TELEGRAPH.
BY W. B. WILSON, ESQ.

A PROMINENT SCOTCH-IRISHMAN.
BY R. J. HOUSTON.

HISTORY OF THE DONEGAL CHURCH.
BY DR. J. L. ZEIGLER.

LANCASTER, PA.
REPRINTED FROM THE NEW ERA.
1896.

The People who Made Lancaster County,
    By W. M. Franklin, Esq., ... 181

Early Industries on the Octoraro,
    By Dr. J. W. Houston, ... 204

Some Helffenstein Letters,
    By Dr. Jos. H. Dubbs, ... 218

The Early Telegraph,
    By W. B. Wilson, Esq., ... 226

A Prominent Scotch-Irishman,
    By R. J. Houston, ... 251

History of the Donegal Church,
    By Dr. J. L. Zeigler, ... 258

The People Who Made Lancaster County.

It is a rather singular feature of most educational systems that a knowledge of the people and nations of remote regions and by-gone ages is deemed of primary importance, while the historic drama moving in the world immediately around us, and in which our own people have been, through successive generations, the actors, attracts but little notice.

The knowledge of our own country and our own people is an educational factor too much neglected and too often treated as a secondary and inferior accomplishment. Every organized community has a history that is significant and more or less important, and it is impossible to fully understand a people, to discern their true spirit, and be in complete sympathy with them, without adequate knowledge of their history, which reveals the hidden sources of their individuality, the origin of their peculiar modes of thought and action and the formulating factors in their social development.

From this standpoint, and from what our early annals reveal, the history of our own State, and particularly of our own county, is most interesting and important; and as illustrating the results of what may be achieved by men and women of earnest purpose and resolute devotion to duty, it is not only instructive but most inspiring, and well calculated to awaken a sense of gratitude and arouse a feeling of genuine patriotism.

It is a lesson of deep importance for us to learn that what we are and what we possess in this great State and county we owe to the bravery, the self-sacrifice, the prudence, the far-seeing enterprise, the indefatigable energy, added to the patriotic public spirit, the high standard of morality, the rigid integrity, the broad charity and religious enthusiasm of our ancestors. To them we are indebted for this goodly heritage, and it is our obvious duty and should be regarded as a most grateful task, in the light of what we now enjoy, to study the early conditions of our county and the character of her pioneers ; what was the impelling cause of their migration here, what was the spirit that animated them after they came, and what were the purpose and tendency of their lives in these new conditions. It is only after such study that we can truly understand our people and comprehend the real foundations of their success; and the more we contemplate their life and character, their struggles and achievements, the more profoundly do we respect and reverence those brave men and women who made Lancaster county, and, passing to their reward, left it a rich inheritance to their children.

Wealth of the County.

Lancaster county is the richest agricultural county in the United States. It has an area of 973 square miles, or 623,720 acres, of which more than 500,000 acres are cultivated land, divided into 9,000 farms, whose assessed valuation in 1896 was $87,262,990, and the annual products, according to the census of 1890, aggregated $7,057,790.

It is interesting to note that the county second in agricultural wealth in the United States, St. Lawrence county, New York, as revealed by the census of 1890, produced crops valued at $6,054,160, or $1,603,630 less than Lancaster county ; and our adjoining county of Chester ranks third in agricultural wealth in the United States with annual products valued at $5,863,800; and our neighboring county of Bucks is fifth, with annual products valued at $5,411,370. The amount of money returned to the assessors as invested at interest by the people of Lancaster county and liable to State tax in 1896 amounted to $21,427,601, and the amount of taxes collected in Lancaster county in that year was $955,965.24. There are twenty-eight national banks whose combined resources of capital, surplus and deposits aggregate over $12,000,000. The county expended $53,136.70 in 1896 for the poor, and over $300,000 for the maintenance of its 700 public schools, whose average attendance exceeds 30,000 pupils. There are 300 Sunday-schools in the county, with an average attendance of 38,136 pupils.

In enumerating the present resources of the county, it is important to bear in mind that all that we possess and all the favorable conditions that surround us in this great county, represent what has been accomplished within a period of less than two hundred years.

Early Settlers.

While it has been ascertained, through the researches of Dr. J. H. Dubbs, Professor of Archæology in Franklin and Marshall College, that the first white creature that settled on the soil now comprised within Lancaster county was John Kennerly, a Quaker, who came over the border-line in the year 1691 and located in what is now Sadsbury township, a mile from Christiana, yet it is well known that the first real settlements of consequence were made in 1709 by the Swiss Mennonites and French Huguenots, who were followed by the refugees of various German sects, and later still by the Scotch-Irish and the Welsh with a goodly number of English, including a large proportion of Quakers.

The county was organized on May 10, 1729, and the county seat, originating with a wayside tavern, that, with the addition of a few dwellings, was called Hickory Town, was organized into a Borough on May 1, 1742, and chartered a city on March 20, 1818.

The first settlers were refugees from the terrors of European tyranny. Towards the end of the seventeenth century Protestant Christians in nearly every country on the continent of Europe were subjected to the most cruel persecutions. The Edict of Nantes, which had granted toleration to the Huguenots, or French Protestants, was respected for about ninety years, but was revoked in 1685 by the decree of Louis XIV., when the floodgates of persecution were opened and the most barbarous acts of cruelty were perpetrated. According to the historians of that dreadful time the French provinces and the Palatinate, or provinces on the Rhine, the most fertile and best cultivated region of Germany, where the doctrines of Luther and Zwingli took firm root, were "again and again overrun by a fierce and dissolute soldiery, who offered the alternatives of recantation or extermination. In midwinter, while deep snow covered the ground they laid waste the fields, destroyed the vineyards and burnt the dwellings of 500,000 people, who were left shelterless and starving."

Under this fiery ordeal the Huguenots who escaped death fled in vast numbers, some of them across the British channel and others into parts of Germany. The bloody hand of persecution was not less active in Switzerland and extended into the communities of Simon Menno. The Mennonites fled into Holland and Germany, but they were followed relentlessly into Germany and were finally driven to encounter the terrors of the sea and sought refuge in the wilds of the Western Hemisphere.

Dr. William H. Egle, State Librarian of Pennsylvania, writes concerning the persecutions of the Mennonites, that "there were more people of that sect who were put to death in one city, Antwerp, in one year, than there were martyrs in all England during the time of Queen Mary."

The Swiss Mennonites landed in considerable numbers in 1709, and, pressing into the interior towards the Susquehanna river, settled in the territory now comprised within the boundaries of Lancaster county.

It is scarcely possible for us to fully realize the hardships endured by the pioneers in these primeval forests. They were obliged to grope their way through the woods and thickets along narrow Indian paths, and they were not only surrounded by the gloom of the dense forests and deprived of all the accompaniments of civilization, but they were obliged to encounter the terrors of wild beasts and reptiles, and of savage tribes whose vandalism and thefts and murders fill the annals of the times with unutterable horror.

So late as 1763 it is recorded that "the reapers of Lancaster county took their guns and ammunition with them into the harvest fields to defend themselves from the Indians." An autobiographer, referring to the days of his youth, passed in the early period of our history, relates that "in attending school he was compelled to walk three miles through a deep and tangled forest infested with wolves, wild cats, snakes and other animals."

But the early settlers were equal to their vast undertaking. They lost no time in proceeding to clear the forests. They discovered the soil to be of more than ordinary fertility. The ground was broken up and assiduously cultivated, habitations were erected, in the course of time roads and bridges were constructed, settlements were established, villages were laid out, and then began to appear the village school house and the village church—evidences of the true aim and the sacred purpose of the sturdy people who laid the foundations of the prosperity that we now enjoy.

Period of the Proprietorship.

After the pioneering period, with all its terrors and hard experiences, and the vast labor of establishing homes and settlements and organizing communities, grave troubles arose at an early period from the proprietorship of the land being lodged in foreigners. There was a sense of uncertainty and insecurity in regard to title. Suspicions and jealousies were engendered, especially after people of different nationalities came to swell the population in considerable numbers—a state of feeling that seemed inevitable among people who in their parent country were for centuries accustomed to regard all strangers as enemies. But this gave way in the course of time, as the relations of proprietorship and title were adjusted and became better understood. As might have been expected, these earnest people, of widely different nativity but of the same aim and purpose, under the favoring influences of freer conditions, were brought into closer intercourse, they developed a kindred spirit, a sense of mutual regard for one another, and doubtless this early experience in the amalgamation of various nationalities through the fire of pioneer hardships was the basis of the American idea of brotherhood, of equal opportunity, of individual liberty and of union.

The Spirit of '76.

Later came the period in which English oppression aroused "the spirit of '76," and forced on the Revolution, that bloody conflict through which was established the independence of the American people; and from the provisional association of the colonists under the Continental Congress, after passing through the experiment of a Confederation of the States, came finally this great independent nation based upon the broad foundations of a Constitutional Government.

Who that studies the conditions and events of all these early periods, and recalls the hardships and the heroism of the brave people who took their part so nobly in shaping the destinies of our country, is not thrilled with admiration and a profound sense of gratitude! For it is the more impressive when we reflect that the lives of these sturdy men and women were so supremely unselfish that there was no prospect and no hope at any time of themselves ever witnessing the ultimate results of their trials and sacrifices, or enjoying the fruits of their labors. All was suffered and endured for the benefit of their posterity.

Much was accomplished in developing the resources of Lancaster county by the early settlers during the pioneering period and during the years prior to the Revolution, as the population became augmented from time to time by those hailing from various quarters of the European world, who, of course, bore all the characteristics of their different nationalities— French, German, Scotch-Irish, English, and Welsh, including among them the Episcopal, the Lutheran, the Reformed, the Presbyterian, the Moravian, the Quaker, the Baptist and the Mennonite elements.

It was not, however, till after the Revolution, and the organization of a form of government and institutions suited to the new conditions, that a marked impetus was given to the energies of the people towards undertaking larger aud more permanent improvements, especially of a public nature.

Conditions at Time of the Revolution.

At the time of the Revolution the population of Lancaster county, and indeed of the whole country, was sparse. There were few towns or villages, the highways were few and generally wretched, the people had but limited means, and the methods of business and ordinary conditions of social life were most primitive. McMaster, in the "History of the People of the United States," narrates that the farmer who witnessed the Revolution ploughed the land with a wooden plow, sowed his grain broadcast, and when it was ripe cut it with a scythe and threshed it with a flail. The farmers' houses were poor structures, scantily furnished and with no articles of adornment. In many instances sand sprinkled on the floor did duty as a carpet. There was no glass or china. A stove was unknown, coal was never seen, and matches were not heard of. Many of the vegetables now in common use and most prized were not only uncultivated, but entirely unknown, such as the tomato, egg plant, cauliflower, okra, rhubarb, sweet corn, head lettuce, cantaloupes, and some of our most cherished flowers, as geraniums and verbenas.

The boundaries prescribed in the treaty of peace signed at Paris on the 30th of November, 1782, and ratified by the representatives of the thirteen States assembled in Congress on July 14, 1784, were very different from those that now skirt our vast domain. The area of the country was only half its present extent, and the historian points out that a narrow line of towns and hamlets extended, with many breaks, along the coast from Maine to Georgia, and the country extended westward across plains of marvellous fertility into regions yet unexplored by man. The whole was little better than a vast wilderness. The population numbered three and a quarter millions, and more were in the Southern than in the Northern States. Virginia alone contained a fifth, and Virginia, with Maryland, the two Carolinas and Georgia, held almost one-half of the whole population of the country.

Contrast With the South.

Pertinent to this fact of the predominance of the population being in the South is the extraordinary contrast between the people of the North and those of the South, in respect to material wealth, thrift and enterprise, which is to be attributed not to any circumstance relative to locality, but wholly to the moral character of the people. Noting this contrast, the historian already quoted relates many things concerning the social life of the people in the South. They were not content to enjoy the simple, homely pleasures of our frugal ancestors, with their house-warmings, spelling-bees and huskings, barn-raisings and tea-parties. "No pastime could flourish among them that was not attended with risk. They formed hunting clubs......they gambled, they bet, they gathered in crowds to see cocks cut each other to pieces with spurs made of steel. Many of the lower caste played cards, particularly faro; they wrestled, and seldom went home without a quarrel or perhaps a brutal fight. The combatants coolly agreed before the fight began whether it would be fair to bite off an ear or gouge out an eye, or maim in some other terrible way. Gouging out an eye was always permissible. Every b lly grew a long thumb nail or finger nail for that very purpose, and when he had his opponent down would surely use it unless the unfortunate man cried 'kings cruise' or 'enough.'...... The practice was long a favorite one, and common as far north as the Maryland border." Dr. Ramsey, in his history of South Carolina, declares that "betting and gambling were, with drunkenness and a passion for duelling and running in debt, the chief sins of the Carolina gentleman," and adds that "duels take place oftener in South Carolina than in all the nine States north of Maryland." Another historian, telling of the clubs that flourished in the City of Charleston in the early days, remarks that "the life passed in them may be judged from their names—the Ugly Club, the Jockey Club, the Hell Fire Club, and others."

McMaster gives us an insight into the life of the young Southerners, which he pronounces a strange mixture of activity and sloth. "When they were not scouring the country in search of a fox, riding twenty miles or more to a cock fight or barbecue, they indulged in supreme idleness. Travellers were amazed to find a man in the best of health rise at nine, breakfast at ten and lie down in a cool place in the house to drink toddy bombo or sangaree, while a couple of slaves fanned him and kept off the flies."

There is perhaps nowhere a more obvious lesson to be gleaned from the pages of history than that which contrasts the spirit and purpose and manner of life of the people of the South with what characterized our ancestors here in Lancaster county, and the contrast should at all times awaken in us, who have received from them this rich heritage, the deepest respect and unbounded gratitude.

Added to a profound sense of gratitude for our inheritance of what may be deemed, in large measure, material advantage, though based on the sound foundations of correct living and a high standard of moral character, we are entitled to entertain just pride in the accomplishments of our forefathers in the higher ranges of human activity.

Our Early Settlers Not Illiterate.

It is an erroneous impression that the early inhabitants of Lancaster county were ignorant and illiterate. On the contrary, there were among them men of learning, and many men and women of education and culture and refinement. Not, indeed, that veneer of refinement or affectation of polish that is so often presented as a substitute for the genuine quality, which reposes not less in the most homely than in the most attractive personality. They were a plain, sturdy rural folk, calm and thoughtful, with serious purpose, enterprising but prudent, often shrewd and calculating, but honest and trustworthy, with a high ideal of manhood and citizenship, an ardent public spirit, and a zeal and enthusiasm in religion that was constant and practical.

The Swiss and German refugees, who were the most numerous of our early settlers, exhibited a wonderful amount of enterprise and established a literary centre here, of which we may be justly proud. Prior to the Revolution there were more printing presses operated and more books published by the German portion of our ancestry than in the whole of New England, with all its boasted culture. The first book printed in German type in America appeared in 1739, ten years after our county was organized, and contained a collection of the hymns of the Ephrata Brethren. The Ephrata Brethren had a complete plant for a printing establishment. They made all their own materials, they had their own paper mill, type foundry and bindery, and they printed and published probably more than a hundred books in the past century. The Bible was printed by our German ancestors in their own language three times before it was ever printed in English in America, and the New Testament was printed by them seven times before it was printed in English in this country.

Judge Samuel W. Pennypacker, LL. D., of Philadelphia, who has made a life-long study of the history of the Pennsylvania Germans, is authority for the statement that to them must be awarded the credit not only of publishing the first book in America, but also of producing in America the earliest essays upon music, bibliography, pedagogy and astronomy. He also notes the interesting fact that "down to the time of the Revolutionary War, there were eight newspapers published in Pennsylvania in English, and there were ten newspapers published in Pennsylvania in German. What is true of the East is also true of the West. The first time that a Bible appeared west of the Alleghenies it was published in 1814, in German, at Somerset."

The first genealogical work printed in America and the first work on pedagogy were issued from the Ephrata press, and the first stereotyping in America was done at Ephrata, and also the first printing in oil colors. A book of common prayer, believed to be the first that was ever published in this country, was printed at Ephrata in 1767. It is now in the possession of the Historical Society of Pennsylvania, and its title page bears the following inscription : "The Family Prayer Book, Containing Morning and Evening Prayers for families and private persons. To which are annexed Directions for a devout and decent behavior in the public worship of God ; more particularly in the use of the Common Prayer appointed by the Church of England. Together with the Church Catechism. Collected and published chiefly for the use of the Episcopal Congregations of Lancaster, Pequea and Cærnarvon. 'I will pray with the Spirit; and I will pray with the understanding also.' I Cor. 14 : 15. Ephrata. Printed for William Barton, 1767."

It is an interesting historical fact that George Washington was first called "The Father of His Country" in a German almanac, printed at Lancaster, for the year 1779. The almanac has a full page frontispiece containing an emblematic design with the figure of Fame holding in her left hand a portrait inscribed "Washington," and in her right hand a long trumpet with the words issuing forth, inscribed on a scroll, "Des Landes Vatter." As this was printed in the fall of 1778, the expression "Des Landes Vatter," "The Father of His Country," dates back to that year.

Dr. David Ramsey, who has been called the "Father of American History," was born in Little Britain township, on April 2, 1749. He removed to South Carolina, and to the labors of an active medical practice he added those of a voluminous historical writer. He published a "History of the American Revolution," a "Life of Washington," a "History of the United States," a "History of South Carolina," and other important works. Dr. Ramsey was the first person who took out a copyright under the laws of the United States.

Lindley Murray, who may be justly called the "Father of English Grammar," was born in Lancaster county in 1745, at Swatara, in a part of the county that was carved out to form Dauphin county. His

["Grammar of the English Language," published in 1795, became the standard authority and is the basis of all the grammars that have since been published, and his "English Reader" and "English Spelling Book" were popular through several generations.

The first Pharmacopœia ever published in America was the work of Dr. William Brown, published at Lititz in 1778, and printed in Philadelphia by Christian Seist.

Many other authors have been given to the world by Lancaster county, but it is not designed to go into this phase of our subject exhaustively, and our necessary limitations have allowed only a brief mention.

Records of Early Patriotism.

We have every reason to be proud of the records of the patriotism of our ancestors. Pennsylvania, with its capital "City of Brotherly Love," was conspicuous among the colonies as the home of American liberty. Founded in 1681, she was, with the exception of Georgia, the youngest of all the thirteen original States, and under the liberal policy which was inwrought in her constitution and laws, through the Quaker influence, and which was gratefully accepted and firmly supported by the Germans and the Scotch-Irish, this youngest of the colonies advanced to the front rank. It was regarded throughout the world as the most successful experiment of practical freedom, and the character of the people is reflected in the remark of Voltaire, "Their colony is as flourishing as their morals have been pure."

Pennsylvania had the first representative form of government in the new world. It was the first of the States to adopt the Constitution of the United States, and it was the vote of Pennsylvania that made the Declaration of Independence possible.

Judge Pennypacker, in writing of the Convention that assembled in Philadelphia in 1787, to pass upon the adoption of the Constitution, states that "after the Constitution had been framed it was still a matter of grave doubt whether it would be accepted by the States. It is generally conceded that the adoption of the work of the convention was due to the early action taken by Pennsylvania. She was the first of the great States to declare in favor of it. When the question of the adoption of the Constitution arose in the Pennsylvania Assembly there was the greatest diversity of views, and the contest became heated and earnest. In that eventful crisis the very earliest effort in behalf of the new government came from the Germans."

Not only was this timely patriotic spirit manifested in the adoption of the Constitution, but with equal truth may the same be said regarding the Declaration of Independence. Hon. Geo. F. Bear, LL. D., of Reading, in a public address in the Court House at Lancaster in 1891, speaking to representatives of the German counties of Eastern Pennsylvania, and referring to the fact that at the time of the Declaration of Independence nearly one-half of the population of Pennsylvania was German, declared that the Germans were the potential factors in securing the essential vote of Pennsylvania for the Declaration of Independence. Under the proprietary rule only those could vote who were natural born subjects of England, or duly naturalized after swearing allegiance to the King, and possessing certain property qualifications. Comparatively few Germans qualified themselves to vote. In 1775 the Pennsylvania delegates to the Colonial Congress were instructed by the General Assembly to vote against separation from Great Britain.

The situation was most critical. Independence and union were impossible without Pennsylvania. It became necessary to secure the enfranchisement of the Germans. A provincial convention was called and met in Philadelphia on June 16, 1776, to frame a new government, and through this really revolutionary proceeding, as Bancroft expresses it, "the Germans were incorporated into the people and made one with them." The 19th of June, 1776, enfranchised the Germans and made the Declaration of Independence possible.

It is by no means strange that this patriotic spirit should have been called forth at two such important and critical periods of our history. When it is remembered that Pennsylvania enjoyed the first representative form of government in the new world, and philanthropy was one of its chief corner stones, it will be seen that it was eager for the blessings of liberty to be spread abroad through the land. In none of the colonies did liberty take such early root as here. As has been truthfully recorded by an accomplished writer on early Pennsylvania history, Benjamin M. Nead: "It found no foothold on Puritan soil, for the blight of intolerance was there. Roger Williams, in insisting on the freedom of conscience, was compelled to risk the stake. South of Pennsylvania the feudal idea governed in its stricted form."

It is an interesting matter of local history to know that a native of Lancaster county, Dr. David Ramsey, was President pro tem. of the Continental Congress during the illness of John Hancock, and General Mifflin, who lies buried in Trinity Lutheran Church yard, in Lancaster city, presided over the Continental Congress at Annapolis when Washington resigned his commission as Commander-in-chief.

General Edward Hand, whose remains lie buried in St. James' Church yard, in Lancaster, was a gallant soldier of the Revolution, a close, confidential friend of Washington and Adjutant General of his staff. Close by the tomb of General Hand is that of Edward Shippen, prominent in colonial and revolutionary times, whose son became Chief Justice of the Supreme Court of Pennsylvania, and one of his daughters, Peggy, in her eighteenth year, became the second wife of Benedict Arnold in April, 1779.

Early Abolitionists.

The abolition of slavery in this State in 1780 was due to the controlling power of the elements of our population whom we have described as having made Lancaster county; and it is interesting to know that of all of the societies for promoting the abolition of slavery the oldest was formed in Pennsylvania. It is recorded that a protest against slavery was made by the Society of Friends at Germantown as early as 1688, and "five days before the battle of Lexington an anti-slavery society was formed in the old Sun Tavern at Philadelphia, which was reorganized after the Revolution, when Benjamin Franklin became its President, and from 1784 it had a long career of usefulness."

It was a Lancaster countian, William Wright, who first suggested the "Underground Railroad," or systematic concert of action to aid escaped slaves to safe refuge. The first conflict and bloodshed in the United States under the Fugitive Slave Law, passed by Congress in 1850, occurred in Lancaster county, near Christiana. And it was the representative from Lancaster county in Congress, Thaddeus Stevens, whose influence and leadership accomplished the enfranchisement of the emancipated slaves.

Free Education.

The same dominant spirit, in his earlier legislative career, prevented the overthrow of the Liberal School Law, and firmly established the free school system of this Commonwealth. It is a fact for every Pennsylvanian to be proud of that we have had free education from the beginning of the Commonwealth. In New England one of its foremost States had not a free school system till within the present generation. And we may boast not only of the liberality, but also of the gallantry of our Commonwealth, for we have never in Pennsylvania denied to females equal rights with males in our schools. It was very late until they came to that idea in New England, where the girls could go to school only when the room was not needed for the boys.

The first school in Lancaster county was established as early as 1712 by Swiss Mennonites in the Pequea Valley, near the present site of Willow Street. They erected a log house to serve for their religious meetings on Sunday and for school during the week.

The first Sabbath-school in this country was opened in Lancaster county by Ludwig Hacker in 1740, more than a generation before Robert Raikes started Sunday-schools in England in 1780. This enterprise for the religious instruction of youth was conducted on Saturday afternoon, the Sabbath of the Seventh Day Baptists. It continued prosperously for thirty-seven years until 1777, when the Battle of Brandywine turned the school house into a hospital for wounded troops. Judge Pennypacker has a collection of 381 tickets that were used in this Sabbath-school, printed in 1744, on every one of which is printed in German a text of Scripture and a religious verse.

In 1791, under the patronage of the

celebrated Dr. Benjamin Rush, the first non-sectarian Sunday-school in this country was commenced in Philadelphia, and it is curious to learn that their founders were reviled as Sabbath breakers. There are now in Lancaster county 308 Sunday-schools, with an attendance of 33,288 pupils.

Pennsylvania may boast of being the home of Presbyterianism in America, and it was here that the first American Presbytery was organized in 1705.

The first scientific society in America was founded here in 1744 at the suggestion of Benjamin Franklin, who was afterwards succeeded by David Rittenhouse, the great astronomer and mathematical genius, among whose inventions of great practical value was the metallic thermometer.

The researches of F. R. Diffenderffer, Secretary of this Society, reveal that the third public subscription library that ever existed in the United States was that of the Lancaster Library Company, established in 1759. Its name was changed four years later to The Julianna Library, in honor of Lady Julianna Penn, daughter of the Earl of Pomfret, and wife of Thomas Penn, one of the proprietors.

It was a Pennsylvania botanist, John Bartram, who first described the plants of the new world, and a Pennsylvania Scotch-Irishman, Alexander Wilson, who was the first American ornithologist. The celebrated scientist, Dr. Joseph Priestly, sought refuge from English intolerance and spent the last ten years of his life in the freedom of Pennsylvania, making his home in our neighboring county of Northumberland.

The Pennsylvania Hospital, established in 1752, was the first hospital founded in this country, and connected with it was the first asylum for the insane that ever existed in America.

The first bank that was ever established in the United States was a Pennsylvania enterprise. Prior to the Revolution nothing of the kind was known in this country, and we are indebted for the first bank to Robert Morris, under whose commanding financial genius the Bank of North America was chartered on December 31, 1781. Not until three years later did any rival appear, when the Bank of Massachusetts was organized in Boston, and a few months later the Bank of New York and later still in the same year the Maryland Bank in Baltimore.

The first turnpike in the United States was the Lancaster Turnpike, extending from Philadelphia to Lancaster, which was commenced in 1792. It is estimated that there are now more than 400 miles of macadamized roads in Lancaster county. And it is a point of historical interest to the people of Lancaster county to know that not only did they have the first macadamized highway in their county, but also the first railroad of any considerable length, that which was built from Philadelphia to Columbia, a distance of eighty miles.

In connection with the subject of transportation, although this is an inland county, we are reminded that the world is indebted to Lancaster county for the man who first successfully introduced the application of steam to navigation. Robert Fulton was born in Little Britain township in 1765, and the old stone house where he was born and reared is one of the famous places of pilgrimage in the county. His boat, "Clermont," was launched on the Hudson river in 1807. He had previously invented a torpedo or submarine boat when abroad, and in 1801, under the patronage of the French Government, while making a public test he remained an hour under water and guided the torpedo around the harbor of Brest. Fulton was an accomplished artist, and with his pencil succeeded in providing means for his education. When he went to England he made his home with his fellow countryman, Benjamin West, the first great American painter, who was a native of the adjoining county of Chester.

Benjamin West executed at Lancaster, in 1752, for William Henry, a gunsmith, a picture representing the death of Socrates, which contained the first figure he ever painted from life. This painting is in possession of a descendant of Henry living near Bethlehem. Henry afterward became a Justice of the Courts. He was a man of enterprise and refined culture, and he extended the hospitalities of his house to many visiting foreigners and men of letters and science of his own country. It was during a visit to his house that Thomas Paine wrote a portion of "The Crisis" over the signature "Common Sense." His son, John Joseph Henry, who lies buried in the Moravian burying ground, in Lancaster, became the President Judge of the Courts of Lancaster county in 1781, and he was distinguished not only for his legal learning, but also for his mechanical genius. He was the inventor of the screw-auger.

Lancaster county has given to the world a great number of important mechanical inventions. Among them was the steam plow, which created a great sensation, invented by Joseph Fawkes, who was born and reared in Bart township, and is now living retired and greatly respected in California. He was the inventor of a number of agricultural implements, and his steam plow was first exhibited on the Fair Grounds at Lancaster in August, 1859, and the next month a practical test was made at Freeport, Illinois, where he was awarded a prize of $3,000.

Another important Lancaster county invention, now in universal use among agriculturists, is the double corn shovel harrow, patented in 1869 by Jacob Mowrer; and his son, Nathaniel Mowrer, when a lad of only eighteen years, invented the corn-cob crusher and the degerminating machine for extracting the eye out of corn before grinding.

In his valuable paper read before this Society, William B. Wilson, of the Pennsylvania railroad, whose early experience in the telegraphic service was with Col. Thomas A. Scott, during the early days of the Rebellion, says: "Lancaster city has the honor of hearing the first click of an electric telegraph instrument on the first telegraph line built for commercial purposes in this country......The first fruit of the experimental telegraph line built for Professor Morse between Washington and Baltimore was a line built between Harrisburg and Lancaster, along the tracks of the Harrisburg, Portsmouth, Mount Joy and Lancaster railroad, which was completed November 24, 1845, and the first message was transmitted on January 8, 1846."

Many more facts of a similar kind might be gathered from our local records in illustration of the mental activity, the patriotism, the industry and thrift of the people whose names are identified with our early history, and all these points and incidents of our history are interesting and instructive as evidence of the character and condition of our ancestors, whose lives and achievements, the better we know them, are calculated to deepen our respect for them and make us all the more zealous in fostering a just local pride.

The lesson that is most impressive from

this glimpse at the early history of our county, and the perils and hardships endured by our forefathers, their heroic self-sacrifice and patriotism is this—that as in those pioneer days they endured hardships and suffered untold miseries to build the foundations of a social structure they could not expect themselves ever to enjoy, laboring wholly and unselfishly for their posterity; and as they wisely built on the sure foundations, the solid rock of sound morality and religion, on faith, and in hope, and for charity, illustrating in their life and character, in their aims and purposes and in their culture and achievements, the elements and types of genuine manhood and true citizenship—so now we, who are in possession of this magnificent heritage, have every inspiration to meet the present conditions and solve the problems of the present time ever in the same spirit, with the same bravery, standing firmly on the same solid rock and illustrating in our life and conduct, to the utmost of our ability, the sturdiness of character which so happily distinguished them and cause us to feel so justly proud of our ancestors.

In the words of Edward Everett: "Characters, like those of our fathers, services, sacrifices and sufferings like theirs, form a sacred legacy, transmitted to our veneration, to be cherished, to be preserved unimpaired, and to be handed down to after ages."

Early Industries on the Octorara.

The subject assigned to me for investigation was the "Eastern Branch of the Octorara and its Tributaries," with their present and extinct industries as far south as the hamlet of Steeleville.

I have carefully examined the geography and history of this region and find much that is inaccurate and many important landmarks missing. Although I have personal knowledge of nearly half a century of this territory, and have heard many of the traditions relating thereto, both historical and biographical (some of the yarns rather tough ones), yet I am not self-confident that my work is perfect, having to cull from a mass of contradictory traditions from equally reliable traditionists, who evidently are impressed by that biblical text found in Second Thessalonians, second chapter, and fifteenth verse, which reads, "Stand fast and hold the traditions which ye have been taught." I have endeavored to verify the results of my investigation which I now have the honor to present to this learned society.

Here I desire to extend my thanks to Hon. Wm. McGowan, Postmaster John Borland, both of Christiana, and to 'Squire H. H. Bower, of West Grove, Chester county, for valuable assistance rendered in compiling and collating this record.

I also want to enter my protest against a very common spelling of the term Octorara. The ending of the last syllable should be an a and not an o. The name Octorara is of Indian origin and was used to designate a sub-tribe of Indians, having a village or encampment near the eastern banks of this stream on lands now owned by Lewis Newcomer, of Upper Oxford township, Chester county.

History and traditions are alike silent as to whether they belonged to the Shawanese or Delawares. The term is also applied to the entire southeastern slope of Lancaster county, which is drained by this stream. The name has also been appropriated by at least five churches. The post-office at Andrews Bridge is named Octorara, and numerous beneficial and social organizations have borne this title.

The Eastern Branch of the Octorara is formed by the union of the waters of Buck run, Williams run, Pownall's run and Pine run. Each of these streams has its source near the watershed of the Mine Hill range.

This region, in which are found the many sources of the numerous tributaries contributing to the formation of this romantic and beautiful stream, is now included in the township of Sadsbury, where the first settlements, in what is now Lancaster county, were made while the territory was yet in the mother county of Chester previous to the organization of Lancaster county in 1729. This territory on either side of the inter-county line was largely settled by Friends, they being induced to locate here because of the Penn reservation of one thousand acres of land, which was here established immediately south of what is now the Gap station, on the Pennsylvania Railroad. This reservation was surveyed at the time Wm. Penn visited King Wopaththa, of the Shawanese Indian tribe, A. D. 1700. This tract of land is still known as Penn's Manor, the name being perpetuated through title deeds, notwithstanding Penn named the reservation Springtown, a very appropriate name.

Several of those who accompanied

Penn on this occasion, serving as staff officers, as it were, to the proprietor, also pre-empted tracts of land in this vicinity some of which were in the Pequea Valley, then known as Conestoga, and others on the southern slope of the hills extending south of and embracing the ground upon which Christiana now stands.

To return to the subject proper, I think I can truthfully assert that no stream within the boundaries or confines of Lancaster county can show such utilization of its water power in the past and present as the Eastern Branch of the Octorara and its tributaries from the diverse sources to its mouth. Particularly was this true during the early half of the nineteenth century. The longest tributary to the Eastern Branch of the Octorara is known as Buck run. It is an intra-county branch, and rises on the southern slope of the Mine Hill ridge, on the farm owned and operated for years by Hon. Wm. Hamilton, recently Senator, representing Lancaster county in the General Assembly. This branch, about three miles long, meanders through the farms known as Maxwell's, Webster's and others, receiving contributory branches. Where it enters the farm of Jacob Townsend it is now, and has been for more than a half century, under contribution by the Townsend saw mill, which was built in 1841 by John Townsend, father of the present proprietor. Near to the saw mill is the Smyrna creamery, recently erected. One-half mile down the stream we find a flouring mill, known as Spring mill, in good condition. It was built by John Townsend, Sr., in 1841, and is now owned and operated by John F. Reed. Along the road leading from Smyrna to Christiana the stream was again four decades since laid under tribute by one Christopher Corbett, a peculiar character, who may have been an ancestor of the noted pugilist.

He erected mills for sawing timber and cleaning cloverseed, but their existence was of short duration, and even the ruins have been obliterated. On this stream, in the western part of Christiana, stands an unused flouring mill, which was erected A. D. 1816 by Dr. Robert Agnew, father of the late Professor David Hayes Agnew, M. D., who for years was professor of surgery in his alma mater, the University of Pennsylvania. The quaint old farm house, in which the professor was born, is still in good repair. For years the driveway leading to the farm buildings was on the embankment of the mill pond.

This mill was known as Earnest's, and later as Hanway's, but the power has been abandoned and decaying walls guard the site. If you will pardon the digression I will state that this mill was the scene of the premeditated, atrocious, diabolical violation of the constitution of these United States, by which act one Reuben Chambers, although not specifically mentioned in that instrument, nevertheless was entitled to all the rights and immunities guaranteed to citizens of this nation, yet, notwithstanding this assured protection, he was deprived of valuable property, to wit: sundry bags of sumac tops and berries, as depicted by a former narrator. Although foreign to my subject, yet, following closely the text of his biographers, permit me to assert that the world may never know what was lost to humankind by this wanton destruction of Rhus Glabrum, since Reuben was famed for manufacturing and compounding medicinal preparations unthought of by the medical profession.

Reuben, alone of all the great army of veterinarians, could provoke emesis in equines. I think 'Squire Evans' Brackbill's gray mare was the subject of the experiment at a period after her subjugation by means of the blue horse cart, which was loaded with stones.

The Williams run rises on the Maxwell farm a few hundred yards from the source of Buck run, and passes through the farms of Rea Moore, Calvin Carter and Isaac Slokom, and then forms a junction with Buck run on the western border of Christiana.

The Pownall run rises on the Hathaway farm, runs a southerly course, crossing and recrossing the Pennsylvania railroad, and empties into the Williams run near the confluence of that stream with Buck run. After the union of these waters the stream enters the Noble mill pond to contribute to the formation of the East Branch of the Octorara. The inter-county stream, known as Pine run, continues as the eastern boundary of Lancaster county for one and one-half miles north of Christiana, when the inter-county line leaves the stream on the farm of Benjamin Pownall and bears off northeast to the course of the stream. Pine run rises near the site of the former Asbury Methodist Episcopal Church, on the farm of Mrs. Shaw, on the southern slope of the Gap hills. One-half mile south of its course are found the ruins of Lear's mills comprising flouring, sawing and clover mills. These mills were formerly Gest's mills. Continuing south, near to Sadsbury meeting house, thirty years ago, was the Amos Townsend saw mill. Below these ruins we find the site of the Denny machine shops, unused for years.

Within the borough of Christiana water power was furnished by Pine run, which was utilized for nearly sixty years to furnish power for the foundry and machine shops now operated by the Christiana Machine Company, but the power has not been used for eight years, having been supplanted by steam power.

The head waters of Pine run are now utilized by the borough of Christiana in furnishing the water supply to her inhabitants. The water is conducted by small pipes leading from springs to a common reservoir or basin, from which it flows to the borough through larger pipes by gravity, a distance of two miles. Within the borough there is a head pressure of one hundred and sixty feet, rendering fire engines unnecessary. The water is generally distributed through the town and is assuredly an excellent system of water supply, furnishing as it does to Christiana the most potable water of any borough or town in Lancaster county. Neither mud nor microbes need apply.

After the confluence of Buck and Pine runs in Noble's dam, the name of the Eastern Branch of the Octorara is given to the stream. This dam is in the southern part of Christiana and furnishes power to drive a flouring and feed mill. Years ago there were saw and plaster mills attached. These mills are yet known as Noble's mills. Forty years ago they were owned and operated by Thomas Whitson, of anti-slavery fame, the father of Thomas Whitson, Esq., of the Lancaster Bar. These mills are now in the occupancy of Henry Rakestraw, who also operates a creamery nearby. South of Nobleville, on the old Noble farm, now owned by Henry Rakestraw, are found the ruins of a woolen factory which was burned fifty years ago.

Near this locality the stream is reinforced by the waters of Valley run, which rises in Bart township, flows in a southerly course past Bart meeting house, then adopts an easterly direction to its mouth. The first utilization of its waters was sixty years ago, when Rood's tanyard exacted tribute. Only tradition can point the site.

Journeying down the stream, we find

the chopping mill and creamery of Cyrus Brinton. This building a half century ago was a woolen factory known as Rose Hill. Later, lime spreaders were here manufactured. Both enterprises were managed by Lewis Cooper.

One mile east of this plant we find the ruins of the Burnt Mill, formerly known as the Brick Mill, built by Samuel Irwin in 1825, and for years owned by his son, Ellis Irwin; then later the property of Wm. Spencer. In 1853 it was burned; the site alone remains. This mill was being operated during the time of the Christiana riots by Castner Hanway, who, with Elijah Lewis and Jos. Scarlet, was tried for treason to the United States by reason of being implicated in this first battle of the great American conflict for human liberty and the emancipation of the American slave. The scene of this resistance to tyrants in obedience to God was on the south bank of this stream, about two miles distant from Christiana.

Near the confluence of this stream from the west the East Branch receives a tributary from the mother county, known as Glen run, evidently a token of maternal love. This stream rises in Sadsbury, Chester county, flows southwest through the borough of Atglen, immediately north of the Pennsylvania railroad. On this stream, years ago, was the Buckley forge, known as Greenwood. The buildings are now used as a foundry for manufacturing iron novelties, especially Mrs. Potts' sad irons. The Chalfant Company operates the works.

In the southern part of the town are found the ruins of Crawford mill. Glen run supplied the power. This mill furnished great quantities of cornmeal for export during the time of the famine in the emerald of the ocean.

When her children like lost Israel's tribes
　　were scattered as the leaves,
Yet round every standard but their own
　　are twining laurel wreaths.

On a branch of Glen run, flowing from the east, the ruins of Boyd's mill are found. A creamery occupies the site.

Near the confluence of this stream with the East Branch a flouring mill, late known as Ann's, now Ferguson's, is being operated. Below this mill we come to Mercer's dam, which, like all dams on the East Branch, is long and rather narrow. A half century since this dam furnished power for two flouring mills, which were built in the last century by one Downing, saith tradition. Evans, in his "History of Lancaster County," says by Sterrett Brothers in 1781. These mills ground much of the wheat raised in Pequea valley on its way to the Wilmington market. They were also used to grind corn for Ireland during the famine, at which time they were operated by John Mercer, father of Captain John Q. Mercer, late of Lancaster city. Years since one of these mills was converted into a paper board mill, but this industry is on the wane.

Flowing into Mercer's dam from the Chester county side is an unnamed stream on which forty years ago was a tilt-hammer shop for the manufacture of mowing and cradling scythes operated by James Moore. Here at Mercer's mills a covered bridge spans the stream. The road leads toward Cochranville, Chester county. From Mercer's mills to Steelville, a distance of three miles, the east branch flows through what a Western cowboy would denominate a mountain gorge, bounded on either side by ranges of lofty hills, broken at intervals by canons through which some tributary flows. The rocky ledges and stony character of the soil, with a forty-five degree elevation of the hillsides, renders any attempt at cultivation impossible until the table land is reached. These hills, covered as they are with a foliage presenting all the varied tints of the rainbow, present to the lover of natural scenery a panorama wonderful to behold.

Here in these mountain fastnesses nature has hidden many of her choicest floral germs. Here in the sweet seclusion of nature's first temples such eminent botanists as H. H. Bower, Esq., of West Grove, Chester county, and the late Howard W. Gilbert, formerly of the Lancaster city High School, received the inspiration which carried them into the front rank of scientists.

The grandly natural picturesqueness of the scenery along this part of the stream from the great valley to Steeleville is without rivalry in Lancaster county.

Twenty years ago, through the persistent efforts of Hon. Marriott Brosius, ably supported by the foreman of the road jury, the late lamented George W. Hensel, father of our own General W. U. Hensel, the Lancaster county court opened a driveway along the western bank of the stream from Mercer's mills to Steeleville, which is largely patronized by lovers of natural views, which are here beheld in all their pristine beauty. Here during the summer months are found camps of those desiring seclusion and restful enjoyment. Here picnickers abound and fishing parties are in evidence to catch the gamey bass, with which the stream was stocked twenty years ago.

This was the hunting ground of that famed trio of Nimrods, Prof. Hall, of Lancaster; George Pownall and William H. Sproul, of Christiana, and woe betide the unlucky grouse, quail, rabbit or squirrel that became the object of their unerring aim.

Down the stream from the Mercer mills, along the Brosius road, are found the ruins of Sadsbury Forge No. 1, known as the upper forge, and Sadsbury Forge No. 2, known as the middle forge. They were purchased by James Sproul (who moved there from White Rock Forge, Little Britain township, A. D. 1828), from John Withers, who also owned and operated Mount Eden Furnace in Eden township.

A half mile down the stream we come to a break in the Lancaster county range of hills which led to the Sproul mansion, near which on the surrounding plateau were erected barns and stables required to accommodate the great number of horses and mules used in transporting the smelted iron from Lancaster to the Sadsbury forges and to return the finished bar iron to water transportation. This was before the era of the Pennsylvania railroad. Teams were also necessary to haul the charcoal for the surrounding country to the forges, where it was consumed in the reduction of the iron.

I well remember, during the boom of 1844, of seeing processions of six to eight six-horse teams all engaged in hauling the product of a single furnace plant to the Pennsylvania railroad.

Near to the headquarters mansion the No. 2 Sadsbury Forge, known as the middle forge, was in operation, No. 1 forge furnishing chafery iron, which was manufactured in No. 2 forge into octagonal bars, and were largely sold to a New England company, the Whitney, to be used in manufacturing gun barrels.

After Mr. Sproul's death, which occurred in 1847, No. 1 forge was unused. Mr. Goodman and son continued the bloomery enterprise at No. 2 forge for some time, but the scarcity of charcoal, and their efforts to manufacture coke having failed, this forge was also abandoned and only ruins remain.

Journeying southward the next utilization of the stream was without doubt the first effort to manufacture iron on the East Branch and probably was inaugurated by one Duquesne. Evans says by Michael Withers about the middle of the last century. This forge afterward became the property of James Buckley, who purchased a large tract of land in this locality, a portion of which became the property of James Sproul, A. D. 1837, he having purchased it from the Buckley brothers, sons of James Buckley.

Years ago, when writing up the local history of Chester county, I received the above tradition from Dr. A. V. B. Orr, who was closely identified with this locality from his birth, in 1809, up to his death, in 1880. Even the ruins of this forge are almost obliterated, a high stone wall, part of a coal house, alone remaining to mark the site of the Duquesne forge.

A half mile down the stream we come to the ruins of Ringwood forge, which was built by the Buckley brothers early in the present century. John McGowan, father of Hon. William McGowan, became proprietor of the forge in 1837 and here manufactured forge iron until 1848. Charles Cloud, of the Pennsylvania railroad, was engaged here for some years as proprietor, when Thomas Bailey succeeded to the business. Bailey attempted to manufacture iron from the slag of former operators, but failed. His assignee, Wm. Borland, however, was successful in the enterprise. Twenty-five years ago a freshet tore out the plant, which was not rebuilt. Three-fourths of a mile below Ringwood forge, through a rift in the Lancaster county hills, a stream known as Knott's run contributes its waters to the swelling East Branch. On this run General Steele built a large cotton factory. The stream, though not abounding in water, furnished ample fall to guarantee sufficient power. This enterprise was a failure, and for years only stone walls remained to tell the tale of the General's venture. Thirty years ago a paper board mill was erected on the site, but this attempt was abortive, and crumbling walls alone appear in evidence.

The water, after operating the large factory during the Steele administration, was conducted around a spur of the southern range and by means of an aqueduct was again required to furnish power for a less pretentious cotton factory, but in after years this building was converted into a dwelling, and as such is in fair repair at present time, though lacking modern improvements. Thus far the waters of the East Branch and tributaries in their journey to the Susquehanna, except Glen Run and the Tilt-hammer stream, have only furnished power for present and extinct industries on the Lancaster county side of the stream. Now the sites of decaying industries as we enter Steeleville (so named by General Steele) are only found upon the Chester county side. Covered bridge, No. 2, is found here. Steeleville three score and ten years ago was a place of moment. The busy mart for the entire region, it was not only a business centre but it was a social and political centre also. Her business men were of the most enterprising type. Her politicians were patriots. Two of her citizens were Colonels in the Continental Army, Colonel Taylor and Colonel Thompson, and General Steele served his country with distinction during the war of 1812. Her matrons and maidens were amongst the fairest of the fair and the hands of the latter were sought in marriage by the gifted and educated at home and abroad. But Steeleville's prowess is no more ; it is only a country cross-roads post-office villa, fast hastening into obscurity. Business activity is lost. The dignified citizen has departed. Science no longer has a foothold.

The lyceum, which numbered amongst its members men who have adorned the professi ns, men who have given to the scientific world gems from nature's hidden stores, men who have contributed to the ennobling of humanity, has long since ceased its meetings and crumbling walls which once echoed in response to oratory alone remain.

Here in this comparatively deserted hamlet we view the site of a former paper mill built by General Steele and successfully operated by him for many years, but the industry ceased shortly before his death, fifty years ago, and only vestiges of the plant are found.

To the antiquarian is shown the site of a tanyard built and operated by Thos. Woods for decades, but in consequence of the scarcity of oak bark and new methods in competition this industry was discontinued.

The only present industry is a flouring mill owned and operated by John Evans, which supplies the demands of the surrounding farmers.

Tradition tells of a copper mine once worked in Steeleville at a time unto which the memory of the oldest inhabitant runneth not back, traditions all fixing the time previous to the revolution. Twenty-five years ago a weak effort was made to locate and reopen the mine, but beyond locating and finding evidence of the existence of former shafts and drifts, nothing was accomplished; no ore was found.

This gorge, through which the East Branch flows from the great valley to Steeleville, was at one time, early in the present century and even as late as forty years ago, as my day book shows, dotted with tenement houses wherever it was possible to erect a dwelling with safe ingress and exit. There were nearly two score of them on the hillside tenanted by the employes of the various industries. For years these buildings have been deserted, and those not razed by the hand of time are fast crumbling into ruin. The only habitation except the old cotton mill on this stretch of three miles is the Goodman mansion, erected on the lawn of the former Sproul home and which is now owned by Thomas Griest, a brother of our townsman, Ellwood Griest, editor of the Lancaster *Inquirer*. Thomas Griest owns and operates a large farm on the table lands adjacent to the mansion house.

The southeastern slope of Lancaster county drained by the Octorara has not only been celebrated in the past and present for its industries and agricultural production, but the people comprised within its area, principally descendants of English Friends and Scotch-Irish Presbyterians, are noted for industry, integrity, intelligence and piety; imbued as they are with a love for civil and religious liberty, their patriotism is intertwined with their religious convictions, and their sympathies reach out to other lands less fortunate in their forms of government.

In conclusion, permit me to say in personification of our good old city of Lancaster that no brighter jewels bedeck her starry crown, as you well know, than some of the gems gathered from the valley of the Octorara.

Still laughingly on the East Branch flows,
By the haunted dell where the hazel grows;
Ever onward, never finding repose,
  For its waters so sparkling and clear;
Enriching the verdure on its sinuous shores,
Willingly giving of its bounteous stores,
As it hastens along o'er its pebbly floors,
  A creation of God for his children so dear

SOME HELFFENSTEIN LETTERS.

The Reverend John C. Albertus Helffenstein was pastor of the Reformed Church of Lancaster from 1776 to 1779. He was born in the Palatinate, February 16, 1748, and died at Germantown, Pa., May 17, 1790. He was the son of the Rev. Peter Helffenstein, Superintendent of Churches at Sinsheim. In 1772 he came to America, accompanied by his half-brother, the Rev. John H. Helfrich, and the Rev. J. G. Gebhard. Helfrich settled in Lehigh county and his charge has ever since been occupied by one of his descendants. Gebhard became pastor at Claverack, N. Y., where he founded a literary institution. Helffenstein died comparatively young, but was a celebrated preacher, and several volumes of his sermons were published. Seven Reformed ministers were his descendants and bore his name.

While Helffenstein was pastor in Lancaster he was an earnest patriot. It frequently became his duty to preach to the Hessian prisoners who were kept here. On one occasion he preached on the text, Isaiah 52 : 3—"For thus saith the Lord, Ye have sold yourselves for nought and ye shall be redeemed without money." This sermon caused a good deal of excitement and offense among the captives. On another occasion he preached a discourse in the evening on the words : "If the son shall make you free ye shall be free indeed," when the excitement became so great that it was deemed necessary to accompany him home with a guard. Once he preached to the American soldiers on their departure for the scene of conflict from the words : "If God be for us who can be against us?"

Some years ago it was my privilege to visit Sinsheim in the Palatinate, where I saw the old church in which the Helffensteins preached. About the same time I found, in this country, a number of letters written by the members of the family who remained in Europe to their brother in America. As early letters of this kind are extremely rare, it has occurred to me to translate several specimens, and I offer them to the Historical Society in the hope that though antiquated they will not be found uninteresting.

The first is a letter from the father to his son in America:

SINSHEIM, June 3, 1772.

MY DEAR SON: Though it grieves me greatly to live separate from you, and that I can entertain no hope of ever visiting you in America, I yet rejoice in your fortunate change of circumstances. May God grant us all a new heart so that we may walk in his fear! Beware of sectarians and remain faithful to the true doctrine to which thou hast sworn.

If the Lord suffers me to live awhile longer you shall find in me a true and faithful father, who will not suffer you to want if it is in his power to prevent it. In the package you will find: 1. Du Bosc's sermons in 4 to; 2. Stackhouse's "System of Doctrine," seventh volume. If you should receive the part in which one of the sheets is defective suffer it to remain unbound until I have an opportunity of supplying a complete copy. 3. Saurin's sermons in six volumes; 4. Dunckel's "Funeral Sermons;" 5. Gronau on the Twenty-fifth Psalm; 6. "Theologia Pastoralis Practica," four volumes bound and one unbound; 7. A package of underwear. In the sealed book I have placed a gold piece with which you may pay the freight. I would gladly have sent more, but the price of grain is very low and I have had to send all I had for sale at great expense to Heidelberg, as it is now illegal to sell grain anywhere but at the grain market. If you can indicate a reliable means of conveyance I will send you a package of books every year; and if you are in need of anything write to me promptly...... I have written to Pastor Weyberg and he will send you my letter.

Your brother will not remain in the Palatinate, and if I can get a position elsewhere I shall also leave my fatherland. I release you from your promise to Louisa the more readily because I can see no way of coming to you. When you make up your mind to get married consider virtue first of all, but also give some consideration to property; for a minister who does not secure some possessions by marriage is sure to suffer all his life.

If there is anything which you desire do not hesitate to write. I must now close—more another time. God be with you and with us all! I remain

Your faithful Father,
P. HELFFENSTEIN.

The second letter of the series was written six years later by a brother who remained in the fatherland. In the translation I have considerably abridged it, but all that is of general interest has been preserved.

DEAREST, BEST, MOST-BELOVED BROTHER: Providence has at last afforded me an opportunity of writing to you to inform you that your excellent father, your sister and I are still in the land of the living. But what shall be the fate of this letter? What distant lands, what nations will it have to visit? Perhaps my prayers will pierce the clouds and ascend to Him who loves to hear them, when they are sincere, so that my letter may finally reach you. Are you still alive, O dearest brother? Or has death gathered you with the thousands that have fallen before his sickle? How sad it is to live in such uncertainty concerning our dear ones! O, would that you were still in your fatherland with me in our quiet, peaceful cottage—how joyously would the stream of time flow on!

How shall I begin and what shall I first tell you? I can relate but a few of the important events that have occurred since last I wrote to you and these but briefly. A year and a-half ago the worthy pastor at Wissloch, Sauerbrunn, passed away, and the Church Council called our father to be his successor; the Court, however, interfered and granted the position to Inspector Hasse, of Lautern. The result was a law suit. Our father had an interview with the Prince Elector and it was finally determined that he was to receive 200 thalers annually from Wissloch (by way of compensation) in addition to his previous salary. Now we are comfortable in Sinzheim. Wirt has been called to Lautern, and Koch, rector of Bretten, has become the assistant pastor at this place.

Your correspondent has been for three months pastor at Hilsbach; but is required to pay to the superannuated minister Braun 500 thalers annually, to his wife, if she should survive him, 150, and after her death 50 to their daughter, who suffers from epilepsy. His engagement with Fraulein von Schmidt was broken at her request, and he is married to the daughter of Captain Baunegis, now a member of the Council of Administration, bearing the title of Government Councillor.

The winter of 1776–7 was for me very depressing. I suffered from a nervous disease which brought me near to death and did not leave me until spring. I am again restored, but am very nervous and must be very abstemious, especially in labor. I must beware of everything that might prove exciting, and unless I am particularly well dare not venture to read a tragedy or an affecting story for fear of suffering the most painful consequences.

Our sister has been married, and to whom? I am sure you cannot guess! It is our cousin Helffenstein. He is pastor at Schoenau, two miles from Heidelberg. He has already greatly improved in disposition. I hope our sister, who has much spirit and is fully able to control him, will be able to effect still further improvement. Our cousin Louise is also married. Her husband's name is Weidenhahn. He owns a linen factory and has the title of Commercial Councillor. She corresponds with me and, besides her sister, is my dearest friend.

In the Reformed Church of the Palatinate revolution follows revolution. A year ago the entire ministry agreed, on account of present conditions, to appoint five of their number deputies and to grant them a printed power of attorney to act in their name. These five men have not as yet accomplished a great deal, but order has been restored in the Council and no one is oppressed. Appointments are granted without the payment of money, and the administration of the church is more economically conducted. The Commission consists of Pfaltz, French pastor in Manheim; Herzogenrath, French pastor in Manheim; Kling, inspector in Neustadt; Kilian, Superintendent of Schools in Ladenburg, and our father. This commission is to be permanent and is to have entire control of the Reformed Churches of the Palatinate; if any one of the members should die the survivors are to choose his successor.

In Germany a fire has been started; it

is yet only glowing, but the blaze must come ; and then alas ! for us. Its cause is the recent death of the elector of Bavaria. The Queen or Austria and Bohemia has seized some territories to which our sovereign, as the nearest relative, is held to have a prior right, and this the other States will not suffer. The preparations for war between Austria and Prussia are terrible, and streams of blood must flow unless the angel of peace should extend the olive branch between the contestants, and clear up the heavens that are now pregnant with terror.

I have to inform you that we have become interested in a silver mine, only six miles distant from this place. Our prospects are pretty good, for after the present year we are promised from 25 to 30 reichsthaler monthly per share. Of course, we have had to pay assessments for two years, but the returns of a single month will reimburse our expenses. Father has two shares, and my sister and I each have one.

A truce to all this, which must remind you of the style of the newspapers, and which gives me so little satisfaction. Let me devote the present hour to something that is better. How are you prospering, my dearest brother? Friendship and love, I seem to hear you say, transform my days into an everlasting spring ; my faithful wife and the pledges of our love are a never failing fountain of the purest joy. When I return from the labors of my profession my wife's greeting and the innocent prattle of my children cause me to forget the troubles of the day. A knock at the door announces a visitor and Helfrich or my faithful Gebhard hastens to my embrace. O, that such bliss might long be yours ! May there be no dark days in your spring, no thunder clouds in your blessed summer.

Do you ask how I prosper? Dearest brother, I cannot speak of my own existence in such exalted terms. My path is not strewn with roses, but I am not often pricked by thorns and am contented. Solitary walks through the valley or across the smiling fields—some beautiful book—the care of my flowers and other rustic employments, these are my most pleasant recreations; and thus my days pass quietly away. Sometimes, it is true, I feel greatly depressed, but religion, reason and the power of will soon restore my courage.

* * * * *

January 2, 1777. During the past year I have suffered many trials, and I pray that you and yours may have been protected in the midst of danger......"O, mighty ruler of the universe, direct the sword to return to its scabbard. Grant peace to the countries which suffer from the scourge of war. Bless especially my brothers and my friend Gebhard! If it is Thy will—if it is for their welfare—bring them back to their fatherland; or at least suffer me to behold their face before I close my eyes in death." These are the prayers which I offer to Heaven at the beginning of another year.

* * * * *

[Here follow four pages of extracts from the diary of the writer. They are beautiful and tender; but as they are purely personal they may be omitted.]

The writer concludes:

"Dear brother, when may I expect to receive a letter? Three years have passed since last we heard from you. Our dear father expects you to write often—do not disappoint him. He wants to know how many grandchildren he has, and sends his blessing to them all. Many friends desire to be remembered.

"Dear brother, tell us about your circumstances. We should also be glad to know your opinion of the war that is now raging in America. Perhaps it is not safe to write about such matters, but you will at least join us in our prayer for the speedy restoration of peace.

"Once more, farewell! Do not forget those who so often speak of you—who long to be with you—and who think of you daily. Especially remember him who will love you as long as there is a drop of blood in his veins. Do not forget

Your most faithful brother,

HELFFENSTEIN."

SINSHEIM, April 21, 1778.

THE EARLY TELEGRAPH.

A few weeks ago, upon the suggestion of my friend, William U. Hensel, I accepted an invitation to come to Lancaster and read my historical paper on "The Telegraph in Peace and War," as it contained some historical matter of local interest to Lancastrians. Upon more deliberate consideration, however, I concluded that it would be imposing too much upon your indulgence to read it in its entirety, and that it would be better to cull from it those portions relating to this locality and add material in my possession which would interest you. This I have done, and in doing it been enabled to bear testimony to unrecorded deeds of some Lancaster men, and put in shape for preservation by your society some events in which Lancaster city and county were the fields where they occurred.

A portion of this material I have had in type for limited circulation, but the major part is now presented for the first time and the whole of it put in form to be of interest, if not of value.

The recent destruction of the Columbia bridge prompted my writing a sketch of it, so that there might be a record made of its continuous history, and I will open this paper with that sketch :

"The Columbia Bridge," whether in the singular or collective sense, has encountered as much, if not more, disaster than usually falls to the lot of such structures. Its history, beginning in the first and now running in the declining half of the last decade of the nineteenth century has been marked by financial and physical woes, and yet, as one element after another has tried its destructive powers upon it, it has nobly turned from its tribulations and offered fresh defiance to its foes.

The success of the Philadelphia and Lancaster turnpike road between those two cities, and that of the Lancaster and Susquehanna, completed in 1803, between Lancaster and Columbia, gave an impetus to turnpike road construction and bridge building, and stimulated the formation of companies to accomplish those results. As Pennsylvania was the centre of the progressive transportation movements of the time, it became also the centre for the promotion of those companies, and gave freely of its means to aid in advancing their projects. Not the least of the projected public improvements was the bridging of the Susquehanna at Columbia. That enterprise found life on the 28th of March, 1809, when Governor Simon Snyder approved an act, entitled "An act authorizing the Governor of Pennsylvania to incorporate a company for the purpose of making and erecting a bridge over the river Susquehanna, in the county of Lancaster, at or near Columbia." In that act Stephen Girard, William Sanson, James Vanuxem, John Perot, Henry Pratt, Thomas McEwen, Martin Dubbs and Thomas S. Lewis of the city of Philadelphia; John Hurley, Absaham Witmer, Casper Shaffner, Jr., Jacob Strickler, James Wright and Samuel Miller, of the county of Lancaster, and William Barber, John Stewart and Godfrey Lenhart, of the county of York, were appointed commissioners to receive subscriptions to the capital stock, which was placed at $400,000. This was a great undertaking for those days; the length of the proposed bridge was unprecedented, the risks were hazardous, and the consequences of these conditions was a hesitancy on the part of the public to subscribe. Although the limit to be reached in the number of shares at par value of $100 each before letters patent could issue was only 1,200, it was not until November 19, 1811, that the commissioners could certify that such subscriptions had been made. On that day the Governor issued the letters, and created the corporation under the name and style of "The President, Managers and Company for Erecting a Bridge over the Susquehanna River, in the County of Lancaster, at or near the town of Columbia." In pursuance of that authority, the stockholders met December 11, 1811, and elected William Wright as president ; William P. Beatty treasurer ; John Barber, secretary ; Thomas Boude, Samuel Bethel, James Wright, Samuel Miller, John Evans, Christian Breneman, John Forrey, Jr., Abraham Witmer, Henry Slaymaker, William Barber, Jacob Eichelberger and John Tomilson, managers. One of the provisions of the act authorizing the construction of the bridge was that work upon it should begin in three and be completed within fifteen years. The Legislature, by the act of April 2, 1811, authorized a State subscription of $90,000 to the stock, half of which was to be paid upon the completion of the abutments and piers and the other half upon the completion of the structure.

At a meeting of the board on December 26, 1811, they provided for soliciting bids for plans and the erection of the bridge. Quite a number of plans and proposals were submitted, out of which those of Henry Slaymaker, Jonathan Wolcott and Samuel Slaymaker were selected, and on July 8, 1812, they were awarded the contract for erecting the bridge on the Burr plan, and in accordance with their bid upon stone piers forty feet long, ten feet wide at the top, and twenty feet high from low water mark, for the sum of $150,000. The site selected, and upon which the bridge was erected, was about 1,000 feet feet farther up the stream than the site of its successors.

The amount of stock subscribed by individuals at the time was but $150,000, whilst that by the State was provisional. The board and contractors thought they could save money by going on with the abutments, piers and superstructure all at one time, and still obtain the State's subscription. In this they counted without their host. After expending $78,000, all that was realized from individual subscriptions, and an additional amount nearly equal to that of the State's first installment, they found that the Commonwealth's subscription was unavailable under the provisions of the law, and when they attempted to obtain legislation to alter the terms of payment upon which the subscription was based, there developed an opposition which was strong enough to prevent the alteration. The company's and contractors' funds having all been expended in the incomplete work, and financiers refusing to loan any money upon such kind of security as the unfinished bridge, the board in its dilemma, and to save the enterprise from ruin, on July 5, 1813, determined upon a banking scheme as an aid in constructing the bridge. Out of this transaction came the funds for the completion of the bridge and the payment of the State's subscription of $90,000.

The title of the company was changed on the 29th of March, 1824, to "The Columbia Bridge Company," and the legislation which authorized the change also authorized the company to carry on a banking business. The previous banking operations of the company had been carried on without legislative consent and brought it into a conflict with the authorities. From the business thus authorized was evolved what is now "The Columbia National Bank." After a quarter of a century of banking and bridging combined, the directors became convinced that the financial standing of the bank was constantly menaced by the hazardous nature of the bridge property, and determined upon disposing of the latter by sale. As early as May 1, 1852, they procured legislative authority to make such disposition of it, but it was not until twelve years thereafter, on the heels of disaster, that the sale was accomplished and the Columbia Bank and the Columbia Bridge Company became two distinct corporations, and their operations confined within the limits of their respective spheres.

The bridge was completed and opened for traffic in 1814. It was 5,690 feet long, between abutments 30 feet wide, 23 feet above the usual level of the water, and composed of 53 arches resting upon stone piers. It was roofed over, and cost $231,771. The amount of capital stock subscribed was $419,000 by individuals and $90,000 by the State. All receipts in excess of cost of bridge were applied to banking purposes.

In February, 1832, a destructive ice freshet occurred in the Susquehanna. A gorge, where huge blocks of ice welded together by friction were piled up thirty or forty feet high, was formed several miles below the bridge, damming the stream, backed the ice and water up over the front street of Columbia and carried the bridge from off its piers. The river, from shore to shore, was filled for days with fields of floating ice, with here and there a span of the bridge eddying through them. On the 3d and 4th of February five spans of the bridge were taken away, on the 7th nine more, and a few days after thirty additional ones followed, and the destruction became complete. It was replaced in 1834 by a structure which cost $129,726.50, with its approaches.

The bridge of 1834 was, wth its approaches, 5,620 feet long, 40 feet wide, with its bottom chords 15 feet above high water mark. It was a covered bridge, had two tracks and divisions for foot passengers, carriages and other vehicles, and two towing paths, one above the other, for the accommodation of Susquehanna canal traffic through the pool of the dam.

When the wave of civil war struck the shores of the Susquehanna by the march of Early's division, of Ewell's corps, of Lee's army of Northern Virginia, the bridge was ordered by the military authorities of the United States to be destroyed, so as to prevent its being passed over by the enemy. In accordance with that order it was entirely consumed by fire on Sunday, June 28th, 1863, and the naked piers were left to mark the most northerly limit reached by the army of the south, which, receding from that limit, moved southwardly until overpowered and disbanded at Appomattox. The sight of the burning bridge was a sublime one. The fire swept along from span to span until the whole structure was one roaring mass of angry flames; blazing timber hissed as they dropped in the stream and floated towards the dam. The Southern soldiers lined the right bank of the river and swarmed over the adjacent hills, interested spectators of the grand display of fire's awful force. Men, women and children crowded the left bank, almost spell-bound, as the fire shaped fantastic colorings on sky, tree and water. Then came panic. Columbia had never before seen such a spectacle. "The retreat of the troops, the firing of the bridge, and shell and shot falling into the river created a panic, and the stampede continued during the night, as the shelling of the town was anticipated."

On the 12th of July, 1864, the Columbia Bank sold and conveyed the bridge franchises, piers and other property to Josiah Bacon, Wistar Morris, Thomas A. Scott, Joseph B. Myers, Edward C. Knight, Herman J. Lombaert and Edmund Smith. These gentlemen had, on July 6, 1864, met and organized the Columbia Bridge Company in accordance with law, and elected Herman J. Lombaert as president and Edmund Smith as secretary and treasurer. On the 6th of September, 1864, they conveyed to the bridge company the property, etc., which they had purchased from the bank. In 1868-69 the bridge company built a new railroad and highway bridge upon the piers. The bridge was a "through Howe truss arch." It consisted of 27 spans, was 5,390 feet long, and roofed and weather-boarded. Subsequently two iron spans were placed in the center of the bridge, so that the possible loss by fire should be reduced one-half. Some idea of the size and weight of the structure can be gained from the bill of lumber which went into it. Without going into details, the lumber in board measure consisted of 3,299,952 feet of white pine, 729,906 feet of white oak, 1,900,000 feet of short joint shingles. It was opened for ordinary travel on January 4, 1869, and partially opened for railroad purposes on March 1, 1869. Including the rebuilding and strengthening of many of the piers, and capping them with dressed stone, the cost reached nearly $400,000. On July 1, 1879, the Columbia

Bridge Company conveyed it to the Pennsylvania Railroad Company.

In the destruction of this bridge it was destined that an element other than those which entered into the destruction of the two preceding bridges was to try its force. Water and fire had had their mad revels, and now the wind was to try one of its most terrific manifestations, having in view the bridge for its most prominent victim. On Saturday, September 26, 1896, a storm was reported as a tropic line moving northwest from the Carribbean Sea, it being southeast of Cuba. During the 27th it passed northwestward into the southeastern part of the Gulf of Mexico, and on the 28th moved northward west of Florida. On the morning of the 29th it was over southern Georgia, and by 8 p. m. of the 29th had advanced to southwestern Virginia. The center passed over Washington, D. C., about 11:30 Tuesday night, the lowest barometer reading being 29.30. During the first three days the storm appeared to have very little energy, but on the 29th developed force rapidly as it moved northward. A velocity of 54 miles occurred at Charleston, and 42 at Wilmington. It reached Columbia shortly after 12 o'clock, mid-night of Tuesday, lashing itself into fury before 1 o'clock Wednesday morning, and leaving devastation in its wake. The Columbia Daily *Spy* of September 30th has this description of its force and effect :

"The disaster was wide-spread and general. The force of the winds was irresistible, and the effects more disastrous than any ever known in eastern Pennsylvania. Thousands of people were awakened soon after mid-night by the fury of the storm and the terror of crashing trees and flying debris from roofs and buildings. Houses were swaped to and fro by the mighty force of the winds. Sleepers were awakened by the crash of window panes or the rocking of their beds, and consuming fear seized many as they contemplated the fury of the storm. To add to the terror of the moment, mill whistles and alarm bells sounded a chorus of distress and summoned the aid of the fire department. This brought hundreds, perhaps thousands, of people to the streets, who wended their way to the scenes of disaster through the debris of the storm, cautious of overhanging roofs, signs and awnings, and fearful of trolley and elecric-light wires. Fortunately there was no fire, and the department apparatus was promptly returned to their quarters.

"The hurricane which was promised for to-day came a little after mid-night with a force and fury unknown to the experience and lives of people in this section. The disturbance was gentle at first, but, increasing with every moment, it soon became a hurricane, which swept over the town and country with resistless force, marking its pathway with destruction and ruin. The climax of the storm's power and fury was the destruction of the Columbia bridge, which for so many years had withstood the force of storm and the power of flood. It is a total wreck. It was struck by the full force of the hurricane, swept from the piers, and thrown into the river, a mass of broken and tangled debris. Nothing remains but a short span at the Columbia end of the bridge, the iron span in the center, and the façade at the entrance on the York county side.

"Pen cannot describe the picture of desolation which the bridge presents, and only actual sight will convey to the mind the effect of the fury and force of the terrible storm. The old bridge was the pride of the town. Now all that is left are the stone piers, with straggling timbers hanging on them. In place of the bridge there is nothing but a stretch of wreckage. We all loved to speak of it as the longest covered bridge in the world, a distinction generally accorded to it, though sometimes disputed by like claims for a similar bridge across the Mississippi river recently completed."

Turning from bridge to wire, Lancaster city has the honor of hearing the first "click" of an electric telegraph instrument on the first telegraph line built for commercial purposes in this country.

After encountering opposition and nearly endless obstacles, Professor Morse, when hope had almost deserted him and poverty stared him in the face, received governmental aid for the construction of an experimental line of telegraph between Baltimore and Washington. Then, as the lamented Blaine so eloquently said :

"The little thread of wire, placed as a timid experiment between the National Capital and a neighboring city grew and lengthened and multiplied with almost the rapidity of the electric current that darted along its iron nerves, until, within his own life-time, continent was bound unto continent, hemisphere answered through ocean's depths unto hemisphere, and an encircled globe flashed forth his eulogy in the unmatched eloquence of a grand achievement."

The first fruit of that experiment's success was a line built between Harrisburg and Lancaster, alongside the tracks of the Harrisburg, Portsmouth, Mount Joy and Lancaster Railroad.

No sooner had the practicability of Morse's invention been proven than the patentees made numerous contracts for the construction of lines throughout the country, and the most valuable, important and generous of them was given to Henry O'Reilly, of Rochester, N. Y.

Under this contract it became necessary to construct a line between Harrisburg and Lancaster on or before January 1, 1846, to connect at Lancaster with a line to be constructed by the Magnetic Company between Baltimore and New York, on a route via York, Columbia, Lancaster and Philadelphia. The route of this latter line, however, was changed so as to cross the Susquehanna at Port Deposit instead of Columbia, and O'Reilly subsequently connected his Western line with it at Philadelphia. He did not lose any time in performing his part of the contract, but with the aid of Bernard O'Connor, of Lancaster, completed the line to Harrisburg on the 24th of November, 1845. It was a primitive affair. Small, unbarked chestnut poles were planted about one hundred yards apart, so as to make eighteen poles to the mile. Through the top of each pole was inserted a turned black walnut cross-arm, the ends of which were covered with gummed cloth. The conductor was a No. 14 copper wire attached to the poles by giving it a double twist around the gummed cloth ends of the cross-arm. The gummed cloth not proving satisfactory as an insulator, insulation was somewhat improved by replacing it with a cotton cloth dipped in molten beeswax.

There was a good deal of enjoyment among the builders, notwithstanding the difficulties with which they were surrounded. The planted the poles whilst singing this refrain :

"Sink the poles, boys, firm and strong,
  Short and close together;
Solder the joints of the mystic thong,
  And let it stand forever."

The instruments arrived about January 1, 1846, and were placed in circuit by James D. Reid, who possessed some telegraphic knowledge obtained from his friendship with Professor Morse and by his experience on the experimental line. The relays, enclosed in large walnut boxes, weighed 250 pounds each, and required the strength of two men to lift them onto a table. The reason for this heavy weight grew out of the theory of Professor Morse and Alfred Vail that the wire of the relay should be of the same size as that of the line, and consequently they covered theirs with No. 14 copper wire wound with cotton.

After the instruments had been put in circuit and the battery located at Harrisburg, the operators, David Brooks and Henry C. Hepburn, at Lancaster, and James D. Reid and H. Courtney Hughes, at Harrisburg, settled down to hard work in their efforts to open up communication between the two offices. With the exception of Reid, none of the party could read or write the telegraphic alphabet without constant consultation with a copy of it printed in a little book of instructions by Alfred Vail, which they kept open before them.

For a week they pounded and adjusted, adjusted and pounded, without any intelligible signals reaching either office. At last, however, on the 8th of January, 1846, just as despair was on the point of supplanting patient endeavor, whilst practicing writing the alphabet by pressing the finger against the armature of the relay, and Hepburn was drumming on the key, Brooks made the startling discovery that the armature of the relay had, under certain conditions, a motion corresponding to that made on the key. Turning to Hepburn, he made known his discovery, and told him to wait a moment and he would so adjust the armature that writing upon the register could be done by simply manipulating the key. Brooks made the adjustment, when the armature began to work apparently of its own volition and the pen-lever of the register responded. Starting the paper to see what marks or impressions would be made on it, they had the great satisfaction, after comparing the marks with their copy of the alphabet, to read, after a long line of dots, the following words: "Why don't you write, you rascals?" These few words, written by James D. Reid on that Jacksonian anniversary, formed the first intelligible message ever sent upon a line in Pennsylvania, and gave to the line itself the distinction of being the first in operation after the Washington-Baltimore experimental line of Professor Morse.

There was great rejoicing in Harrisburg when it was found that instantaneous communication could be had with Lancaster. People flocked to the offices to see the wonder of the age, but made no material use of the line, the patronage being confined to writing names in telegraphic characters on the paper ribbon with written letters underneath in explanation. Such was the only source of revenue. The revenue, as will be readily perceived, was small, even from that source, for the first day's receipts at Harrisburg were 10 cents and at Lancaster $6\frac{1}{4}$ cents. In 1852 James D. Reid, speaking of the line, said: "The first day's receipts of the great national office in Washington were one cent, but Harrisburg, brighter than Washington, saw the clear visage of a dime whilst sober-sided Lancaster gloried in the possession of a 'fip.'"

Although the line was not a financial success, it furnished additional proof to the value of Professor Morse's invention. The relays were difficult of adjustment, and would not remain adjusted for a period of five minutes.

The line itself worked only in clear, cold weather, and then very irregularly. Breaks were of daily occurrence, and so certain were they to happen that Brooks went to the Lancaster office every morning at half past 4 to test for current, and it was the exception when he found it. Finding no current, he would shoulder a bundle of copper wire and start out to find and repair the "break," taking passage on the night line, a train which passed Lancaster at 5 o'clock in the morning on its way from Philadelphia to Harrisburg. This train, climbing over the Conewago hills, made the distance from Lancaster to Harrisburg, thirty-seven miles, in from four and a-half to five hours.

Reid and Hepburn left the line in February, 1846. James M. Lindsay was sent from Baltimore to succeed Reid, and he at Harrisburg and Brooks at Lancaster continued for a few weeks to operate the line. As narrated before, the only revenue accruing to the line was derived from sending the names of the curious over it. The novelty of that patronage wearing off, patrons ceased to materialize, and cash receipts failed to appear. There being no other available revenue, and the line constantly breaking, O'Reilly ordered Lindsay to Philadelphia and Brooks to take down the wire, sell it for old copper, and apply the proceeds to paying the operators' boarding and washing which were in arrears and had been accruing from the time of their arrival. By March 1, 1846, this initial commercial line had passed into history. The money for its construction was furnished by a Rochester, N. Y., company, known as "The Atlantic, Lake and Mississippi Valley Telegraph Company."

The line formed the link in the great chain of protected telegraphs, which in less than twenty years from the time of its completion was to bind in indissoluble bonds the Atlantic to the Pacific and in less than thirty years was to unite four of the grand divisions or continents of the world together, bringing all languages to a common center, benefiting commerce, trade, science, art, invention, agriculture and literature, and proving itself an invaluable factor in producing the remarkable and progressive age in which we live and which marks the closing hours of the nineteenth century with ineffaceable distinctness as civilization's most advanced period since the opening of the Christian era.

During the short life of the line it created quite a stir in the sister counties of Dauphin and Lancaster. The copper wire conductor, stretched tightly between poles, gave the wintry blasts the opportunity of producing somewhat musical, weird and fantastic sounds that could be heard for some distance, to the great discomfort of the rustics. The public mind having somewhat of a superstitious bend, many people in the neighborhood of the line, alarmed by the sounds proceeding from the wire as the wind swept over it, would walk a very considerable distance out of their way, often placing themselves at great inconvenience, particularly after sundown, to avoid passing under or near it. Many dismal stories were told of its supernatural powers, and one woman actually fenced in a pole to prevent her cow rubbing against it, fearing that the milk might be spoiled.

Then in rural communities, when any question excited the public interest, the people would congregate at the "store," or "the Squire's," to gather news and interchange views. I might say that the custom is still in vogue, and has its imitation in the town meetings of their city cousins, who are so fond of pow-wowing over the public weal. Right here let us take a look at the village. The village, a child of convenience, sprung from the loins of necessity at the call of man's herding inclinations, was mostly an unincorporated community; ordinarily the center of a township clustered around an inn, a blacksmith shop, a cross-roads store and a meeting house, finding its highest expression of political importance from being the residence of the Township Supervisor and of that august specimen of the minor judiciary, "the Squire." The population made up principally of farmers and farm hands, found days pass less wearily by dwelling closer together than was permissible by the territorial limits of farms. The great events were mostly the arrival of the semi-or tri-weekly mails at the post office, a fresh invoice of goods at the store, and of incipient statesmen, bearing the burdens of State, at the inn. Those events brought the community together at one of the places named to discuss whatever questions the arrivals suggested, or to exchange gossip. Their pleasures were few and simple, the checker board and card table furnishing most of them, whilst occasional quoit-throwing at the blacksmith shop and the spelling bee and the mock-court at the school house varied the monotony of their lives. "Let not ambition mock their useful toil, their homely joys," for it was from just such villages as those that Hampdens rose and Lincolns expanded into greatness, reaching up to originality of thought and expression by having Nature for a tutor and being so surrounded that their education became something more than the absorption of other men's written ideas, thoughts and opinions.

But all this is changing, and the villages of the long-ago, which were bowers of rustic beauty and the abodes of health and contentment, have passed or are passing away. Their doom had been sounded; the rushing, dashing, flashing spirit of progressiveness which rules this age is the cause. The rustic, but romantic, peaceful edging which the villages gave to the picture of Pennsylvania life is threatened with a change. Already electric lights have deprived them of the softened shadows so comforting to a purturbed spirit on a moonlit night, and the tocsin has sounded announcing the approach of the trolley roads whose entree to those charming localities will forever eliminate their quiet, dreamy, mid-day life. The gas pipe, the water pipe and electric light have invaded the quiet village, the trolley lines in the foreground, and sewers, paved streets, curbed sidewalks, and the woodman's axe in the perspective admonish us that the view is changing, that the dreamy village life will soon be o'er and the village lost in the municipal maelstrom which is engulfing it. But to return to the telegraph and its advent in the village.

One Saturday afternoon, shortly after the line was in operation, a gathering assembled at the "store" in one of the villages, and the all-absorbing topic of conversation was the "telegraph" The "big man" of the vicinity was there. For two terms he had represented his district in the lower house of the Legislature, and he now felt it his duty to express his opinion on the subject, which he did by saying : " This telegraph is a great thing. When I had the honor of representing you in the Legislature I often thought about it, and having turned the subject over in my mind the conclusion reached by me in regard to it is that it will do well enough for carrying letters and small package, but it will never do for carrying large bundles and bale boxes."

David Lechler, a well-kept and humorous man, was the proprietor of "The North American House," where the office in Lancaster was located, and made the telegraph the basis for playing many pranks upon the public. At this day few can credit the curiosity and credulity which characterized the people in connection with the telegraph, and how few had even an idea of the principles governing it. Lechler, discerning the trend of the mind of the people, turned it to advantage in fun-making, and undertook to unfold the mysteries to those who visited his house. It was his great delight on market mornings to gather a crowd of countrymen and women in the barroom, and then explain to them in Pennsylvania Dutch the wonders of the great invention. There was no story that he could invent or apply, or that credulity would accept in connection with the telegraph, that he did not relate. As soon as his harangue had raised the curiosity of his hearers to the highest notch he would hurriedly enter the room where the telegraph office was located and immediately returning, would show a pair of hose, a handkerchief or a newspaper, which he had previously punctured with holes, as specimens of the telegraph's possibilities, at the same time gravely saying: "I received these in just forty seconds from Philadelphia." There were none to doubt Lechler's word or to take into consideration that the line did not extend to Philadelphia, but all, with open-eyed wonder, tried to account for the articles passing over and around the cross-arms. They were satisfied, however, with Lechler's explanation, that that process was the inventor's secret which he dared not divulge.

Whilst the line was taken down and sold the instruments were allowed to remain. Those at Lancaster were used in a telegraphic school, whereto intended telegraph operators from different parts of the country were sent to be taught the mysteries. The teacher was William Johnson, then, as now, a respected resident of Lancaster. Many men, who afterwards became prominent in the telegraphic profession, went out in the telegraphic world with Billy's diploma. Among the number was Anson Stager, who became the manager of Western Union interests that insured the great success that company has scored. Mr. Stager during the war was appointed a quartermaster and detailed to the Military Telegraph Department, in which he rose to be a brigadier-general. The United States Military Telegraph Corps received its first recruits from Pennsylvania and its first line builder was a Lancaster man.

On April 17, 1861, I went with Thomas A. Scott to Governor Curtin's office, at Harrisburg, and there, with a relay magnet and a key placed on a window sill, opened the first military telegraph office on this continent. In the same office, on the 25th of April, 1861, on the call of Mr. Scott, there reported for orders David Strouse, from Mifflin; D. Homer Bates, from Altoona; Richard O'Brien, from Greensburg, and Samuel Brown, from from Pittsburg, four of the best operators on the Pennsylvania Railroad Company's telegraph line.

But of the nucleus formed by the little

band of Pennsylvania railroad telegraph operators grew a wondrous military telegraph corps, in which were enrolled during the war twelve hundred young men, telegraph operators, whose ages ranged from sixteen to twenty-two years—boys in years and stature, but giants in loyalty and in the amount of work they performed for their country. They did not plan campaigns nor fight battles, but amid the roar of conflict were found cooly advising the commanding general of the battle's progress. They formed the corps that was the very nerves of the army during the war, and so considered by all those who came in contact with it, and yet it was not, and has not been, recognized as an integral part of that army.

Their position in the army was a peculiar one, whether as enlisted men or volunteers, and there were both classes in the service; they were not subject to the orders of its active officers, but came under the immediate direction of President Lincoln, as commander-in-chief, through the Secretary of War. They were in effect field couriers, with enlarged responsibilities. The secrets of the Nation were entrusted to them, and the countersign of the army was often in their possession a week or more in advance of its promulgation. All the movements of the army, all the confidences of the commanders were entrusted to them, and yet not one was ever known to betray that knowledge and confidence in the most remote degree.

A hundred nameless graves throughout the battle-fields of the Union attest their devotion unto death to the sublime cause in which they were engaged, and yet the government they loved and labored for never as much as thanked them for their services!

Every nation, ours among the number, has now a military telegraph corps as an integral part of its army, and yet, before the Civil War in the United States, such an arm of the service was practically unknown. It was reserved for mere boys— American boys—to inaugurate that arm of the service, demonstrate its value in actual war, and for so doing, become the recipients of the monumental ingratitude of the nineteenth century!

As the war progressed the corps developed and equipment for field work was perfected.

Whilst Line Builders Paul D. Connor, Charley Noyes and Dave Carnathan were the first to extend the military telegraph lines from Washington into Virginia, it was reserved for Parker Spring, of Lancaster, Pa., to head the first telegraph construction corps for the United States Army. Before Captain R. F. Morley, of the 17th Infantry, and formerly superintendent of the Allegheny Valley Railroad, was specially detailed in September, 1861, as general manager of government railroads and telegraphs, men for construction work were picked up as needed wherever they were to be found. Captain Morley in perfecting the organization selected Parker Spring, an experienced operator and builder, to take charge of the telegraph construction corps. The initial party of the corps was composed of twenty-two men, divided into gangs of "climbers," "pole-cutters," "diggers," and "laborers," with intelligent foremen over each gang. Spring picked his men for being steadfast, reliable and hard workers. They were drilled daily and kept under military discipline. The party was provided with tents, horses, wagons, and a full complement of implements for their work. The work was laborious; at all hours of the day or night they were liable to be and were frequently called upon to meet some exigency of the service. But no matter if they were called from sleep when midnight had thrown its dark shroud around earthly scenes, or in the dawn of the morning, their answer to the summons was made with alacrity and good cheer. In constructing new, tearing down and rebuilding old lines, they were at times compelled to plod through snow and mud, in rain, over hills, across rivers, and to pick their way cautiously through forests and swamps. Frequently the work would go in tracts of country from whence civilization had apparently departed, and where the only sounds to be heard were the notes of their own industry. At other times their work would carry them so close to the enemy's lines that with only a rivulet between they could hold converse with the Rebel pickets. It was a varied and picturesque life, as well as one of excitement and danger. Spring and his men were entitled to great credit for their fidelity and trustworthiness in rapidly extending the telegraph lines to meet the needs of the government in the direction of more speedy means of communication.

I cannot allow this opportunity to pass without making record of heroic service in the face of the enemy of two other men from Lancaster—William Johnson, already mentioned, and Strickland Everts. In the campaign of 1863, when the Southron invaded Pennsylvania, marching almost unimpeded down the Cumberland Valley, these men kept the telegraph lines up and in operation, and were driven step by step down the valley, and as the enemy withdrew returned in their immediate wake and made repairs before the clatter of the swords of the cavalry had died away. On the first of July I saw these two men driven into Carlisle by the advance of General J. E. B. Stuart, and standing on the main street, in front of Dr. Stevenson's house, which was struck by a shell, taking the bombardment as coolly as seasoned campaigners. One of them picked up a fragment of the shell and afterwards sent it to Dr. Stevenson, who cemented it in the breach in his wall, weere it remains to-day.

The city and county are connected with many interesting railroad and canal events, some of which I have recited in my historical sketches of the Philadelphia and Columbia and Harrisburg and Lancaster railroads, but here, and in conclusion, there is one I desire to incorporate in this paper

Early in this century the restless spirit of American progress and adventure, not quieted by extending through the Louisiana purchase the boundaries of the United States across the Mississippi, cast its eyes beyond the Sabine and toward territorial expansion in the land of the Aztec, with its wealth of precious stones and metals. Imperial expansion with imperial power and luxury was an ever-present dream with the highly cultivated people, scions of aristocratic stocks. In the Southern States of the Union, and it is not surprising that the emigration to that part of Mexico now known as Texas was largely made up of educated emigrants from that section, nor that those emigrants should at an early day throw off their allegience to the unstable government of Mexico and establish a government of their own. Without sufficient strength to establish a strong centralized government on an aristocratic basis, there was nothing left the people of Texas after the independences of that Republic was acknowledged and established but to favor annexation to the United States. Annexation was consummated on the 29th of December, 1845. General Taylor, in command of a small American army, left New Orleans in July, 1845, to occupy Texas. On the 8th of March, 1846, he crossed the Neuces and marched toward the Rio Grande, occupying the disputed territory between those rivers. That occupation brought on the Mexican War. Whilst General Taylor was waiting for the orders from Washington to begin his march reinforcements were being pressed forward to him. In the winter of 1845 and 1846 part of these reinforcements passed westward from Philadelphia via the Philadelphia and Columbia railroad. They reached Dillerville in comparatively good time. As the trains left Dillerville, drawn by the "David R. Porter" and "Henry Clay," two eleven-ton engines, to pass over the Harrisburg and Lancaster railroad for the former town a snow storm came up and soon the rails were covered with snow an inch or two in depth and sufficient to stall the trains. That was an unexpected and consequently not-provided-for dilemma. 'Tis true that the hickory brooms placed in front of the truck of the locomotive for the purpose of removing obstacles from the rails were in position, but they only tended to pack the snow harder. At this point American ingenuity and American pluck came to the front and improvised a snow plow to throw the snow from the track as the engine proceeded. This improvised plow consisted of plain boards held in hand by two men sitting on the bumper. The boards were used to push the snow to one side, and were raised and lowered whenever they came in contact with "broken" joints.

Practically, it was shoving the snow off the track. John Keller was one of the two men so engaged, and in the fourteen hours that it took these trains to reach Harrisburg from Dillerville he stuck to his post, displaying those powers of endurance and loyalty to duty that have characterized his career and made it successful.

WILLIAM BENDER WILSON,
Holmesburg, Philadelphia, 1897.

A PROMINENT SCOTCH-IRISHMAN.

In the early settlement of the territory now included in Lancaster county, the portion north of the Mine Ridge was occupied mainly by those speaking the German language, while those speaking English "took up" the portion south of that ridge and familiarly known as the "lower end." Of these the emigrants from the north of Ireland, usually termed "Scotch-Irish," from their Scottish ancestry, were the most numerous, the English Quakers coming next in point of numbers.

Subsequent settlers naturally divided in the same manner, each family trying to locate among those speaking a familiar language; and this rule holds good in the main to this day.

Early in the spring of the year 1796 Charles Sproul, a native of county Armagh, in the north of Ireland, with his wife and family sailed for Philadelphia, his son, James Sproul, the subject of this sketch, being then a lad of eleven years of age. The whole family, including father and mother, would seem to have been liberally educated for that time, and with a rigid regard for the Bible and its teachings, as understood by the Scotch-Irish pastors of the Covenanter and Presbyterian churches of one hundred years ago.

After the usual stormy passage of nearly three months they arrived safely in Philadelphia and located in that city; but not liking the city, they soon removed to Spring Mills, in Montgomery county, where James supplemented his Irish education with a winter or two in the not very promising country school of that day. That James made the best use possible of these limited opportunities to secure an education cannot be doubted in view of his subsequent career.

He was anxious, however, to get to work, and being a born mechanic had a strong desire to deal with and manage machinery. His only opportunity for this near his home was in a country mill, so he prevailed on the miller to take him as an assistant.

In a few months he had so mastered the details of the mill that it is said he knew more about the machinery than the owner and made small repairs that the owner could not have done; but the mill needed greater repairs than he was capable of making, so a millwright was secured and James became his helper. In this position he was entirely at home and became so useful and efficient that the millwright determined to secure him, and between them they procured the miller's consent to his leaving to learn the trade of a millwright.

In this he rapidly became an expert, and followed it for several years, working along the Schuylkill river and its tributaries, on all kinds of mills and on all sorts of machinery propelled by water. While here he assisted in building the first mill for rolling iron erected by the Phœnix Iron Company, on the grounds where their present enormous plant is located.

On leaving the Schuylkill he came to Doe Run, in Chester county, and formed a partnership with the Clarks, a firm of contracting millwrights, but the war of 1812 to 1815 was now on and the price of iron was advancing rapidly, and young Sproul thought he saw a fortune in the business.

He accordingly formed a partnership with a Frank Paik, and together they erected a forge at White Rock, on the east bank of the west branch of the Octorara, in Colerain township, this county, near where White Rock station now stands. Before the forge was ready to operate Paik got tired of the venture and withdrew from the firm, but Sproul stuck to it, probably receiving some financial assistance from the Colemans, who were also Scotch-Irish, from the county of Donegal.

On the completion of the plant the price of iron was falling and the war was nearing an end, so that the venture was not nearly so profitable as he had hoped, but he had a good, well built forge as compared with others and he ran it quite successfully for some twelve or thirteen years, making considerable money. While here he secured quite a large interest in Black Rock Furnace, four miles up the stream from White Rock. He was also interested with Edward Coleman in the Conowingo Rolling Mill, on the site or near the Conowingo Furnace, and with one of the Grubb family in the forges at Codorus, York county, Robert Sproul, a younger brother of James, managing them.

By this time Sproul had established quite a reputation as a successful iron master, and he determined to concentrate his operations, which, in his opinion, had become so much scattered that he could not personally supervise their workings. He leased his White Rock Forge to John Alexander, another representative of the Scotch-Irish of Lancaster county, and purchased from John Withers a large tract of land with three forges on it, in Sadsbury township, on the west bank of the east branch of the Octorara, so fully described in an article just read. He removed to these forges in 1828, and after enlarging and improving the same commenced operations.

His intention now was to make a very superior iron and sell the same for special uses, at a price considerably above ordinary hammered iron, and in this he was fairly successful. The forges were known as the upper and lower Sadsbury forges and the Ringwood forge. The upper forge was arranged to refine the iron and make it into what was known as anconies, when it was transported to the lower or chafery forge, where a higher welding heat was given to it and it was hammered into the required shapes.

The pig iron was boiled or puddled in much the same manner as now, but the process was very crude, much longer, more laborious and less productive of finished iron than now. Very much of the iron passed off as cinder in the operation and every forge had large banks of cinder around it. Mr. Sproul knew that large quantities of iron remained in this cinder, and therefore built an addition to the upper forge expressly to deal with these immense cinder piles, and was successful in reclaiming about 40 per cent. of the weight of this cinder in iron, though the quality of this cinder iron was not nearly so good as the other iron.

This cinder addition, however, was very profitable and all the cinder on the ground and all that was made was put through this process. This gave Mr. Sproul quite a variety of irons at a variety of prices, so that he could accommodate all customers, and he did quite a thriving business.

He sold considerable iron to the hardware stores and manufacturers of Lancaster, Wilmington and Philadelphia; but his best customers were Whitney & Co., of Hartford, Conn., who were large manufacturers of firearms. He hammered this gun iron into octagonal shapes, from $\frac{3}{4}$ to $1\frac{1}{2}$ inches in diameter, and while it was necessary to take only the very best stock, employ only the most skilled workmen and exercise the greatest care in making it, the buyers were willing to pay a good price for it and Mr. Sproul found it profitable to strive for their trade, which he secured almost entirely and continued to hold until his death. The raw material he found best adapted to his use was the Cornwall and Colebrook pig iron with a small percentage of good wrought scrap.

As soon as his business got to running smoothly he purchased what was known as the Hamilton tavern, on East King street, this city, which occupied the ground on which the house of George Nauman, Esq., and the two houses next east of it, are built.

He reserved a portion of the yard of this tavern for his own use and made arrangements that the sellers of the pig iron should deliver to that point, where his teams loaded it and hauled it to the forges. Sproul's wagons were drawn by six mules or horses and made as a rule two round trips per week, though in seasons of great activity sometimes three trips were made. Their load was 1½ to 2½ tons, according to the condition of the roads. The teamsters carried hay and feed for their teams and bedding for themselves.

When there were orders from Lancaster parties for finished iron the teams would have loads both ways, but more frequently they went to Lancaster empty.

When Mr. Sproul came to Sadsbury he was over forty years of age and unmarried, having always been too busy to marry, but in 1830 he was married to Miss Annie Johnson. Seven children blessed this union—Charles N., now living in Philadelphia and unmarried; James C., died in infancy; Margaret A., married to

Robert H. Hodson, and living near New London, in Chester county; William H., married to Dora Slokom, daughter of the late Samuel Slokom, of Christiana, now living in Chester, Delaware county, Pa.; Mary D., married to John T. Dewitt, and living in Cecil county, Md.; James, married to Mary R. Slokom, daughter of Samuel Slokom, and living in Chester, Delaware county, Pa.; and Robert C., living in New London, Chester county, and unmarried.

Whatever Mr. Sproul forgot or neglected by reason of his active, busy life, it cannot be said that he forgot or neglected his early Irish religious training and the Sproul mansion, we are assured, was rather a doleful place on Sunday to the houseful of youngsters named above. The place was quite secluded and they were not permitted on that day to go visiting, or to leave the house except to go to church. Newspapers, of course, were wholly unthought of and the only books permitted were the Bible, the larger and shorter catechisms, Fox's "Book of Martyrs," Baxter's "Saints' Rest" and his "Call to the Unconverted," supplemented by the "Westminster Confession of Faith" and perhaps a volume or two of carefully selected sermons of the seventeenth century. "The Pilgrim's Progress" was not quite orthodox, not being of Presbyterian origin. It was rather tough on the rising generation, but since they have grown up it cannot be said that they were hurt by it.

The story frequently told of James Sproul that while a young man, employed as a wood chopper by the Colemans, he secured his first promotion by sending in an order from the woods to the store so beautifully written that he was at once sent for and put into the counting room, seems to be like so many similar stories, wholly without foundation. He was never employed by the Colemans in any capacity, though they were always his fast, firm, unwavering friends, and on more than one occasion, when things went wrong with him and he was in great danger of failing, came to his assistance. For many years preceding his death, however, it cannot be said that he required any financial aid. He died January 7, 1847, aged 62 years, possessed of quite a large estate.

After Mr. Sproul's death, the forges were rented to different parties who ran them with varied success. Some of them ran at times until the close of the war of the rebellion, but the expensive hauling by wagons, the growing scarcity of charcoal, the cheapness and general introduction of steam power as a motor, the immense rolling mills that grew out of this, and perhaps above all the more scientific manipulation of the iron in immense quantities, were too much for the country till hammers with their single advantage of a cheap water power, so they gradually faded away and are gone.

The reader claims no credit for the above sketch. The subject of it died fifty years ago. To-day none of his active contemporaries can be found, and his living children were all too small in his life to understand or remember much of his varied operations, so that it was extremely difficult to trace his career with accuracy. It may be said to be the joint contributions of his descendants, mainly of Wm. H. Sproul, of the firm Sproul & Lewis, wholesale grocers, Chester, Pa., who is his third son.

HISTORY OF THE DONEGAL CHURCH.

The early history of Donegal Church is involved in obscurity by reason of the fact that none of the records prior to 1786 can be found, and those immediately subsequent are only fragmentary; all that can be authenticated is to be gleaned from the records of Presbytery.

When we consider that Donegal Church was founded less than a score of years after the organization of the first Presbytery, the country at the time being thinly settled, the facilities for communication between neighboring settlements difficult and often dangerous, organization and the means for the preservation of records incomplete, and also the turbulent and unsettled state of the country, the paucity of data becomes obvious.

The aim of the historian should be to present facts, such as can be substantiated by documentary evidence, and such as have been derived from personal observation. Much that has been written concerning Donegal Church is unreliable tradition, therefore it is not the purpose of the writer of this sketch to mingle facts with traditional evidence.

Modern history hardly affords a parallel to the cruelty and oppression which caused the early Presbyterians to flee from the continent of Europe and seek an asylum in the wilderness of the New World. Even here persecution followed them, so that the trials and struggles of the early settlers were almost unendurable. Their ministers, ever in the van of the cause of liberty and freedom of conscience, stood as a bulwark against the oppressor. Though but few in number, we are to-day enjoying the rich blessings of a free government, the seeds of which they planted and nurtured until it has grown into a vast nation of freemen such as the world has never witnessed.

For the purpose of a better apprehension of the first pastorate of Donegal Church, and the relationship which it sustained to the First Presbytery of the Church in America, it may be well to invite attention to a brief outline of that organization.

"The first leaf of the records of the first Presbytery being lost, the book opens with the brethren in session at Freehold on a Thursday engaged in examining Boyd for ordination. They held 'sederunt 2nd' on Friday, sustained his trial and on the Lord's Day, December 27th, 1706, his ordination was performed at the meeting house in this place before a numerous assembly."—*Webster's History of the Presbyterian Church in America.*

"The original members, as far as can be ascertained from the Minutes, were Francis Makemie, Jedediah Andrews, George McNish, John Hampton, John Wilson, Nathaniel Taylor and Samuel Davis. To these may be added John Boyd, who became a member by ordination in 1706."—*Charles Hodge's History of the Presbyterian Church, page 94.*

The second meeting was held in Philadelphia. We will pass over the subsequent meetings, except to say that aid was solicited from Europe and that with the cheerful concurrence of the brethren, some of them at various times made application to different places. In 1710 "Wilson and Anderson wrote to the Synod of Glasgow."—*Webster's History, page 94.*

You will observe that the name of Anderson is mentioned the first time in the history.

The intercourse of the brethren during

nine years was harmouious and happy. Quiet, steady growth in numbers marked each successive meeting.

The Presbytery of Philadelphia met in that city on Tuesday, September 18, 1716. On Friday, the 21st, they resolved to divide themselves into subordinate meetings or Presbyteries which consisted of first, the Presbytery of Philadelphia; second, the Presbytery of Newcastle; third, Snow Hill and fourth, Long Island.

The following were the members of the Presbytery of Newcastle, viz.: Messrs. Anderson, McGill, Gillespie, Witherspoon, Evans and Conn. The name of Anderson again appears.

The ministers who served as pastors of Donegal Church will be noticed in the order of their ministrations. The first pastor, the Rev. James Anderson, was born in Scotland, November 17, 1678; he was ordained by Irvine Presbytery November 17, 1708; he arrived in this country April 22, 1709; he settled in Newcastle; he was called to supply a church in the city of New York, where he remained until 1726; he was called September 24 to Donegal on the Susquehanna and accepted it; he was installed the last Wednesday in August, 1727."

The Donegal Presbytery held its first meeting October 11, 1732, and consisted of Messrs. Anderson, Boyd, Orr, Thompson and Bertram. As early as September, 1735, the emigration to Virginia attracted the attention of Thompson, of Chestnut Level, and he proposed to Donegal Presbytery to employ an itinerant in Virginia. In April, 1738, Anderson was sent to Virginia bearing a letter to the government of Virginia, soliciting its favor in behalf of our interests. The Synod provided supplies for his pulpit, and allowed for his expenses in a manner suitable to his design.

"Anderson performed his mission satisfactorily."

"He married Mistress Suitt Garland, daughter of Sylvester Garland, of the head of Apoquinomy, February, 1712–13. She died December 24, 1736. He married Rachel Wilson December 27, 1737. Anderson died July 16, 1740. His son, Garland Anderson, was one of the witnesses of Andrews' (Jedediah Andrews) will in 1742. He married Jane, daughter of Peter Chevalier, of Philadelphia; he died early. His daughter (James Anderson's), Elizabeth, married Samuel Breeze, and resided in New York, a woman of great excellence." (*Webster History*). The following is the inscription on his tombstone in Donegal Burial Ground:

>Here Lyeth the Body of the
>REV. JAMES ANDERSON,
>Late Pastor of Dunnigall,
>Who departed this life ye 16th of July, 1740,
>Aged 62 years.
>Also His Wife,
>SUITT ANDERSON,
>Who departed this life ye 24th December, 1736
>Aged 42 years.

After the death of the Rev. Anderson the congregation was supplied by the Paxtons, senior and junior, and other ministers until "1748, when the Rev. Joseph Tate was called, who was received as a licentiate by Donegal Presbytery...... On the 14th of June he was called to Donegal, and soon after the Rev. Andrew Bay, of the New Side Presbytery of New Castle, accused him of having preached false doctrine at the Three Springs (Big, Middle and Rocky). He was acquitted October 25th and accepted the call from Donegal, they giving 70 pounds to buy a plantation and 70 pounds salary. He was ordained November 23d, 1748......Immediately after his installation he was married, December 15th, 1748, to Margaret, the eldest daughter of Boyd, of

Octorara. Her father gave her, besides a silk gown, a bed and its furniture, a horse and saddle and nearly every article for housekeeping; all of which are carefully entered in his book......He died October 11th, 1774, aged 63 years."—*Webster's History.*

He is buried at Donegal. The following is the inscription on his tombstone:

In Memory of
JOSEPH TATE,
Late Pastor of this Congregation for 26 years,
Who departed this life 11th October, 1774,
In the 63d year of his age;
and also in Memory of
His Wife, MARGARET,
and Daughter of the Rev. Adam Boyd,
Who departed this life 13th of May, 1801,
In the 75th year of her age.

Also on separate tombstones:
In Memory of
ADAM TATE,
Son of Rev. Joseph Tate,
Pastor of Donegal Church,
Who departed this life the 9th day of
February, 1827,
In the 74th year of his age.
In Memory of
SARAH TATE,
Daughter of the Rev. Joseph Tate,
Who departed this life the 15th of
August, 1780,
In the 30th year of her age.

The records of the interval of three years after the death of Rev. Joseph Tate are not extant. The near approach of our Revolutionary struggle may account for it ; as well as for the meagre account of the early part of the pastorate of the Rev. Colin McFarquhar, who was installed in 1777 and resigned in 1806.

Rev. McFarquhar's name appears on the records of the church as President of the Board of Trustees. In an N. B. to a receipt dated May the 7th, 1806, he says: "My pastoral labors in the church of Donegal terminate at the above date, and therefore the above is a receipt in full for all my pastoral services in said church.

"[Signed]   COLIN McFARQUHAR."

His wife is buried at Donegal, as the following inscription on her tombstone testifies :

In Memory of
ELIZABETH,
Wife of the Rev. Colin McFarquhar, minister of the Gospel in Donegal;
Who departed this life on the 6th of August,
An. Dom., 1805,
In the 64th year of her age.

One year after the resignation of the Rev. McFarquhar, the Rev. William Kerr "was ordained and installed May 1st, 1807 at a salary of $400 yearly until May 1st, 1814, and at $600 per annum," which was continued until his death, which occurred September 22, 1821. Mr. Kerr was much beloved by his parishioners and the people of the neighborhood. There are those still living who remember Mr. Kerr. His son, a much esteemed and eminent physician, a member of the York County Medical Society, died at York, Pa., June 10th, 1889, aged 76. One of the Rev. Kerr's daughters was the wife of a distinguished lawyer of Harrisburg, Mr. Herman Aldricks. Dr. H. L. Orth, the present Superintendent of the Pennsylvania State Lunatic Asylum, is a grandson of Rev. Mr. Kerr. He and two of his children are buried at Donegal. The inscriptions on their tombstones are as follows:

In Memory of
WILLIAM KERR,
Who Was 14 Years Minister of the Gospel
of the Congregation of Donegal.
Born the 13th Day of October, 1776, and Died
September 22, 1821,
In the 45th Year of His Age.

In Memory of
JOHN,
Son of Wm. and Mary Kerr.
Born Jan. 12, 1811, Died Nov. 16th, 1813.

In Memory of
CLAUDIUS B.,
Son of William and Mary Kerr.
Born Nov. 1st, 1820, Died Jan. 24th, 1821.

After an interval of a year the Rev. Orson Douglas was unanimously elected pastor December 2, 1822, and installed the following spring. He served the congregation fourteen years. He resigned in 1836 and removed to Philadelphia. At the close of Mr. Douglas' pastorate the records of the Session were lost. The Rev. Thomas Marshall Boggs was called to Donegal in 1836 and was installed April 27, 1837. He resided at Mr. John Clark's (now Hon. Don. Cameron's) place. He removed to Marietta and subsequently to Mt. Joy, where he died November 10, 1850. Mr. Boggs preached at Donegal, Marietta and Mt. Joy. He was much beloved by his parishioners and greatly esteemed by the community as a sincere Christian in all his walks and conversation. He married Miss Amelia Jane Cunningham, of Chester county, and had two sons and one daughter. His daughter became the wife of the late Rev. John Edgar, President of Wilson College, at Chambersburg, Pa.

Shortly before his death the Rev. James L. Rodgers assisted Mr. Boggs in his ministrations with the view of becoming co-pastor, as the duties of Mr. Boggs were too laborious. At the time (1837) he assumed the labors of the pastorate of Donegal the separation of the Old and New School was being accomplished. Many of the churches throughout the country were more or less agitated by the New School schism, especially that portion of the Donegal congregation residing at Mt. Joy (about three miles east of Donegal). Marietta (about three and one-half south of Donegal) was at that time a distinct church organization under the pastoral care of Mr. Boggs, in connection with Donegal. Mt. Joy had no organization, but had a building in contemplation, and had purchased a lot for that purpose, which the distraction consequent to the separation of the assembly into two bodies frustrated. The Old School party purchased an interest in the Lutheran Church of Mt. Joy, thus securing a place of worship alternately with the Lutherans.

The New School party proceeded to erect a place of worship, which they accomplished in 1840. At this time the Rev. N. Dodge's Ceder Hill Seminary for Young Ladies and Mr. John H. Brown's Mt. Joy Institution for Boys were in a flourishing condition and both Principals associated themselves with the New School party.

Mr. Boggs coutinued his pastoral services at Donegal, Marietta and Mt. Joy until his death.

He and his wife are buried at Donegal. Their tombstones are inscribed as follows:

REV. THOMAS MARSHALL BOGGS,
Pastor of the Presbyterian Congregation of Donegal and Marietta for fourteen years.
Died, November 10, 1850.
Age 1 37 years.
AMELIA JANE,
Widow of Rev. T. Marshall Boggs.
Died, August 25, 1869,
Aged 55 years.

The Rev. James L. Rodgers, who had been supplying the pulpit since the death of Mr. Boggs, "was ordained and installed pastor of the Donegal congregation by the Presbytery of Donegal, Thursday, the 21st day of August, 1851." The Marietta congregation about this time became self-sustaining and with the consent of Presbytery called a pastor, thus severing its connection with the mother church.

During the first year of the pastorate of Mr. Rodgers proposals for union between the Mt. Joy members of Donegal and the New School congregation of Mt. Joy were made and mutually agreed to; whereupon the Mt. Joy members sold their interest in the Lutheran Church to that congregation and appropriated the funds obtained to the liquidation of the debt remaining on the Mt. Joy Presbyterian Church. In 1852 the New School (with the consent of their Presbytery) organization united with the Donegal members residing in Mt. Joy and vicinity (forming what has since been known as the First Presbyterian Church of Mount Joy) under the pastorate of Mr. Rodgers, who continued his ministrations to the congregations of Mt. Joy and Donegal every alternate Sabbath morning until his resignation in September, 1856. Mr. Rodgers' resignation was very much regretted. He was a successful preacher and a very cheerful and lovable Christian gentleman. He removed to Springfield, Ohio, where he died January 25, 1895.

After the resignation of Mr. Rodgers the congregation of Donegal would not consent to the previous arrangement of every alternate Sabbath morning services, but insisted on having every Sabbath morning. To this the Mount Joy people could not agree, as they had the largest congregation and good prospects for a self-sustaining church, to maintain which, at the time, would be a very heavy burden without the aid of the Donegal fund, (the invested fund of Donegal at the time was about $8,000), of which they deemed themselves entitled to a share as the offspring of Donegal, and as they (the Mt. Joy people) constituted one-third of the membership.

The result was that Donegal called the Rev. John J. Lane, who was installed May 14, 1859. He served the cogregation until 1868, when he resigned. He died in 1893. The Mount Joy congregation called the Rev. James Smith, who, on account of declining health, resigned in 1868. Both congregations now being vacant, the former difficulty was amicably adjusted and Rev. John Edgar was installed May 12th, 1869, who served both congregations until 1870, when he resigned to accept a call to New Bloomfield, Pa., where he preached until chosen President of Wilson College, where he died June 5th, 1894.

The Rev. William B. Brown served both congregations from September, 1872, until April, 1880, as stated supply, when his services were discontinued. At the special request of Mr. Brown he was not installed, as he had in view the restoration of Cedar Hill Seminary, which, if successful, he would devote all his time to that object. His efforts not meeting with sufficient encouragement, it was abandoned, whereupon the arrangement with the congregations was continued until 1880, as above stated. He died June 23, 1892.

In 1881 the Rev. Cyrus B. Whitcomb, a Congregationalist, from Connecticut, preached a few Sabbaths as a candidate at Donegal and Mount Joy. He was called by both congregations. His installation was deferred until the meeting of Presbytery, at Columbia, the following spring, when Mr. Whitcomb applied for installation.

A Committee of Presbytery was appointed at Columbia to install him on the following Sabbath after the meeting, at Donegal in the afternoon and Mt. Joy in the evening, June 13th, 1882. The Donegal people secured his dismissal at an adjourned meeting of Presbytery held at Mt. Joy a short time after his installation. At the fall meeting of Presbytery held at Union Church, his relations were dissolved from the Mt. Joy Church.

The installation of Mr. Whitcomb at Donegal deserves special notice as it was unique, if not unprecedented, in the annals of Presbyterianism. Mr. Whitcomb preached the greater part of a year from the date of his call to the 13th of June. In the meantime the Donegal people had unanimously changed their opinion of Mr. Whitcomb's orthodoxy. They all agreed upon a course of action at the installation. The Elder and one of the Trustees were delegated to state the facts to the Committee of Presbytery and request a postponement of the installation, to which the Committee refused to accede; whereupon they were handed a paper (with the request that it be read from the pulpit), the purport of which was that no one should give their assent or dissent to the questions asked by the committee, except those who are eligible according to the charter of the church and the confession of faith; and that the members be permitted to rise in response, instead of raising the right hand as is customary. The paper was read from the pulpit and after the preliminary exercises the Moderator proceeded by asking Mr. Whitcomb the usual questions, after which he turned to the congregation, who were expected to answer in the affirmative by rising. The first and second questions were asked without any one rising. The Moderator asked, "Is there no assent to these questions?" and the congregation responded, "No." He proceeded to ask the remaining questions without receiving any assent from the congregation, when, turning to Mr. Whitcomb, he said: "Notwithstanding the extraordinary circumstances which have occurred to-day, I declare you pastor of this church." After this the congregation was dismissed.

The Rev. Robert Gamble was appointed by Presbytery to supply the now vacant churches. Both congregations united in giving Mr. Gamble a call which he accepted. He was installed October 11th, 1883. In 1886 Mr. Gamble requested the congregations to unite with him in asking Presbytery to dissolve the pastoral relation. After hearing Mr. Gamble's reason they consented. His resignation is dated April 12th, 1886.

The Rev. Edward A. Snook was installed April 5th, 1887, pastor of Donegal and Mount Joy, and on February 23d, 1889, he resigned to accept a call to Williamsport. The Rev. David Conway was installed October 7, 1890, and is the present pastor.

In what year was Donegal Church organized? When was the present building erected? and, as is supposed, there was a building before the present one, where was it located?

These are questions which can only be answered approximately, if at all, and I do not believe that any record, traditional or otherwise, is in existence that will answer these questions definitely. The fact that 175 years ago there was preaching at Donegal, and that there was a place of worship is not to be disputed. Other facts we have show that the country around Donegal was settled by the Scotch-Irish, who fled from persecution in the old country to seek an asylum where they might worship God without molestation, and they constituted the Donegal congregation. Many of their names are recorded in yonder silent abode of the dead. Some of their posterity still worship within the sacred precincts of the structure which their ancestors built. In view of these certainties, why need we premise, suppose and conjecture concerning which we know nothing, the numerous traditions to the contrary nothwithstanding?

The first intimations of a church organization at Donegal we find as follows:

"In 1714 the tide of emigration, following up the eastern side of the Susquehanna, had reached the Valley of Chiquesalunga, now in Lancaster county, where Donegal Church was organized in that year."— *West's Origin and History of Donegal and Carlisle Presbytery.*

And again: "Application was made by Andrew Galbrath to New Castle Presbytery, Aug. 1st, 1721, for supplies for Chick's Longus (Chiquesalunga), and Gillespie and Cross were sent. Roland Chambers renewed the request next year. In May, 1723, Conestoga applied; but Hutcheson failed to go, being unable to obtain a guide thither. In the fall he and McGill were sent to Dunngaal. In 1725, Donegal obtained one-sixth of Boyd's time, and he served them till they called Anderson."—*Webster's History.*

From these extracts we can readily infer that there was an organization at Donegal earlier than has been heretofore recognized. Andrew Galbrath's land adjoined the Glebe land and his application for supplies indicates a deep interest in matters pertaining to the church, but we will not conjecture; let each decide for himself.

On the 4th of June, 1740, two hundred acres of land were deeded to the "Rev. James Anderson, pastor, John Allison, James Mitchel and David Hayes, Elders of the church, by Thomas Penn, by the powers and authority to him granted by the said John and Richard Penn and of his own right."* (Church records.) This

---

*From this we learn that the congregation had probably occupied the land about twenty years before obtaining a patent. The reason for this delay is obvious when we recall the fact that William Penn founded the colony in 1681, and that some time elapsed before the machinery of government was sufficiently established and that delay was encountered between the application and the granting of

was bounded on the north by the land of James Stevenson and on the east by Andrew Galbrath's, on the south by Mary Modrel, or Motheril, and on the west by Ephraim Moore's land. One month after the receipt of the patent the Rev. James Anderson died.

September 11th, 1786, a charter was granted to the Rev. Colin McFarquhar, John Baille, James Baille, James Anderson, Robert Spear, Brice Clark, Samuel Woods, James Muirhead and Joseph Little as trustees and their successors.†

Nine members constituted the Board of trustees, until March 29th, 1805, when an act was passed reducing the number to three.

On the 28th of February, 1787, the Trustees, according to the action of a meeting of the congregation held January 8th, 1787, exposed at public sale the Glebe land, reserving thirty acres for the use of the congregation.

On the 23d of March, 1787, the trustees met "for conserting with James Muirhead, the purchaser of said Glebe, the proper measures for conveying the said land to the said purchaser, and for receiving from him, the said purchaser, a satisfactory security for the same."

---

a deed. It may not be out of place to presume that the permanent church edifice was not erected until after the patent was granted. There were no trustees then, as the deed is in the name of the Session, as being the only representative of the church.

†The congregation no doubt progressed quietly and peaceably (as the long pastorate of twenty-six years under the Rev. Joseph Tate indicates) without any organization but the Session. They found it necessary to have a charter in order to sell part of their land, which they did immediately on the receipt of that instrument. This also accounts for the beginning of the trustees' records in 1786. Prior to this date their records were probably kept by the session, and are lost.

(Church records.) There is no account of the sum for which the land was sold, only that the purchaser is to pay six per cent. interest. There are many entries in the records of the trustees that might be interesting, but our history would be too lengthy. An item from the accounts may be a historical reminiscence: April 16th, 1787—"The trustees took under their consideration a certain donation that was lodged in the hands of James Work, for the use of the congregation of Donigall, by a certain William Moor, deceased, which we find was lost by Continental Money ; therefore, the trustees do acquit the aforesaid James Work of the aforesaid donation.

"JOSEPH LITTLE, Secretary."

Preparation was made to build the grave-yard wall July 29, 1790, by appointing a committee of three, viz : "Richard Keys, James Cook and James Wilson, and to see that it is finished." It appears to have been finished in 1791, as on the 9th of April a committee of the trustees was appointed to meet and settle with the committee appointed to build the wall.

The following minute is recorded April 28, 1795 : "The minutes of the last meeting being read and the reason of the trustees not meeting according to adjournment was the call of the militia to quell the insurrection in the four back counties about fort pit."

The first election for trustees, under the supplement of the charter reducing the number to three, was held May 14, 1805. Those elected were Brice Clark, John Whitehill and Robert Spear. The auditors were John Watson, Joseph Little and John Pedan. The first account of dollars and cents is dated November 30, 1807. The accounts prior to that time were kept in £. s. d., until June, 1809,

when the £. s. d. were entirely dropped.
The Study House was built in 1810-11. The only record is the receipts for material and work, and are dated September, October and December, 1811. This was subsequently altered into a dwelling house, and is at present occupied by the sexton.

An extension to the graveyard was made in 1834, of which there is no record except credits paid for material for the wall. There are some of the members of the church living at the present time who remember the building of the extension wall.

At a meeting of the congregation held June 6, 1851, the trustees were unanimously authorized and instructed to sell all the land belonging to the church west of a line about sixty feet from and parallel with the western wall of the graveyard; and that part of the proceeds arising from the sale of the said land be applied to repairing and remodeling the church edifice; and that the plan of repairing and remodeling be left to the trustees. At the same meeting land was granted for the purpose of erecting a school house thereon. This was built and occupied for a number of years. When the Directors of East Donegal township purchased a plot a short distance southeast of the church they removed the house on the church ground, and built the present structure. The action of the congregation was ratified by the session, which consisted of the following members: Rev. James L. Rodgers, pastor; John Clark and Col. James Patterson, Elders. The trustees for 1851 and who did the remodeling were Dr. Nathaniel Watson, John M. Hoover and James A. Patterson.

Before the remodeling the exterior of the church was not plastered; the windows and doors were arched; there were three entrance doors, one on the south, one on the east and one on the west end of the building ; the aisles leading from these doors were paved with brick ; four large pillars supported the ceiling (these may still be seen at Mt. Joy on the east side of Mr. Newcomer's hardware store); the pulpit with the precentor's seat on its front, and a high sounding board over head, was on the north side ; the walnut wood pews were of the high, square, box variety, in which "tired nature's sweet restorer" found little comfort.

It is sad to see all these old memorials changed and passing away. The ruthless hand of modern improvement spares not the haunts and loved objects of our boyhood days. Possibly it is well, lest we find our minds too much engrossed with perishable things, to the neglect of the weightier matters awaiting our future existence.

In remodeling the old building the large pillars, pulpit, pews and brick-covered aisles were removed; the interior was laid with a substantial board floor; a vestibule divided off at the east end ; the south and west end entrances were closed and a new one made in the east end in addition to the one already there; square windows and door frames were substituted for the old arched ones, and the exterior was plastered to hide the unsightly joints of the old with the new wall, so that nothing remains to remind us of the ancient structure except the hip roof. The material of the old pulpit and pews was used in their reconstruction, but so much changed that one unacquainted with the alteration would not recognize it.

Tradition says that the first church edifice stood in what is now the grave yard, as the foundation walls are still visible. If such is the case, all that can be said respecting it is that our ancestors must have been much discommoded for the want of room, as the enclosure is only 10x16 feet, inside measure.

It is said that the congregation (sometime during our Revolutionary struggle) surrounded the large white oak tree, which stands near the east end of the church, and swore allegiance to our Government. The account differs somewhat, but is true in its main features. This tree has always been regarded as a memorial by the descendants of the congregation.

The history of the early families who settled around Donegal may be traced from the old land titles, wills, the tombstones in the burial ground and their descendants who are still living and worshiping in the old church.

Of Andrew Galbrath, who owned the land contiguous to the Glebe, and whose name first appears in the history of Donegal, little is known, except his application to Presbytery for supplies for the church. Some of his descendants are buried in the northeast corner of the grave yard. The name of Bertram Galbrath appears in the church records in 1790 as an Auditor and subsequently as a Trustee, indicating that the family took a prominent part in church affairs.

The name of James Stevenson, who owned the land (now Cameron's) north of the Glebe, has recently been honored though the elevation of one of his descendants to the highest office of the nation. This is known from the following partial genealogic account: James Stevenson's second daughter, Hannah, married John Gray, whose daughter, Sarah Gray, married David McKinley, who was born in York county, Pa., May 16, 1755. His son, James McKinley, born September 19, 1783, was an Elder in a Presbyterian church in Ohio, and his eldest son, William McKinley, is the father of Major William McKinley, President-elect of the United States.

The Patterson family contributed a large (probably the largest) number to the silent inhabitants of the old burial ground. Their ancestor, Arthur Patterson, of Scotch descent (born 1697, died July 3, 1763, in the 66th year of his age), was one of the early settlers along Big Chiques creek three miles southeast of Mt. Joy. His descendants at one time occupied a large extent of land north, east and south of Mt. Joy; they took a prominent part in National affairs and for many years a conspicuous interest in Donegal Church. The great grandson of Arthur Patterson, Mr. James Agnew Patterson, is the present and only Elder of Donegal, and is in his eighty-seventh year. The late Judge Patterson, of Lancaster, was a great-grandson. His great-great-granddaughter is the wife of Judge John B. McPherson, of Harrisburg, Pa. Major James Patterson, Samuel Smith, Thomas J., James M., William, Alexander, Douglas, Arthur and John, his sons, Samuel and John, daughter Mary Ann, now Mrs. Shock, Phœbe Mrs. Moore, Martha Sterrett, Mrs. Barr Ferree, Mrs. Rebecca Spangler, Mrs. Hatfield, descendants of Arthur Patterson, were personally known to the writer of this sketch. A history of their connection by marriage with the Scotts, Watsons, Pedans, Hatfields, Spears, Sterretts, Agnews, McJirnseys, Hays, Moores, Ferrees, Hendersons, Spanglers and others would fill a volume.

The Watson family resided on what is now the Cameron farm (originally James Stevenson's). They occupied their homestead until 1872, over 100 years. It came into their possession by John Watson, who married Ann, the oldest daughter of James Stevenson, whose son, David Watson, was the father of Dr. John Watson, who had four sons and four daughters, whom the writer knew personally, except Mrs. Boyd. The grandchildren of Dr. John Watson yet living are James P. Watson, Mrs. Charlotte Herr, Mrs. Henry H. Wiley, Miss Harriet P. Watson, Henry Watson, of Williamsport; Dr. Belle Watson and Miss Mary Watson, of Lock Haven; James A. Patterson, Miss Rachael J. Patterson and Mrs. J. L. Ziegler, of Mount Joy; Watson Ellmaker, of Lancaster, and Mrs. Lucy Walker, of the Gap. The family always took a deep interest in Donegal, and the larger number of the grandchildren attend Donegal Church at the present time. There seemed to be an hereditary inclination for the medical profession. Dr. John Watson had two sons physicians, Dr. David C. and Dr. Nathaniel; two grandsons, Dr. David H. and Dr. Belle Watson, of Lock Haven; two great-grandsons, Dr. James P. Ziegler, of Mount Joy, and Dr. Walter M. L. Ziegler, of Philadelphia. The two latter are the great-great-grandsons of Arthur Patterson.

The name Clark appears early on the church records. Brice Clark, one of the charter trustees, took an active part in its affairs, and Mr. John Clark was long an Elder. Many of the family are buried at Donegal. They resided (long before my recollection) on what is now Hon. Donald Cameron's place. Mr. John Clark was a celebrated surveyor, and one of his grandchildren, Miss Martha Clark, is a member of the Lancaster Historical Society.

The Sterretts, a very prominent and large family, were connected with the church. Mr. Patterson Sterrett, an Elder in the Presbyterian Church of Marietta, is a descendant. The Whitehills were active members. John Whitehill's name appears as a trustee in 1788 and later Mr. John M. Whitehill, the father of Mrs. Redsecker, who with her family are living at the present time in Columbia and attend the Donegal Church. Her father during his lifetime was prominent in the church. Many of the family are buried at Donegal.

The Lytles, whose ancestor was one of the charter members, trustee and for some years Secretary of the Board, were prominent in the church. His descendants, Mr. S. S. P. Lytle, daughter and son, Dr. S. P. Lytle, a successful dental practitioner, reside at Mt. Joy at present. The family was large in its connection with the Scotts and Pedans.

Of the Lowries, the name of Alexander Lowrie first appears on the records as an auditor in 1789, subsequently as a trustee. The names of the Spears, Bailles, Muirheads, Woods and Moores appear on the records as early as 1786. The Pedans, Hays, Clingans, Wilsons, Scotts, Moores, Houstons, Mehaffys and many others, and some who rest in unmarked graves, were those who constituted the early congregation.

The oldest legible tombstone inscription is that of

THOMAS JAMIESON,
Son of John and Agnes Jamieson,
who departed this life on the 3rd day of February, 1732,
In the 32nd year of his age.

This probably was a relative of David Jamieson, who left a legacy to the church, and who resided at Conewago.

This inscription taken from a tombstone may be of some interest :

In memory of
WILLIAM McDOWELL,
Late of Conocheague,
Who was a tender parent, careful instructor
and an example of piety to a
numerous progeny.
When the settlement was obliged to fly by
the barbarous Indian War. He deceased
in these parts, so was interred here
September 12, 1759,
Aged 77 years.

The writer spent many pleasant hours in the bright summer days, during his pupilage, around the grounds, springs and burial ground of Old Donegal.

The unlettered tombstones, how many! What a history! What trials and labors, patience and endurance, faith and hope, lie buried there!

"Death is not rare, alas! nor burials few,
And soon the grassy coverlet of God
Spreads equal green above their ashes pale."

PAPERS READ

BEFORE THE

LANCASTER COUNTY HISTORICAL SOCIETY,

ON FEB. 5, 1897.

THE GAP COPPER MINES.
By R. J. HOUSTON.

OLD MILLS AND COUNTRY ORDINARIES.
By SAMUEL EVANS, ESQ.

LANCASTER, PA.
REPRINTED FROM THE NEW ERA.
1897.

The Gap Copper Mines,
 BY R. J. HOUSTON, ... 283

Old Mills and Country Ordinaries,
 BY SAMUEL EVANS, ESQ., ... 299

THE GAP COPPER MINES.

Through the kindness of Dr. Wm. H. Egle, State Librarian, which I thankfully acknowledge, I am enabled to give from the official records in the Land Department at Harrisburg the earliest ownership of the land constituting the Gap mines property.

The first paper is endorsed "An Acc't of Lands surveyed to divers persons, who purchased of James Steel in right of the original purchase of William Bacon," and reads: "William Penn, Esq., Proprietary and Governor of Pennsylvania, by deeds of lease and release bearing date the 11th and 12th days of October, A. D. 1681, did grant and convey to William Bacon, of ye Inner Temple (London), Gent., 5,000 acres of land in Pennsylvania, and the said William Bacon, by like deed, etc., dated 19th and 20th days of February, 1718, did release and confirm the said 5,000 acres to Humphrey Murry and John Budd, and the said Proprietary's Commissioners of Property did grant to the said Humphrey Murry and John Budd two warrants, one dated ye 5th, 3rd mo., and ye other 28th, 6th mo., 1719, for the laying out to said Murry and Budd 4,920 acres. And the said Murry and Budd by deed, dated the 26th of March, 1720, did sell to James Steel, Gent., 1,500 acres. In right whereof there was surveyed to the said James Steel—

"800 acres sold to Samuel Gouldin.

"300 acres sold to Herman Godschalic and Leonard Henrickson.

"100 acres sold to Martin Kolph and John Ledrak.

"200 acres sold to George Rough.

"100 acres mine land at Octorara retained by said Steel, making in all 1,500 acres."

The second paper is a record of a warrant for the 100 acres mine land retained by Steel. It is endorsed "Return 100 acres Octorara," and reads: " By virtue of a Warrant from the Commissioners of Property dated the 5th day of the third month, 1719, surveyed and laid out unto James Steel, of the city of Philadelphia, in right of William Bacon's original purchase, a certain tract or parcel of land scituate in Chester county. Beginning at a corner marked Black Oak on the East side of a Branch of Octorara Creek, from thence North by a line of marked—— 106 perches to a post, then West 160 perches to another post, then South 106 perches to a third post, then East 160 perches to the place of beginning, containing 106 acres. Surveyed the 21st day of December, 1722. Certified by me,

"JACOB TAYLOR,
"Surveyor Gen'l."

It will be remembered that six acres were given with each 100 acres for roads, so that the above tract only made 100 acres.

The third paper is endorsed, "James Steel, 150 acres on a branch of the Octorara," and reads :

"James Steel's Land, situate on a Branch of the Octorara Creek in the County of Lancaster. Beginning at a Black Oak, being a corner of a tract of land surveyed for said James Steel the 21st day of December, 1722, thence by the same North 48 perches to a White Oak, thence East by vacant land 26 perches to a White Oak, thence South by vacant land 158 perches to a White Oak, thence West by vacant land 220 perches to a post, thence North 110 perches to a post, thence East by said James Steel's other land 194 perches to the place of beginning, containing 150 acres and the allowance of six acres per cent.

"Surveyed the 9th of 10th mo., 1730.
"JOHN TAYLOR."

This last purchase by James Steel was not a part of Bacon's 5,000 acres, but was secured from a William Markham, who seems to have owned the land adjoining the Bacon tract on the south, as will be seen from the draft and the following record in the State Land Department. In a volume labeled "Old Rights" there is in favor of James Steel this information:

"No. 42. Return of 250 acres in Lancaster county surveyed the 9th of November, 1730."

This document reads as follows:

"November 9th, 1730. Surveyed and Laid out for James Steel, of the City of Philadelphia, Gent., a tract of land on a Branch of Octoraroe, in the County of Langcast'r. Beginning at a White Oak marked for a corner, thence by a line of marked trees East 26 perches to another White Oak. Then South by a line of marked trees 158 perches to a third White Oak, then West by a line of trees 220 perches, then North by a line of marked trees 110 perches, then by a line of marked trees East 34 perches, then North by line of marked trees 106 perches, then by a line of marked trees East 160 perches, then by a line of marked trees South 58 perches to the place of beginning, containing 250 acres with allowance of 6 per cent. One hundred acres thereof in right of Wm. Bacon by a Warrant from the Commissioners of Property, dated the 21st day of December, 1722, and 150 acres in right of Wm. Markham.

" Certified by Jacob Taylor."

This paper is endorsed on the back: "James Steel 250 acres in Langcast'r County, the Gap Mine Land, now belonging one-sixth part to the honorable Prop'r Thos. Penn, one-sixth part to Andrew Hamilton, one-sixth part to James Logan, or assigns, one-sixth part to Wm. Allen, one-sixth part to Thomas Schute, or assigns, one-sixth part to James Steel."

Enclosed in this is a draft of these 250 acres, with the same endorsement, with the words added, "Surveyed November 9th, 1730. JACOB TAYLOR."

Known at an Early Date.

From the above it seems clear that the existence of valuable minerals on the Gap mine tract was known as early as 1720, or, at the latest, 1722, as between those years James Steel sold 1,400 acres of his 1,500 acre purchase, retaining 100 acres, marked on the record "Mine Land at Octorara." It is barely possible that the tradition printed in Everts & Stewart's Historical Atlas of this county, that some Marylanders discovered the mine in 1718, is correct; but it seems hardly probable that Sir William Keith drove the Maryland people away and worked the mine in 1719, spending much money in opening it and being stopped by the proprietors. As a sane man he would doubtless have tried to secure the property before going to much expense, and it was then for sale, Murry and Budd having secured it in February, 1718, and sold it to James Steel, of Philadelphia, in March, 1720.

It would seem more likely that, while much prospecting by digging pits, etc., was done before, the first regular and systematic working of the mine was after Steel secured the 150 acres of the Markham tract in November, 1730, when the whole 250 acres was divided into six equal shares, Thomas Penn taking one share.

There can be no doubt that these six men, who were all wealthy, proceeded to work these mines as well as the limited possibilities of that time would permit, and by themselves, their heirs or assigns continued to operate them with more or less persistence, at least until 1763, for on November 7 of that year the Hon. John Penn issued an order to John Lukens, Surveyor General, which, after reciting the above facts as to the 250 acres, directs him to survey to the "Gap Mine Company" 300 acres additional, part of which they were already using.

The reason given for this order is that "the said company have at great expense erected divers buildings and other works for the carrying on of the said undertaking and for the use and benefit thereof, as well on the said 250 acres as on the said 300 acres."

The order also directs the Surveyor General to survey both tracts and make return of the same that they may be "confirmed to William Allen and others, the said Gap Mine Company, on the common terms of 15 pounds 10 shillings per 100 acres and the quit rent of one half penny sterling per acre for the whole from the first settlement of the mine tract."

In pursuance of this order the Surveyor General reports that he surveyed the same, "including such surplus as was clear of the lines of the claimers of adjoining lands on the 6th, 7th, 8th, 10th and 11th days of September, 1764, and found it contained $780\frac{3}{4}$ acres." So the surplus clear of adjoining claims must have been about 230 acres. The draft of this whole tract in the Land Office is so torn that no copy can be made.

There is also a record of a re-survey of some of this land made March 15, 1786, which mentions William Allen (probably a descendent of the William Allen of 1730 and 1763) as an owner.

A Valuable Pamphlet.

Of the actual working of these mines in the last century, however, no written history on record seems to have been made, or, if made, was not preserved, so that our only dependence is on the uncertain and frequently contradictory traditions of the neighborhood. So much of these as seemed reliable were gathered up by Capt. Charles Doble, the active and efficient manager of these mines for nearly forty years, but his efforts were not very satisfactory to himself until he recently secured from a former owner of some of the land a pamphlet of twenty pages. For the loan of this, as well as much other valuable information, I desire to make this public acknowledgment of my thanks. I am willing that the members of the society should see this ancient book, but I want them to "handle with care," for to me it seems invaluable. It is the nature of what we would now call a prospectus for the formation of a mining company, but gives a vast amount of the early history of the mine, which I have, so far as possible, compared with information from other sources without once finding it in error. This pamphlet is one hundred years old and, so far as I know, no part of it has been reprinted in this century. I have, therefore, deemed it advisable, in the interest of the future historians, to make copious extracts from it. The title page reads:

"A plan with Proposals for forming a Company to work mines in the United States, and to Smelt and Refine the ores, whether of Copper, Lead, Tin, Silver or Gold, by Benjamin Henfrey. The original can be seen at the Philadelphia Library, No. 91,025. Printed by Snowden & McCorkle, No. 47 North Fourth street, Philadelphia, 1797."

The first paragraph of the preface reads:

"I conceive that it is totally unnecessary for me to make any comment upon the great advantages it would be to this country to be supplied with all the useful metals from its own mines, to purchase which an immense sum, every one knows, is annually sent to Europe." (A terse statement of the great American doctrine of protection, which he evidently wrote for the especial benefit of Brother Hensel.)

The preface is dated, "Gap Copper Mines, Lancaster county, Pennsylvania, March 27th, 1797."

Then follows what he calls "Proposals, &c.:"

"The first mines I would recommend are situated in Lancaster county, Pennsylvania, five miles from Strasburg, thirteen from Lancaster, thirty-five from Wilmington, fifty from Philadelphia, and only two miles from a turnpike road.

"They were discovered by a German by the name of Tersey, in or before the year 1732, and in that year Hon. John Penn made a grant of the land where the mine was found to the following gentlemen, for the express purpose of having it worked, viz: Governor Hamilton, Judge Allen, James Logan, James Steel and Thomas Schute, Esq., and it also appears that Mr. Penn joined in the expense of opening the mine, etc., in doing which they discovered one of those uncommon vitriolic springs called by the Germans *Ziment wasser*, i. e., water strongly impregnated with the vitriol of copper, or, as some writers have called them, copper springs; but, notwithstanding this invaluable discovery, it does not appear that any of the gentlemen were acquainted with the value of the water, as no attempt appears to have ever been made to turn it to account after the European manner, which I shall have occasion to describe.

But previous, I will, for the satisfaction of those who may wish to forward my plan, state the proofs I have obtained of such a spring having been actually discovered in the Gap mines when first opened. These proofs also fortunately report the quantity and value of the water, and, from the great ability as well as respectability of the men, leave no doubt of the truth of the discovery. The report is as follows:

"'An account of the copper springs lately discovered in Pennsylvania, by John Rutty, M. D., of Dublin, communicated by Mr. Peter Collinson, F. R. S. See volume 49, part 2, page 648. Read May 20, 1756.

"'In the Province of Pennsylvania is a copper mine which affords a Spring that appears to have the same effect as that Irish water lately described by Dr. William Henry and Dr. Bond in the 47th and 48th Volumes of the Philosophical Transactions, but is much sharper, for it will dissolve iron in a quarter part of the time, and we are assured by the accounts transmitted from the proprietors of it of the trials they have made, that it yields the same copper—mud or dust—as our Crone Baun water of the county of Wicklow, Ireland, in this Kingdom (being the water above mentioned), which, being collected from the bars of iron immersed in it for the purpose of extracting the copper from the Pennsylvania water, it produced above half pure copper on being melted in a crucible; an experiment that requires to be repeated in order to ascertain the proportion of copper obtained with accuracy; our copper spring of the county of Wicklow yielding a proportion considerably larger than this, viz., 16 parts of copper out of 20 of the mud.

"'In the neighborhood is a great abundance of the ores of vitriol and sulphur and the Spring comes through an immense body of vitriol ore and the supply of water is very large, 700 to 800 hogsheads flowing in 24 hours. The water is of a pale green color of an acid, sweet, austere, inky and nauseous taste.

"'But the genuine quality as well as large proportion of the impregnating salt will further appear by the following analysis of this water, viz., a pint of it exhaled by a slow fire left 400 grains of solid contents, which were partly green and partly ochre colored, with an intermixture of bluish and a rough sweetish taste like that of Sal Martis and appeared to be chiefly saline, not leaving above four grains indissoluble matter on dissolving 196 grains of it and filtering.

"'Thus it appears that the proportion of vitriolic parts in this water is very large, viz., six drachms to a pint or 3,200 grains to a gallon, and consequently it is a stronger solution of vitriol than sea water is of marine salt, and, moreover, is truly considered the strongest of all the vitriolic waters that have yet occurred to my observation, for our Crone Baun water in the county of Wicklow gives but 256 grains from a gallon; Haigh in Lancashire, the strongest in Britain, 1,920 grains; Shadwell, 1,320; Kilbrew in the County of Mealth, 1,530 from the same quantity, so that besides the copper to be obtained by immersing bars of iron as in our county of Wicklow water, this water offers to its proprietors another peculiar advantage, viz., an opportunity of erecting a copperas works or manufacture of vitriol, especially the vast supply of water and plenty of fuel in the place considered."

Mr. Henfrey now brings great names to his aid, namely, the certificate of Dr. Logan respecting the copper springs at the Gap Mine, Lancaster County:

"I do certify that Dr. Benjamin Franklin, a few weeks before his death, informed me that at the time the Gap copper mine in Lancaster county belonging to James Logan and others was worked, a spring of water was discovered in the same highly impregnated with copper. A bottle of water was sent to him, with which he frequently made experiments with his knife, which, being for a short time immersed in the water, would assume the apearance of copper.

"Signed. GEORGE LOGAN.
"STENTON, March 10, 1797."

Dr. George Logan was quite a prominent man of that time. He was intimate with Dr. Franklin, a member of the American Philosophical Society, and in 1801 was elected United States Senator from Pennsylvania. His home was at Stenton, near Wayne Junction, just north of Philadelphia.

What Old Residents Said.

"The following is the certificate of some old people who remember the first opening of the Gap mines and are still living near them and who are persons of good character and in good circumstances:

"'THIS IS TO CERTIFY, to whom it may concern, that we, the subscribers, were frequently at the copper mines in Lancaster county, known by the name of Gap mine, during the time the said mine was working by James Logan & Company, and from hearing the people often talking of the water put the blades of our knives into the water as it came from the pumps, which in a few minutes would be covered with copper. And we further certify that we have often seen quantities of the ore got in this mine and frequently heard the miners say that it was a very rich mine if the water could be kept down so as they could work constantly. At this time there were eight pumps working in this pit, which turned out so much water that it overflowed a meadow and destroyed the grass so effectually that most of the places the water used to cover are barren at this time. Given under our hands severally this 19th of November, in the year 1793.

her
ELIZABETH X ROCKY,
mark
JOHN SHORTS,

Witness: JOHN BRACKBILL.
ABNER BUFFINGTON,
JOHN HOAR.'"

Then follows a letter to Mr. Honfrey, dated Clay Hill, December 27, 1796, from R. Howell, who seems to be the owner or at least to control the property, and who regrets his financial inability to erect machinery to properly work the mine property and accedes to a sale of shares for a portion of the money needed. Mr. Henfrey then proceeds to give his plans for working the mine. He says: "The works are now in such a state as to require only the aid of a machine of sufficient power to raise the water so as to keep the pits clean. A steam engine of moderate power would be capable of doing this. But there are many objections to erecting a steam engine in this country : 1st, the great expense of erecting one; 2d, the consumption of fuel ; 3d, the frequent repairs, and 4th, the high wages you must give to an engineer to attend the machine. I would recommend that a level should be brought up through a meadow to the mine by which a fall of 25 to 30 feet may be gained and a water wheel of 25 feet diameter will be sufficient to work as many pumps as will clear the mines of the common, and raise the copper water for use. There are three small streams in the mine lands that may be conducted into one reservoir, which would then, I am certain, give as much water as the machine will require to keep it constantly going. The machinery on this plan will be simple and such as may be made at the mines.

"Nor will it be so liable to get out of order as the works of a steam engine. If this plan is put in practice the works may much sooner be made productive, for when the level is brought up, the bed of poor ore before noted will be laid dry, and may be worked to immediate profit much sooner than if we have to wait for the erecting of a steam engine, and at much less expense to the company.

Extent of the Improvements.

"I will now for the information of those persons who may be disposed to join in forwarding the proposed plan acquaint them with the present state of the work at the Gap mines.

"We have built a saw mill, made two dams, and cut a head and tail race.

"There is a large log house for the copperas works and a large lead boiler. Several ley tubs, cisterns, &c. There are a carpenters' and smiths' shops and two log houses for workmen. There is a variety of tools, with pit ropes, windlasses, buckets, &c. Also, a complete set of boring rods, 100 feet long. The two main shafts have been cleaned out, which was attended with great trouble and difficulty, as we were obliged to work night and day on account of the water.

"There is a machine to work the pumps, which will be of great use in getting the water out until a more powerful one can be completed. There are eight tiers of pumps, two tiers deep, all in good working order.

"About fifty tons of ore have been raised and a great deal of other work done. I shall, therefore, only further note that a small part of the level is driven and that two men are now at work on it.

"These various works have cost our company a considerable sum, as will appear by our books, and the company who first opened the mines must, I am certain, have expended at least $30,000, so that the proposed company will come in on very advantageous terms, as by these expenses the mines have been put in a state that they only require a steam or other engine to make them pay the profit I have stated and with the probability of much greater.

Condition of the Mine Itself.

"I will now describe the works below. One of the pits is seven feet square; the other is seven by five. The wide shaft is only about sixty feet deep, but the other is much deeper. The vitriolic water rises fifteen feet from the bottom of the wide shaft, and there is forty feet of common water over it. This I have proved many times by my boring rods.

"When we had cleared the pits of earth and stones, and had the waters out, I went down. I found the main shaft in most excellent order, the frame consisting of squared logs laid close upon each, as in building a house; in short, I never saw such strong work and so well secured in any mine I ever was in before.

"I have now only to beg leave to recommend my estimate and plan to the serious consideration of my readers, and to assure them that the views contemplated by this scheme are fair and honorable."

Estimate of Expense to Complete the Works at the Gap Mines.

1797. To expense of level	$4,000
To machine to work the pumps	1,200
To troughs for copper water	2,000

To finish copperas works.	1,000
To incidental expenses...	500
To manager's salary.....	1,000
To clerk's salary.........	300
	$10,000

Estimate of the Expense and Probable Profit in Working the Gap Mines the First Year.

1798. To expense of completing works as above........	$10,000
To cash for 200 tons bar iron..................	20,000
To 25 workmen at $200 each.................	5,000
To 2 smiths at $300 each..	600
To 2 coopers at $300 each.	600
To 1 clerk...............	800
To 1 manager............	2,500
To incidental expenses...	600
To ⅛ of the net profits to be paid to the lessees of the mines..............	11,612
	$51,712

Contra Credit.

By 300 tons of fine copper to be precipitated from the ziment water which I will value at $400 per ton................	$120,000
By 300 tons copperas at $30 per ton.......................	9,000
By 10 tons fine copper precipitated from ore..............	4,000
	$133,000
Less expense............	51,712
Profit..................	$81,288

A similar calculation for the second year, 1799, makes out a net profit of $256,726.

Tried, But Unsuccessfully.

With this astounding display of profits it seemed to me that Mr. Henfrey must surely have raised his company, and I accordingly wrote to Captain Doble to ascertain whether his subsequent examinations gave evidence of Mr. Henfrey's plans having been put in operation and received the following reply :

NICKEL MINES, January 15, 1897.
R. J. Houston, Esq.

DEAR SIR : In answer to yours of the 12th inst., I have to say that there is strong evidence that Mr. Henfrey's plans or a part of them at least were carried out. The old water wheel that we discovered was about 25 feet in diameter and 20 inches wide, located right on the edge of the old east shaft. This is the shaft Mr. Henfrey spoke of as being so well and strongly secured with squared timbers laid one upon the other and is the one farthest east on the mineral range.

There was a level or tail race some 300 yards in length brought up from the meadow below direct to the water wheel. The bottom of this tail race is about 25 feet below the surface at the point where it reached the wheel. The first 200 yards from its outlet was an open ditch and the other 100 yards was tunneled.

The water to drive the wheel was collected from the springs of three little valleys into a dam one hundred yards north of the wheel, viz., from the springs at the head of the same valley that the wheel was in, from the springs of a little valley eight hundred yards west brought to the dam in an open race, and from the springs in a little valley over a half mile east, brought to the dam in the same way ; parts of these dams and races can still be seen. The springs from these three little valleys are the source or head of this branch of the Octorara.

I never saw any signs of the old mines having reached a depth of over sixty feet from the surface, and only in one place, viz., the East shaft, where the wheel was located, did they reach a depth of sixty feet. But to the depth of from twenty-five feet to forty feet from the surface, they did a great amount of work in the way of sinking pits, tunneling, etc. Much of this work seems to have been done with natural drainage (I mean without pumping), consequently the vertical depths of these workings varied according to the natural rolling surface.

How much, if any, of Mr. Henfrey's plans for the treatment of the "vitriolic" waters were carried out, I do not know. Yours truly,

CHARLES DOBLE.

It would seem from this letter that Mr. Henfrey doubtless organized his company and about equally certain that it was not successful. The difference between the estimated and actual profits of his operation probably did not differ widely from many similar estimates and results of the present day, and Mr. Henfrey, as a promoter of mining companies, need not occupy a back seat even with the experts in his line of a century later.

His operation was the last previous to the recent working which began in 1849, but, as this sketch is already too long, I must reserve that for another paper.

Up to 1785 two parties are named as having operated the mines, viz., "James Ramsey & Co." and later "William Allen and others." Both of these names are among the six original owners. This would seem to render it probable that while some of the six originals had sold out to either their partners or outsiders, others of the originals, or their descendants, were willing to renew the work, and that some of them were the immediate predecessors of Henfrey's company.

[TO BE CONTINUED.]

Old Mills and Country Ordinaries.

The pioneer settlers in the "Upper End" of what is now Lancaster county came from the north of Ireland. A number of them were tenant farmers, who were more or less imposed upon by selfish and greedy landlords, and they were only too glad to seek homes in a land where they could own farms in fee. When they landed at New Castle on the Delaware, they at once struck out for the wilderness beyond the frontier settlements in the Pequea and Conestoga Valleys, and took up the lands along Chickiesalunga Creek, and westward of that. They were self-sustaining from the moment they located their homesteads. I have no doubt they depended the first year almost wholly upon wild game for subsistence. A number of French Indian traders were located a few miles from their settlement, where they had trading stores and kept Indian supplies. I have no doubt many of these pioneer settlers resorted to these posts, or stores, where they bartered furs for supplies.

Many of them embarked in the Indian trade, and became a power in the province, and they were, in a great measure, responsible for the hostility of the French, who sought to control the Indian trade in the far west, which, eventually, brought on a war between the English and French and Indians.

Their dwellings were rude and constructed of logs cut from the surrounding forests. When the timber was prepared for dwellings and barns, neighbors were notified to assemble and assist at the "raisings." One of these gatherings turned out to be of great service to the

Penns. In the year 1735 Blunston and Wright, Esqs., of Hempfield, learned that Colonels Rigby and Hall, of Baltimore county, Maryland, were mustering the militia preparatory to a raid into Pennsylvania. Benjamin Chambers, a millwright, who had been in the neighborhood, was sent down to Maryland by Blunston and Wright to visit the camp of the militia and ascertain the cause of the gathering. He was arrested as a spy, but he escaped and hastened back to Wright's Ferry to warn the settlers of the anticipated raid. Mr. Chambers, hearing of a house and barn raising in Donegal, hastened there and made known his errand. All dropped their work, and, taking their guns, hastened to Wright's Ferry and crossed the river, where they met three hundred of the Maryland militia marching in battle array to the Ferry, under the command of Col. Hall and Col. Rigby. The Donegalians drove them back to Captain Cresap's fort, three miles and a half south of the ferry. Maryland's valiant army retreated gracefully to the land of homing and our friends in the Upper End returned to their usual occupations.

In the year 1720 they formed a Presbyterian congregation and built a log church at the large spring where, or near, the present church stands.

In the same year John Galbraith located along what was then called "Spring Creek," which had its source at the spring at Donegal Church. He selected the land at a point where a new road had been laid out, branching from the Peter's road, a short distance northeast from the present town of Mt. Joy, and which led through the new settlement. This road again branched at Galbraith's, one road going to the river and the other one inclining northwest and connecting with the Peters road near Conoy creek.

John Galbraith in the same year erected the first grist and saw mill above the Conestoga.

The travel over these roads became so great that Mr. Galbraith applied to the Chester County Court to grant him a license to keep an ordinary and brew beer.

The petition for the "ordinary" clearly sets forth the reasons which prompted the application. The petition has a large number of signers for that time. There were a number of other settlers in the neighborhood, who were either not asked, or else they declined to sign the paper.

The paper itself is a matter of some interest. I will add a short sketch of the signers, which may give it additional attraction.

John Galbraith, the petitioner, came from the north of Ireland with his father, James, and his brothers, James and Andrew. He was a member of the first Grand Jury in the county, and was elected Sheriff of the county in 1731. He was a member of Sheriff Samuel Smith's posse who marched to Connejohela Valley, on the west side of the river, and captured Captain Cresap's fort, and took that warrior a prisoner and landed him in the Philadelphia jail. In 1748 he was a captain in his brother's (Colonel James Galbraith) battalion, which ranged along the mountains to protect the frontier settlers from Indian raids. He died in 1753. He had a son named Robert, who died in the year 1747 and left a widow named Rebecca. The widow married Captain John Buyers, who then owned the Jacob Mumma farm. A hundred years ago the Mummas added a story to the dwelling.

Captain Buyers moved to Cumberland

Valley and became a distinguished officer in the Revolutionary War.

Colonel Ephraim Blaine, the great-grandfather of the late Hon. James G. Blaine, married Rebecca, the daughter of Robert Galbraith. They moved to Carlisle. After the death of John Galbraith his lands were divided and sold. That part on the east side of the creek was purchased by Mr. Hiestand, and the grist and saw mill, with the ordinary, and several hundred acres of land, were purchased by John Bayly, who was the son of Thomas Bayly, and was born upon a farm near where Florin is. He married Ruth Anderson. He was a member of the Supreme Executive Council of the State from this county during the Revolutionary War. The mills and ordinary were conducted by him until his death in 1794. He was one of the owners and founders of the town of Falmouth.

A few years after his death Henry Shearer purchased the farm and mills. In the year 1804 he tore the old mills down, and erected a large stone mill on the south side of the road and a large stone dwelling on the hill on the north side. Either then or a few years later a still house was erected near the mill. This was known as a merchant mill. Large quantities of flour from this mill were shipped down the river in arks to the Baltimore market.

James Paterson, the first signer on the petition, married Susannah Howard, and located near Martin Chartier's trading post, in what is now Manor township, in the year 1710. He embarked in the Indian trade and established a store and trading post upon the farm near Washington Borough lately owned by Jacob B. Shuman. He kept many of his pack horses on the west side of the river where they were pastured. When Captain Thos.

Cresap came up from Maryland to Connejohela Valley, in 1730, he and his brothers-in-law shot Mr. Paterson's horses. This caused a conflict between the Pennsylvanians and Marylanders, which culminated in "Cresap's War." Mr. Paterson died in October, 1735. His daughter, Sarah, married Benjamin Chambers, mentioned above, who founded Chambersburg, Pa. His son, James, became a distinguished officer in the Revolutionary war.

Another daughter, named Susannah, married James Lowrey, a celebrated Indian trader, who moved to Frankstown, on the Juniata, in 1750. A daughter, Rebecca, married George Polson, who resided in Lancaster. James Paterson, the oldest of the children, married Mary, daughter of George Stewart, Esq., of Donegal, and moved from the latter place to the Juniata Valley, in 1750. He was a famous captain in the French and Indian wars, as was also his son, Capt. William Paterson.

Thomas Howard was the son of Gordon Howard, and was largely engaged in the Indian trade. The Hon. J. D. Cameron owns part of his land, which extends in the direction of the Harrisburg and Lancaster turnpike.

William Dunlap was engaged in the Indian trade, and resided along the Swatara river.

David McCakarty removed from Donegal and went to Cumberland county.

George Moffet and John Moffet also moved from Donegal at an early day.

James Mitchell, Esq., was a prominent person. He was at this time a Justice of Peace for Chester county and a land surveyor. He lived a mile below Galbraith's mill. He was a member of the Legislature in 1729, and was with Sheriff Smith when Cresap was taken. He was a large landholder.

Thomas Wilkins was the son of Robert Wilkins and was largely engaged in the Indian trade. He owned the farm and built the first story of the dwelling now owned by Mrs. Nissley, along the road leading from Donegal Church to Mount Joy. In 1738 he bought a farm at Canoy creek and leased the ferry of James Logan, now Bainbridge. He died in 1742.

John Burt was an Indian trader, and had his post along the river, near where Harrisburg now is.

David Jones lived near the mouth of Poquea Creek, and owned the land where Colemanville now is. He was the first constable of Donegal township in 1722, which then extended to the mouth of Pequea Creek.

James Galbraith was the brother of John. After his marriage to Elizabeth Bertram in 1733, he moved to Spring Creek, where Derry Church is, and built a grist mill, which he sold to Mr. Garber about 1750. He was Sheriff of this county in 1742-43. He was a Colonel in the French and Indian war and Lieutenant Colonel of Cumberland county during a portion of the years during the Revolutionary war. His sons, John, Bertram, Andrew and Robert, were Revolutionary officers. Judge Gibson married his granddaughter. The late Dr. Carpenter was a descendant of Colonel Bertram Galbraith.

Thomas Bayly lived along the Paxtang and Conestogoo road, near where "Florin" is. He died in 1734 and left a widow and son, the Hon. John Bayly, who bought the Galbraith mills, and a son, James Bayly, Esq., who bought the farm now owned by Mrs. Abraham N. Cassel, in 1761-2. He was a Justice of the Peace and wagon master during the Revolutionary War. He died in 1793. There are no descendants of any of these families in the county.

James Allison resided northeast of the Peter's road, near where the road now leads from Maytown to Elizabethtown. He was a large landholder and a prominent person.

James Moor resided near Chickies creek, on the east side, one mile south of the Paxtang and Conestogœ road.

Hugh Whoit (White) resided along Little Chickies creek near the Paxtang road. He left sons Hugh, John, Henry and Moses. A son of the latter married a daughter of John Allison, Esq. He was the Colonel Hugh White, of the West Branch Valley, in the Revolutionary War.

Willam Buchannan resided near Canoy creek, above the Peters road.

James Brownloo moved to Carolina.

Joseph Worke took up the land on the west side of the Peters road, and east of where Greybill's Meeting House is. He built a tannery near the big spring where Mr. Hostetter now resides. This was probably the first tannery west of the Conestogœ. He was a captain in the French and Indian war, and was at the battle of Loyal Hannon, under Colonel James Burd, when General Forbes' army was marching to the Ohio to capture Fort Duquesne. His son, James, who married the daughter of John Galbraith, was an Indian trader, who settled at the mouth of Canoy creek, and remained on the mansion farm where Mr. Hostetter resides. His sons, William, Joseph and ———, moved to Virginia, and were officers in the Revolutionary Army. Joseph Worke, who was elected Sheriff of the county in 1779, was the son of James Worke.

There was a carding and fulling mill on the lower end of the Worke tract. I do not know the exact date of its erection. Prior to the year 1820 it was owned by Mr. Zook, and within my own recollection it was owned by David Zook. Some years ago it was purchased by an English company and was burned down about ten years ago, and was not rebuilt.

This mill manufactured "Linsey-woolsey" and casinet cloth. I remember when a small boy of taking fleeces of wool to this mill to be carded. Upon one occasion I went to the upper story to see the looms at work. I was surprised to find so many young girls at work. They threw little wads of wool at me, and I hastened out of the mill. When I returned home the back of my roundabout was found to be full of little pieces of wool. This was my first and last visit to the weaving room.

John Tyler lived along Little Chickies creek, near where Myers' stone bridge is.

Michael Carr lived in Derry, and moved to Hopewell township, on the west side of the Susquehanna, where he died in 1746.

John Carr was a brother of the above.

Hugh Moor lived near Big Chickies creek. Afterwards in Hempfield township.

Jonah Davenport was an Indian trader and took 300 acres of land, where Bainbridge now is, in the year 1720. He sold to James Logan, whose heirs sold to the Groffs, Works and Scotts. The latter sold to James Galbraith, father of Colonel Bertram Galbraith. Davenport crossed the mountains to trade with the Indians at the Ohio as early as 1727.

James Cunningham resided at the spring at Donegal Church and was the father of Colonel James Cunningham, who commanded the "flying camp" at the battle of King's Bridge and at the battle of Long Island. He was a member of the Supreme Executive Council from this county. He was a land surveyor, and laid out the soldiers' lands west of the Allegheny. He resided in Orange street, Lancaster, where he died about the year 1801.

William Eben removed from the township.

William Bryan lived along the Peters road and owned the land now owned by the Brandts.

Hugh McKen owned a farm adjoining Bryan's.

William Hoy resided along Conewago creek. He was Major in Colonel Alexander Lowrey's battalion at the battle of Brandywine in September, 1777, and was Colonel Cunningham's Major at the battle of Long Island.

Robert Buchannan resided on the east side of Canoy creek, and was Sheriff of the county in 1732-34. In 1748 he sold his land to Christ. Kauffman, whose widow, Barbara, married Martin Nissley in 1749. The farm then became Nissley's.

James Smith resided along the Peters road near Canoy Creek. He was an Indian trader.

Andrew Galbraith settled below Donegal Church upon land lately owned by Peter Nissley and the Garbers, in the year 1720. He, in connection with Rowyand Chambers, founded Donegal Church. He was a brother of John Galbraith, the miller. After the erection of the county he was appointed one of the Justices of the Common Pleas Court, and in 1732 he was elected a member of the Legislature and was re-elected for a number of successive terms. He married a daughter of James Kyle, who was the ancestor of the Hon. James Kyle, now a United States Senator from Dakota. Mr. Galbraith moved to Cumberland county in 1747.

Ephraim Moore lived near Big Chickies Creek, afterwards in Hempfield township.

John Mitchell resided to the west of where Maytown is. He was a brother of James.

Joseph Cochran lived above Conewago creek.

Gordon Howard was an Indian trader, and resided along the Paxtang and Conestogœ road, about a mile west of where Florin now is. Mr. Hershey now owns part of the land, which extended across into what is now Mount Joy township. The Hernleys bought part of the land. He owned seven hundred and fifty acres. The valley back of Hernleys is called Howard's valley. Gordon died about 1755. Some of his children moved to Guilford county, North Carolina. One of his sons moved up to the Juniata valley.

Patrick Campbell kept an "Ordinary" near Canoy, Indian Town. He was the first constable of Donegal township, after the county was organized. He married Mary, the widow of Captain Samuel Smith, in 173–, and then moved to one of the Smith farms, now owned by Simon Engle, where he kept an "Ordinary," which was kept as such by Capt. Smith for a number of years prior to its occupancy. Being in close vicinity to the Indian Town, and along the Peters road which led to Logan's Ferry, and being surrounded by Indian traders, it became a very important place. It was the custom of the traders to assemble at Smith and Campbell's just before starting with their pack trains for the Indian country. They made things lively while they were there.

They forded Canoy creek at or near where the stone mill stands, in recent years called "Erb's Mill." Samuel and Mary Smith had one son, named William, who moved to Baltimore and embarked in the mercantile business. William Smith had a son named Samuel, who was born in Donegal. He married a daughter of William Spear, who was born at Big Chickies creek. William Spear also moved to Baltimore in 1752. He married Elizabeth Galbraith, daughter of

John Galbraith, Indian trader, and Dorcas, his wife. Samuel Smith, son of William Smith, was a distinguished general in the Revolutionary War, and was a United States Senator from Maryland for fourteen years.

William Patterson, a rich merchant of Baltimore, married Dorcas Spear, daughter of William Spear, mentioned above, and their daughter married Jerome Bonaparte, brother of the Emperor. Descendants of this family reside in Baltimore and Boston.

Isaac Marauda, one of the French Indian traders, had his trading post near Campbell's "Ordinary." His daughter, Mary, married Governor James Hamilton, of Pennsylvania. He died in 1732.

Alexander Hutchinson lived along Little Chickies creek. On the north side he built a grist and saw mill, just above where the iron bridge is, in 1750. A hundred years ago Tobias Miller purchased some of his lands and the mills. It is probable that Mr. Miller built the stone dwelling on the hill and the present mill of stone, which is a very old one.

Robert McFarland settled along Little Chickies creek below where Mount Joy is. One of his sons moved to Virginia. John and James remained on the homestead farm. Thomas Clingan married the widow of James and came to own one-half of the land. Ludwig Lindemuth purchased part of the land. Mr. Zercher now owns part of the land.

Richard Allison owned 600 acres of land along Spring creek and adjoining Andrew Galbraith's land. His land went to his son, William, and his daughter, who married Wm. Miller, and to his daughter, Mary, who married James Sterrett, the grandfather of Hon. J. Sterrett, Chief Justice of the Supreme Court of the State.

Randel Chambers resided near Conewago creek. He was one of the founders of Donegal Church and a ruling elder of that congregation for many years. He moved to Cumberland Valley.

[TO BE CONTINUED.]

BIBLIA,

Das ist:

Die

Heilige Schri[ft]

Altes und Neues

Testaments,

Nach der Deutschen Uebersetzung

D. Martin Luthers,

[mi]t jedes Capitels kurtzen Summarien,
beygefügten vielen und richtigen Parlelen;

Nebst einem Anhang

Des dritten und vierten Buchs Esra und de[s]
dritten Buchs der Maccabäer.

Germantown:
Gedruckt bey Christoph Saur, 1743.

PAPERS READ

BEFORE THE

LANCASTER COUNTY HISTORICAL SOCIETY,

ON MARCH 5, 1897.

OLD MILLS AND COUNTRY ORDINARIES.
By SAMUEL EVANS, ESQ.

THE EPHRATA PAPER MILL.
By JULIUS FRIEDRICH SACHSE, ESQ.

LANCASTER, PA.
REPRINTED FROM THE NEW ERA.
1897.

Old Mills and Country Ordinaries,
  By SAMUEL EVANS, ESQ., ... 313

The Ephrata Paper Mill,
  By JULIUS FRIEDRICH SACHSE, ESQ., .   323

Old Mills and Country Ordinaries.

(*Continued from page 310.*)

Kreybill's mill was located along Spring Creek, about half a mile above Galbraith's mill. The first mill was of stone and two stories high. This mill was probably erected as early as 1730. For some years prior to 1773 it was owned by George Clingan. In the year 1773 he sold the mill and seventy-six acres of land to Abraham Stauffer, who, in the year 1784, sold it to Jacob Kreybrill, miller, of Rapho township, for $3,000. The old stone mill was torn down about sixty years ago. Before that time, in the year 1830, Mr. Kreybill built a three-story brick mill across the road from the old mill. This mill had the reputation of making the best flour in that end of the county. In my boyhood I took many grists to this mill. As early as I can remember, I had curiosity to know what a grist mill was and what was the meaning of tolling the grist. I was told that the miller took out one-tenth of the grist for grinding the grain. Some of the men employed about the farm told me that the miller had a wooden scoop with which he took out the miller's share, after which he threw it against the ceiling. If it stuck fast he did not toll it again, but if it came down, he tolled it a second time to make sure that he got his share. This seemed a strange proceeding to my youthful mind, so I begged to be allowed to take a small grist to the mill and I would wait until it was ground. I watched the miller very closely, but I did not see him take out any toll; and when I came to return I found that the bag I took the grist in would not hold the flour, middlings and bran, and I had to borrow another bag. This was a mystery to me. I asked no more questions about the "grist" or the miller.

This mill is now owned by Mr. Nissly, a relative of the Kreybills. Jacob Kreybill, a grandson of Jacob Kreybill, is living in the West. On the northeast branch of Spring Creek the first mill was

Zook's Factory,

of which I have spoken. A short distance above was Worke's tannery, of which I have also written.

A mile above Worke's is a very old corn mill, built of stone, which was known eighty years ago as Breneman's mill. The mill is very old and probably dates many years beyond the Revolutionary period.

At the head of Spring Creek we find

Nissly's Grist and Saw Mill.

This mill stands upon land taken up by John Wilkins, Indian trader, as early as 1721 or 22. He died in 1741, and his son, John Wilkins, and other heirs sold some of this land to Nissly in or about the year 1762. He built a grist mill about the year he purchased the property. It is still in the name of the family and in full operation.

John Gardner settled at the mouth of Chickies Creek, in 1720, and built a

Hemp Mill,

which stood on the east side of the creek, which was in full operation for a hundred years. The saw mill at the mouth of the creek was built by Henry Haldeman about the year 1826. The large stone merchant mill at the mouth of Spring Creek was built by Christian Haldeman, sixty years ago. Like many other merchant mills in the county, it is idle.

At the junction of Big and Little

Chickies Creeks Henry Shearer built a very large stone merchant mill, also idle. At the lower point of Rapho township, at the junction of the two Chickies creeks, a

Carding Mill

was erected by Christian Martin one hundred and fifty years ago. The ditch for the head race is all that marks the spot upon which it stood.

Half a mile above the mouth of Little Chickies Creek, Abe Hiestand had a

Fulling and Saw Mill

ninety years ago, and it was probably built many years before that time.

Rhoddy's Grist and Saw Mill

were built as early as 1721 or 1722. They stood where Risser's Mill now stands. The present brick mill was built by Mr. Houtz about eighty years ago. The stone building behind the brick mill is part of the Rhoddy Mill, and after the erection of the new mill the old one was used as a clover mill. Joseph Worke, before mentioned, married a daughter of Mr. Rhoddy, who died in the year 1733. He directed his executors to build a grist mill along Conewago creek for his son, Alexander Rhoddy, within two years after his death.

In 1745, James Rhoddy, son of above, sold the mills and 350 acres to John Forry and Joseph Sherrick. The Sherricks owned some of this land until within a few years ago.

Tobias Miller owned the mill above, which I have described. There were seven or eight mills further up the stream which, for want of space, I cannot describe.

Patrick Hays built a

Carding and Fulling Mill,

which stood above the stone arch bridge at Myer's, about the year 1730. A few years ago the stone walls of the old mill fell down, and nothing but the foundation walls mark the spot.

Jacob Brubaker, grandson of the pioneer settler, Hans Brubaker, built a

Fulling Mill

on Little Chickies creek before the Revolutionary War, which stands below Mastersonville.

The first grist mill above Rhoddy's was built by David Hays about the year 1730. John Hamaker, Esq., purchased this grist mill.

In the year 1772 Mr. Hamaker was one of the County Justices and was a prominent man in his time.

This mill was a log structure and is now used in part for a dwelling. John Hertzler purchased the farm and mill about ninety-years ago, and built a new mill of brick four stories high and about seventy feet square. He made a tunnel through solid rock from the dam to the new mill. The Hertzlers sold to Shenk, and the mill is now owned by Michael Moore, who in recent years has converted it into a roller process mill. Under the latter's ownership the mill has done a large business. When other mills were going down this one held its own and prospered.

"Commodore" Greider built a large stone grist mill about the year 1804. This is the first mill above M. Moore's, and is now owned by his brother, John H. Moore.

About forty-eight years ago John Gamber built an

Anthracite Furnace,

which he named Sarah Anne, after his wife. Gamber sold the furnace to David R. Porter, then Governor of the State. A cinder pile and a blacksmith shop are all that remain to mark the spot where the furnace stood. Above this mill was

Musselman's Mill,

owned by him ninety years ago. The date of its erection is much earlier. In late years it was called "Bender's" mill, and still later Barr's mill. The latter also had a distillery in connection with the grist mill.

Above Barr's mill at the crossing of the old Paxtang and Conestoga road Samuel Scott located and built a

Grist and Saw Mill

on the west side of the creek about the year 1729 or 30; after the above road was built, in 1732 he built an

Ordinary,

which became a famous tavern during the French and Indian wars, and during the Revolutionary period. When the officers and troops marched to join Braddock's and Forbes' armies they invariably halted at Scott's tavern to dine, it being a convenient distance from Lancaster. Mr. Scott's first wife was a Miss Boyd. His second wife was Hannah Polk, an aunt of President James K. Polk. He died in 1777. He gave the mills and tavern to his nephew, Captain Hugh Pedan, a Revolutionary soldier.

After Mr. Pedan, the tavern and mills passed to his son, John. The tavern was rented to the late John Guy, who also ran a line of stages from Lancaster to Harrisburg. Henry Shenk bought the mill and water right and built a very fine stone grist and merchant mill on the east side of the creek. The mill is now owned by Mr. Garber, who does a successful business.

The Shawnee Corn and Grist Mill

was built of stone, near the mouth of Shawnee Run, about the year 1730, by Samuel Blunston and James Wright, who settled where Columbia is, in the year 1726. During Braddock's war and afterwards, when General Forbes was organizing his army at Fort Rays, or Bedford, 1758, James Wright supplied these armies with flour packed in kegs and carried to Bedford on pack horses. He also supplied the Indians on Turkey Hill with flour.

An Interesting Legal Case.

Herewith I present to the Society an opinion of the Supreme Court, which gives a history of this mill. In this paper there is much which would interest the legal profession.

In 1796 Samuel J. Atlee built a tan yard a short distance above this mill. Fifty years ago Shawnee Furnaces absorbed most of the land and water belonging to the tan yard. About a mile above the tannery George Getz had a grist mill. I remember when a boy of going into the mill to look at the water wheel and found Mr. Getz treading the wheel. The stream of water was very small. The wheel was about twenty-eight feet in diameter. When the turnpike to Chestnut Hill was built, forty years ago, the mill was torn down.

Abram Hess, of Conestoga, purchased several hundred acres of land from James Logan about the year 1730, which was located along and near the creek, which empties into the river above "Vinegar's Ferry." Mr. Hess, who was a miller, built a

Grist Mill and Saw Mill

soon after his purchase of the land. In the year 1760 he sold the mill and land to John Grove (Groff), miller, also of Conestoga. In the year 1787 John Grove conveyed the grist and saw mill to Henry Grove, a son of John, and in 1795, for £2,800, Henry Grove sold 100 acres and the mills to Abram Shock, who came from Manor township.

After the Revolution, Conrad Ziegler purchased a farm above Shock's Mill.

About fifty-five years ago sons of Mr. Ziegler built a large stone grist mill.

Prior to that Huber had a grist mill at or near where Ziegler's mill is. At or near where Ziegler's mill stands, James Le Tort, Indian trader, had a store and trading post, and was followed by James Lowrey and Captain James Paterson, Indian traders.

In the year 1750 Jacob Downer, the founder of Maytown, built a tannery upon the same stream where the road from Galbraith's mill to Conoy creek crossed.

At the mouth of Conoy creek, a hundred years ago, Melchoir Brenneman, and his son-in-law, John Haldeman, built a large stone merchant mill and saw mill and still house. The grandfather of the late Bayard Taylor did the stone work. The farm and mills are now owned by Henry M. Wiley.

All of the land from the mouth of Conoy Creek, for about one mile and a half, was settled by John Galbraith, Indian trader, before spoken of.

About a mile above the Wiley mill, in the year 1756, Conrad Wolff purchased fifty-four acres from John Galbraith and built a grist and saw mill.

Dewald (David) Wolff, son of above, sold one-third of the mill to George Bambaugh, of Derry, and in the year 1769 Bambaugh sold his interest to Henry Nissly, miller, of Rapho, who sold to John Engle and Adam Brenneman. Engle sold his interest to Brenneman. About the year 1798 Brenneman built a new mill of stone. Of late years it was known as

Erb's Mill.

It has been idle for some years.

Alexander Hutchinson built a grist and saw mill about a mile above Erb's mill. In the year 1749 the Hutchinsons sold to John Wilson, who sold to John Engle in the year 1770. In recent years this mill was known as

Horst's Mill.

A mile further up the stream there was another mill known ninety years ago as

Horst's Mill.

The next mill above was called

Brubaker's Mill.

Next above was

Root's Mill.

Next one

Gish's Mill.

Philip Gloninger built a grist and saw mill on Conoy Creek where either Brubaker's or Root's mill was, as early as 1740. In 1749 Gloninger sold the mill to Martin Nissly.

On the west side of Conoy creek, where Elizabethtown now is, Captain Thomas Harris established an Indian store and trading house, and built a tavern about the year 1730, called the

Bear Tavern.

In the year 1731 or 1732 the Paxtang and Conestoga road was laid out and constructed from Paxtang to his tavern, and in a year or two the road was finished to Scott's Tavern (before mentioned) and extended to Lancaster Townstead in two or three years. This tavern was one of the headquarters for the Indian traders. Harris was Captain of a company of Rangers in the year 1748. In 1749 he sold his farm and tavern to Lazarus Lowrey, another Indian trader, who resided on Senator J. D. Cameron's farm in Donegal. In the same year Mr. Lowrey rented the tavern to Captain Barnabas Hughes, who purchased the tavern and farm in 1750. In the following year he laid out a town and named it after his wife, Elizabeth. Mr. Hughes was Captain and Commissary of Subsistence in the French and Indian wars. He was the first person to bring the news to Carlisle of the disaster to Braddock's army. He was also at the battle of Loyal Honnon in 1758. He moved to Baltimore in the year 1765, and became largely engaged in the iron business. His sons, Colonel Daniel, Colonel John and Colonel Samuel, were all prominent officers in the Revolutionary war. They all became extensive iron masters in Western Maryland and in Harford and Cecil counties. The sons sold the tavern and farm and ground rents in Elizabethtown to Captain Alexander Boggs.

At a point where the road from Hummelstown to Harris' tavern crosses Conewago creek, Captain Harris purchased a

Grist and Saw Mill

from Captain Samuel Smith in the year 1750. The latter moved to the Juniata Valley and became one of the Judges of Cumberland county. The ditch which carried the water to this mill is all that remains to mark the spot where it stood.

The Harris family moved to Deer Creek, Baltimore county, Maryland, in the year 1766. The sons were prominent officers in the Revolutionary War.

The first mill on Conewago Creek was called

Nissly Mill

as early as 1815. There was probably a grist mill there long before that.

The Grubbs built a forge where the Pennsylvania railroad crosses the creek, about the year 1800, and in the year 1820 they built

Mount Vernon Furnace.

Some years later they built a grist and saw mill.

Patrick Allison built a grist and saw mill below where Colebrook Furnace is as early as 1740.

I have only noticed the earlier mills, in a small portion of the county.

There has been a wonderful depreciation in the value of grist and merchant mills within the last fifty years. The water wheels in many of them stand still.

Hemp, oil, clover and carding mills are seldom to be seen.

Another industry has gone the same way. When I was a boy, and driving along the turnpike from Marietta to Lancaster, I could count twenty-three still houses. There is not one to be seen there now.

THE EPHRATA PAPER MILL.

A paper was read a short time ago before the Historical Society of Pennsylvania upon the subject of paper making and the different water marks used by the Willcox family, whose history the learned speaker traced through the several generations down to the present time.

Until within a few years ago the general impression has been, and the idea is propagated even now, that paper making in America had its origin in the Ivy Mills on Chester Creek in Chester (now Delaware) county, Pennsylvania, in the year 1714, and that Thomas Willcox was the first paper maker. This statement has been repeated so often that even standard writers have incorporated it in their works.

Now, the facts of the case are, as shown by the above speaker, that the old Ivy mills of Thomas Willcox were not erected until the year 1729, or shortly afterwards, and from the outset became one of the leading commercial paper factors in the Colonies, he having Benjamin Franklin as a patron, who started his printing office in the same year. One of the specialties of the Willcox Mill was the making of paper for notes or currency, and it has been claimed that they made the first paper of that kind and used for that purpose in this Province—a claim which I will show you cannot be maintained. However, as a matter of fact, the Willcox Mills have supplied most all the paper used for currency purposes from the time when a thick pulpy mass was used for Provincial and Continental currency with its gruesome legend, *to counterfeit is death*, down through all the various conditions of our country; including the peculiar silk "Onion skin" paper of our old State banks as well as the localized fibre paper upon which our national bonds and currency are printed at the present day.

During the course of this paper a statement was made in reference to the watermarks used; further, that they were adopted a few years previous to the outbreak of the Revolution, and that the designs had to be imported from England, as they could not be produced here, until the experiments of Nathan Sellers during the Revolution made it possible.

Now so much for the Wilcox episode.

EARLIEST WATERMARK OF WILCOX PAPER MILL.

As a matter of history, the first paper mill that ground pulp within the American colonies was set up in Germantown, or, more properly speaking, within the German township in Philadelphia county. This was prior to the year 1690. And, what is more, the mill had a special water mark of its own. The founder and originator of the enterprise was one William Ryttinghuisen, now anglicized to Rittenhouse, and I am pleased to say that some of his direct descendants are enrolled among the membership of the Pennsylvania German Society.

An account of this paper mill appears in Richard Frame's poem, "A Short Description of Pensilvania; or a Relation of What Things are Known, Enjoyed and like to be Discovered in said Province." This was printed by William Bradford, at Philadelphia, in 1692. Four years later (1696) Judge John Holme also wrote a poem in the same strain; it was entitled: "A True Relation of the Flourishing State of Pensilvania," wherein the reference to the Germantown paper mill is as follows:

PRINTER.

"Here dwelt a printer and I find
That he can both print books and bind;
He wants not paper, ink or skill,
He's owner of a paper mill.
The paper mill is here hard by,
And makes good paper frequently,
But the printer as I do here tell,
Is gone into New York to dwell.
No doubt but he will lay up bags
If he can get good store of rags.
Kind friend, when thy old shift is rent
Let it to th' paper mill be sent."

Thus it will be seen there can be no question whatever as to the priority of the introduction of paper making into the American colonies. It may seem somewhat strange to such persons who have not devoted any study to this subject, but merely accepted as truth the biased statements as to the ancient mill on the banks of the Chester creek, when they learn that not only was printing paper made at the first Rittenhouse mill on the banks of the Wissahickon, but good writing paper as well, both white and blue, as will be seen from the agreement made in 1697 with William Bradford, the printer.

Then, again, from the earliest establishment of the enterprise the Rittenhouses, father and son, made use of a water mark. The first distinctive one adopted by the Rittenhouses was the word "Company," to designate the original partnership under which the industry was started.

(326)

PENSILVANIA

WATERMARK OF RITTENHOUSE PAPER MILL ON THE WISSAHICKON.

The next water mark used were the letters "W. R." on one half of the sheet, and upon the other half was a clover leaf in a shield surmounted by a kind of a crown, beneath which was the word "Pensilvania." I have here a fac-simile of these watermarks, as they appear upon a deed signed by Francis Daniel Pastorius and Daniel Falkner. Now, so far as currency or money paper is concerned, the first issues of Pennsylvania currency in 1723 were printed upon just such paper, the product of the Pennsylvania Dutch (if I may be pardoned for the use of the term) paper mill on the Wissahickon.

Then if any one wishes to take the trouble to visit the Historical Society of Pennsylvania, or the Ridgway Library in Philadelphia, and inspect the files of the *American Weekly Mercury*, the first newspaper ever printed within the British Middle Colonies, they will find impigned upon each sheet of the early numbers the letters "K. L.," standing for Klaus Rittenhouse, the name of the paper maker.

The second paper mill started in the American colonies was the venture of one William De Wees, a brother-in-law of Nicolas Rittenhouse. This mill was built in the year 1710 on the west side of Wissahickon creek, in that part of Germantown known in early times as Crefeld, near the line of the present Montgomery county.

The third mill within the Province appears to have been the Willcox venture upon the Chester creek.

The fourth paper mill to be set up within the Province, and which was perhaps the most important one in regard to its output, was located upon the romantic banks of the Cocalico, at Ephrata, in Lancaster county.

It is upon this enterprise that I wish to speak, and bring to your notice a few facts which appear thus far to have escaped the attention of local historians and students. *Die Papier-Muhle der Bruderschafft*, like other industrial and commercial enterprises of the Zionitic Brotherhood, originated in the fertile brains of the Eckerling brothers. It was a distinctive enterprise with a dual object.

First. To furnish paper for the publications of the *Mystic Brotherhood* and the various imprints of the Society.

Secondly. It was intended as a commercial venture, to furnish a revenue to the Community.

Unfortunately, no records are known to the writer which would give the exact date of the setting up of the paper mill upon the Cocalico. From the meagre data in the *Chronicon Ephretense* we find an allusion to the grist mill in Chapter 22, which places the purchase of the mill some time prior to the death of Brother Agonius (Michael Wohlfarth), which occurred May 20, 1741. It is but reasonable to assume that the other mills and industrial establishments were set up in rapid succession, and that at the time of the culmination of the trouble between Beissel and the Eckerling brothers and the expulsion of the latter, September 4, 1745, the enterprise of the four Brothers had developed the resources of the mystic Community of the Cocalico until it became the greatest industrial establishment in the American colonies.

Again referring to the *Chronicon*, we learn that on the morning of September 6, 1747, a great calamity overtook the Community. This was nothing less than the destruction of three of its mills by fire.

The annalist of the Community, commenting upon the calamity, writes (Chapter 27) that at that time the Community owned and operated a grist mill, with three runs of stones; a skillfully-built oil mill, with stones the like of which none before existed in America; a fulling mill, a saw mill and a paper mill.

Upon the night in question the grist, oil and fulling mills became a prey to the incendiary's torch. The saw and paper mills were only saved from destruction by the hard labors of the Brothers and Sisters of the Community, with such of the neighbors as were attracted to the scene.

Brother Agrippa adds in a foot note, "That the mill had been of great benefit to the households for the poor Solitary now for nearly fifty years." As this was written in 1785 or 1786, it would place the setting up of the grist mill about the year 1736. The above quotations from the *Chronicon Ephretense* appear to be the only direct official records left to us of the commercial enterprises of the Community, as upon the expulsion of the Eckerlings all records and papers are said to have been destroyed upon the order of Beissel. The only additional data relating to the paper mill known to the writer, and having a semblance to authenticity, are three entries in the diary of Brother "Kenon" (Jacob Funk):

(1.) *1761—Den 26, Juni hat Br : Melchy die Babir Muhl verlassen.*

[(1.) 1761—On June 26, Bro. Melchy severed his connection with the paper mill.]

(2.) *1770—Den 4, September ist oder sind OBADJA und KENAN von der BABIR-MILL gegangen und obadia ist in Verginia gestorben und 1780 im May ist Kenan wider nach EPHRATA geKomen.*

[(2.) 1760—On September 4, Obadja and Kenan left the paper mill. Obadia died in Virginia, and in May, 1780, Kenan returned to Ephrata.]

(3.) *1784—Den, September morgens etwa zwischen 2 und 3 uhr ist das neue Muhlhaus in brand gesteckt worden, aber doch glucklich wider geloscht worden.*

[(3.) 1784—On September 1, between 2 and 3 o'clock in the morning, the new mill building was set on fire, but luckily, the fire was extinguished.]

From the above it would appear that the Funk family, who were practical paper makers, had charge of the paper mill. This family consisted of the father, Martin Funk, his wife, Magdalena, and two sons and a daughter—Samuel, born 1719; Jacob, born March 4, 1725, and Sophia, born 1727. The family first came to Ephrata in 1744 and settled in the immediate vicinity as "Householders." They came from the Conestoga country where they had lived since 1735. The mother, Magdalena, died January 14, 1745-6. Samuel then joined the Zionitic Brotherhood and henceforth became Brother Obadiah. April 20, 1747, Jacob followed his example, and closed his career under the monastic name of Kenon. Upon the following day Sophia became a "Rose of Saron," entered the convent and was enrolled as Sister Genoveva. On April 22 the father was also admitted to the Brotherhood.

Now, in view of certain statements to be found in contemporary records, which set forth that the Ephrata paper mills produced more paper than any similar establishment in the colonies, it occurred to the writer that some notes or data might be found in the periodicals of the day bearing upon this branch of the provincial industry at Ephrata. In the long and persistent search for authentic information upon the subject, several interesting items were discovered.

The first one was in connection with the earliest Bible printed in America. It was, as you all know, a German one, and the title page bears the legend 1743. I allude to what is known as the "Sauer" Bible.

You will naturally ask, what has this to do with Ephrata? Well, I will tell you. This monumental work, which had immortalized the Germantown printer, was printed upon paper made either in whole or part in the "*Bapier muhle der bruderschafft zu Ephrata.*" The edition was bound at Ephrata by the Brotherhood, and I feel pretty certain that if the records could b) found they would show that a great part of the sheets were printed at Ephrata upon the old "Kloster presse," now reposing in the rooms of the Historical Society of Pennsylvania.

Then, again, the fact was brought out that the greater part of the first edition of the American Bible was sold in Lancaster county. It may be well to state at this point that at the time when Christopher Sauer finished his Bible in 1742–3 the bookbindery at Ephrata was the largest and best equipped bindery in the Colonies, and the only one who could undertake to bind an edition of great magnitude.

I will now present to you a few proofs in support of my argument. First, we will refer to Sauer's newspaper:

No. XLIII., dated February 16, 1744. Der Hoch Deutsche Geschichts-Schreiber, Odor: Sammlung Wichtiger Nachrichten aus dem Natur-und Kirchen-Reich.

No. XL., November 16, 1743.

[The High-German news writer or faithful chronicler of important events in Nature and the Church.]

[No. 40—November 16, 1743.]

"Der Drucker (Sauer) Machet bekant weil er siehet, dass sehr wenige sind, welche ungebundene Bibeln begehren, u, er nicht so viel binden kan lassen, als in dieser kurtzen Zeit von ihm begehrt worden ob man wohl gern jedermann so gleich geholffen sahe; Denjenigen welche nicht weit von Ephrata wohnen, die konnen gegen ihre Quittungen und Zahlung des ubrigen daselbst eine gebundene oder ungebundene Bibel finden, und die nicht PRAENUMMERIRT haben, die konnen auch daselbst finden, und bestellen sie wie sie sie wollen gebunden haben, oder finden schon gebundene bey Samuel Eckerling. Von dorten sollen auch in die neue Stadt gebracht warden an H. Rieger, Doct. Med., in Lancaster."

[The printer (Sauer) announces since he finds that there are very few possessing unbound bibles, that he cannot bind them as rapidly as they are required, although he would like to see everyone satisfied. Those who do not live far from Ephrata can procure bound or unbound bibles for their payment and receipts. Those who have not yet subscribed, can procure them and order them bound as they may desire, or may find them already bound by Samuel Eckerling. They can also be procured from H. Rieger, M. D., in Lancaster.]

From the above it would appear that the whole edition of the so-called "Sauer" Bible was at that time in Ephrata, viz., November 16, 1743.

The next interesting item is a notice in the same paper, under date of February 16, 1744:

"Weilen in Ephrata nicht so viel Bibeln konnen gebunden werden, als in Lancaster by Herrn Rieger bestellt werden, so berichtet man, dass nachstans sollen gebundene dahin gesand werden."

[Since there cannot be so many Bibles bound in Ephrata, as were engaged of Mr. Rieger, we suggest that hereafter bound volumes be sent there.]

This notice certainly shows the devout character of the early German settlers of Lancaster county. Two months later, April 16, 1744, Sauer notifies the public that

" Bey H. Jacob Friedrich Rieger in der neuen Stadt Lancaster sind nun auch Bibeln zu haben von verschiedenem Band und Preiss."

[Bibles of different bindings and prices are now to be had of H. Jacob Friederich Rieger in the new State of Lancaster].

This same number of Sauer's newspaper makes mention of the expulsion of the Eckerlings :

" Die Raporte vom Ausgang Verschiedener Bruder aus Zion sind ungleich: Dass beyde Bruder Samuel u Israel Eckerling nebst Alexander Mack dem Getummel der Welt gantzlich zu entweichen und ihrem Puff u Zug gemass in ferne Wusten gegangen, nachdem sie ordentlich Abscheid genommen haben, dass ist gewiss ; dass sie aber heimlich hinweg, und nach Bethlehem gegangen seyn, um sich daselbst Weiber geben zu lossen, a dass ist entweder Missverstand oder beyden seiten zum Spott erdichtet."

[The reports concerning the departure of various Brothers out of Zion differ. It is certain that the two brothers, Samuel and Israel Eckerling, also Alexander Mack, were determined to leave the bustle of the world completely, and accordingly went to the far West after they had taken formal leave. That they went to Bethlehem to procure wives is either a misunderstanding or fiction, created on both sides for the purpose of ridicule.]

We now come to the second item of interest. I allude to the watermarks used by the Ephrata Community, some of which will occasionally be found in the sheets of the Sauer Bible, the paper in which is by no means of either uniform texture or quality.

The product of the *Bapier Muhle des Kloster's* was not limited to coarse printing paper, and what was known as " Macalatur," but they made fine grades of both writing and printing paper as well. All of the latter grades are marked with one of their distinctive watermarks. The ordinary grades of printing paper, such, for instance, as was used in the *Martyr Spiegel*, were made upon plain sieves, without any watermark. I may here state that the wire sieves used in making the various kinds of paper were a local product, being made by one Isaac Langle, of Germantown, who died about the time when

WATERMARK FROM SAUER BIBLE, FIRST EDITION.

the Sauer Bible was being printed. Early in the year 1744 Friedrich Ochs and Johannes Eckstein advertised for sale a "Siebmachers-weberstuhl mit einen dazu gehorigen eisern Sohienen-zug u anders Zugehor."

[A wire-weaver's weaving frame, with an iron apparatus for wire drawing, and other belongings.]

The question of watermarks is a very interesting one, and I have a few here to show you and illustrate my remarks.

WATERMARKS OF THE EPHRATA PAPER MILL SUBSEQUENT TO 1744.

The first one is taken from the fly-leaf of a Sauer Bible. It is a crude home-made affair and was the private mark of the Funk family. It consists of a large figure four, the perfect number, below which are the letters R F.

The same watermark, F B, (Bruder Funk), without the figure "4," also appears in some of the subsequent publications of the Community, as you may see from the specimen I have taken from a page of the "*Theosophische Lectionen,*" which was also printed in the year 1745.

The next one, and by far the most important one from a historical standpoint, is the design adopted by the Zionitic Brotherhood, and was intended for the distinctively mystical publications of that body of religious enthusiasts. It was evidently made at Ephrata, and crude as it is it bears the undeniable stamp of the Mystic Brotherhood. You will observe that it consists of a large Latin cross, surmounted by a scroll with the word "Zion." Two keys form right angles with the upright and arm of the cross. These keys have reference to the *Clavicula Salomonis*, or the "Keys of Solomon," a mystic book of the XVII. century which was held in high esteem by the Brotherhood. The cross, it will be seen, rests upon a panel bearing the legend "Efrata." The whole design is surrounded by an ornamental scroll.

This watermark you will find in the *Hohe Zeugnisse* and a few other books printed at Ephrata up to the year 1745. The paper bearing this watermark was evidently made while the Eckerlings were still in control of the Community, as it does not appear to have been used after their expulsion from the Community. After that unfortunate episode in Ephrata's history, there appear several new watermarks, which were continued in use

WATERMARK OF THE ZIONITIC BROTHERHOOD USED PRIOR TO THE EXPULSION OF THE ECKERLINGS.

for a number of years. The oldest seem to have been a "post horn" and a "heart shape" with the letters "E F" in the centre. These two designs were usually used together upon opposite sides of the sheet. A crude crown was also used frequently in connection with the post horn. Another design was a large "E F" in letters about an inch high, upon a book made of fine writing paper, now in the priceless collection of the Hon. Samuel W. Pennypacker. We find the full word "Efrata" impinged upon the pages of the volume in letters about three-quarters of an inch high.

There are without doubt still other watermarks in existence dating from this old Community, whose glory has long since departed; imprints which may shed still more light upon our subject, and if it were only within the possibilities of the future that some fragments of the commercial records of the Community and escaped the ruthless bonfire made in the meadow on the Cocalico on that September day in the year of grace 1744, to gratify the whims of Conrad Beissel. I say, were such fragments to come to light, they would doubtless show that the *Papier Muhle der Bruderschafft zu Ephrata* was one of the most important enterprises of the Provincial period.

APPENDIX.

The Dr. Jacob Frederich Reiger alluded to in this article as Christopher Sauer's agent at Lancaster was a prominent physician of Lancaster during the middle of the last century. He was born in the Palatinate, and came to Pennsylvania in September 12, 1734. (See Pennsylvania Archives, Second Series, vol. 17.) He was a brother of the Rev. John Bartholmew Reiger, the celebrated pioneer of the Reformed Church in Lancaster County, and who also was a physician, and a graduate of the University of Heidelberg, and who came to Pennsylvania in 1731. No doubt Dr. Jacob Frederich Reiger was also a university man, and this, united with his profession, gave him prominence in the community. The fact that he was Sauer's agent for the sale of his bibles is entirely new. He is best known through the unfortunate duel in which his son, Dr. Jacob Reiger, was engaged with Stephen Chambers, formerly a captain in the 12th regiment of the Pennsylvania line, and one of the leading lawyers of the Lancaster bar. He died on January 2, 1762, aged 87 years. He is buried in the graveyard attached to the First German Reformed Church in Lancaster, by the side of his wife, Jane Reiger, who died January 25, 1773, aged 52 years, and his illustrious brother, Rev. John Bartholomew Reiger, who died March 11, 1769, having been born January 10, 1707. Dr. J. F. Reiger's tombstone states that he was an eminent surgeon.

Dr. Jacob Reiger, who as already stated, fought a duel with Captain Chambers, died October 20, 1793, aged

38 years, and is no doubt buried in the same graveyard, although there is no head stone to mark the spot, but the record of his death appears in the Church register. He died intestate and letters of administration were granted on his estate.

That Dr. Jacob Reiger was the son of Dr. Jacob Frederick Reiger is shown by the following extract from the latter's will, dated December 19, 1761, and probated shortly afterward by Edw. Shippen, Register, and recorded in book B. vol. 1., page 364, etc.: "I give and bequeath all my real and personal property to my wife Jane Reiger and my son Jacob Reiger. If Jacob shall die before arriving at 21 years then I give his share to the children of my brother John Bartholomew Reiger, Philip Gerhard Reiger, Adam Reiger and the children of my sister Catarina Reiger."

Inasmuch as the Reiger-Chamber's duel is said to have been the first one fought in Pennsylvania the facts are deemed of sufficient interest to be added here.

In the "Shippen Papers," under date of May 18, 1789, Col. Shippen writes from Lancaster to his brother, the Chief Justice : " I am extremely concerned to tell you that a most unfortunate duel happened last Monday, May 12, evening, between Dr. Reiger and Mr. Chambers, on a challenge of the former, for an affront received at a tavern. When each had fired one pistol shot without effect the seconds interfered, and proposals of accommodation were made, which Reiger could not be persuaded to agree to ; each then presented a pistol ; Chambers' snapped, but Reiger's discharged a ball through both his antagonist's legs. His wounds bled much, but for two days were considered not dangerous ; a mortification then ensued ; its progress upwards was great and rapid till Saturday morning, May 17, when it extended to his bowels and carried him off, to the most severe distress of the families and friends of both. The procession at his funeral in the evening was truly solemn and affecting. This melancholy subject has already too much agitated my mind to dwell on it longer, by relating the particular circumstances."

The subsequent correspondence which accompanies this letter on the " Shippen Papers " shows that the affront was offered to Dr. J. Reiger at Stokes' tavern, and that the duel occurred in the "Barrack yard at seven o'clock in the afternoon " (evening). The matter is referred to briefly in " Fithian's Journal."

Captain Chambers left a widow and several small children, and was a charter member of Lodge 43, F. & A. M. Stokes' tavern was the "Swan," located in Penn Square, and had formerly been owned by Matthias Slough. The affront offered was to the effect that Reiger was dressed in shabby attire, Chambers being in full regimentals. The duel is referred to in S. M. Sener's " Old Time Hostelries " in Christian Culture, vol. 2, pp 138 ; also in Dr. W. H. Egle's Historical Register, vol. 2, page 279 ; in Dr. Welchans' " History of Lodge 43, F. & A. M," page 207–8; and the Pennsylvania Archives, vol. 10, second series, page 759.

PAPERS READ

BEFORE THE

LANCASTER COUNTY HISTORICAL SOCIETY,

ON APRIL 9, 1897.

EARLY INDUSTRIES ON THE OCTORARA.
By Dr. J. W. Houston.

THE OLD WELSH GRAVEYARD.
By B. F. Owen.

LANCASTER, PA.
Reprinted from The New Era.
1897.

Early Industries on the Octorara, By Dr. J. W. Houston,
continued from page 217

The Old Welsh Graveyard,
By B. F Owen, ... 361

Early Industries on the Octorara.

(Continued from page 204.)

At the meeting of the Lancaster County Historical Society, held in the Iris Club rooms, on the seventh of January last, I had the pleasure of submitting a paper on the past and present industries of the East Branch of the Octorara and its tributaries, from its many sources along the Mine Hill divide and including the entire region drained by this stream, as far south as Steeleville, which hamlet reposes on the Chester county side of this inter-county water line. Progressing southward from Steeleville, along a continuation of the Brosius Heusel road, the valley of the East Branch suddenly expands, by the recession of the bounding hills, until it is one-fourth to one-half a mile wide, without gorge or defile, for a distance of eight miles, near to Pine Grove, where the junction with the West Branch is effected.

In all this region traversed by the historic Octorara only fertile meadows, sometimes guarded by abrupt hills, greet your view. These meadows, during the grazing season, furnish in abundance luxuriant pastures, fully appreciated and appropriated by the many herds of sleek, fat, contented kine, which, after cropping the nutritious herbage during the early morning hours, retire to the cool, inviting shades of friendly groves, and there, protected from the heated rays of the summer's sun, chew their cud in silence and repose, until aroused from their quietude by the familiar voices of the rosy-cheeked dairy maids, each summoning their charge to the scene of the evening milking.

Half a mile south of Steeleville a stream of considerable volume, known as Annan's Run, enters the East Branch from the Lancaster county side. This brook rises on the Wm. Borland homestead and, flowing somewhat south of an easterly course through the farm of David J. Jones, effects its confluence with the absorbing stream.

This Jones property is part of a tract of land deeded by the Penn Proprietors of the province to John Devor in 1734. In 1743 Col. James Taylor, of Revolutionary fame, bought the Jones tract and erected thereon a stone house, which even now at this late day is in quite good condition. The walls of this structure are quite thick. Neither sand nor lime entered into its composition. Clay, properly tempered, was used to cement the stones which were required in the construction of the building.

The house was evidently intended to subserve the double purpose of a dwelling and also as a fortification, within which the inmates would be safe during the frequent Indian incursions. The windows or embrasures were limited to two lights of eight by ten inch glass, one above the other. Some of these loopholes have given place to a more modern style of window, yet enough of the portholes remain to vindicate the date stone in the western gable which bears this motto, "The Lord of all is my *suport*," (spelled with one p). Below the motto appears the date 1743. This date 154 years ago suggests the query : Are there any buildings extant in Lancaster county bearing an earlier date of construction ?

One hundred years ago an oil mill was in active operation near the site of the fortified dwelling. The waters of Annan's Run had been diverted from their natural channel to furnish power for the grinding of the flaxseed. Near these buildings a causeway existed for many years prior to the advent of the white man, evidently built by the Indians, across a swampy piece of ground, to gain access to the flowing waters. Tradition tells of an Indian burying ground on the east bank of the stream.

Twenty years ago Mr. Emmor Jones discovered and developed on this tract of land quite a good quality of roofing slate, but want of transportation to market precluded its utilization. Doubtless future generations will operate these quarries. After traversing southward for a half mile the fertile meadows, recently the property of the late John C. Jones, we come to the Ross fording bridge—an open structure across the stream, which, in the dry seasons of the year, affords a safe, dry-shod crossing, but when there is a rise in the creek the Lancaster county approach to the bridge becomes useless and, to use the language of the gamins, is no good. A few rods below the bridge Lancaster county furnishes Shaw's Run to the swelling stream.

Here on the west bank a rocky ledge fifty rods long looms up to view as the foreground of a high hill. The ledge is known as Wolf Rock, which years ago furnished safe retreats for these animals, from which they made excursions to the neighboring settlers' sheep folds, they being fond of lamb, either chops or cutlets. A long, deep pool, whose waters leave the eastern ledge of the rocky ridge, is noted as a fishing resort, and those who delight in Izaak Waltonian pleasures do here congregate during the open season from the entire region roundabout to catch the wary bass.

On the summit of the Wolf Rock hill a grove of pine trees three acres in extent is found. It is a prominent landmark in this region and is known as Roney's Pines, the grove receiving the name of the proprietor, and is not named for Annie, the sweetheart of Joe. South of the rocks on the Chester county side is a beautiful grove on the farm of the late Hamilton Ross, which was the annual camping ground of the Steeleville Bachelors' Club, with which select society a few favored Benedicts were admitted, after pledging themselves not to divulge the secrets of the organization to their wives. It is needless to say I never became a member, though frequently a guest. The games indulged in were archery and croquet.

Near to the camping grounds Chester county contributes Officer's Run to swell the waters of the East Branch. This stream was extensively utilized years ago from its mouth to its source. Ascending the stream we first find the site of Love's distillery, next Robb's clover mill, of which only landmarks are found; then Rambo's saw mill in ruins on a tributary. Of Robinson's clover mill, the site alone remains. Above we find Hodgson's grain mill in good condition and near the headwaters are the decaying buildings of 'Squire Gilfillin's tan yard. The industry has ceased to exist.

One hundred rods down the stream from the confluence of Officer's Run, on the Chester county side, we come to Pine Hill, on the farm of W. A. Heming. This hill is the especial habitat or home of the red foxes and is celebrated in sporting literature. Those gentlemen who indulge in the manly sport of fox hunting seek the laurel-covered bluffs of this rocky ridge in the early morn, there unleash their hounds, certain before long to rouse reynard from his lair. Soon the baying of the dogs gives evidence that the nimble-footed quarry, with flowing train, is on the alert, endeavoring to outstrip his insatiate pursuers, whose melodious sounds awake the echoes of each surrounding cliff and are enchanting even to the ear of the fleeing fugitive, although he well knows retributive justice is on his track, and, should he be overtaken, his life would pay the penalty for having robbed some farmer's poultry yard the night previous.

Often have we checked our horses, when driving past this sportsmen's paradise, when the hunt was on, to listen to the symphony of the hounds, recalling those lines by the late Hon. J. B. Everhart, whose memory Chester county ever delights to honor as one of her favored and favorite sons. He thus characterizes the music of the chase:

   And surely never yet was heard,
   From tongue of man, or throat of bird,
   From reed or tube, or string or key,
   From all the craft of minstrelsy,
   More stirring, joy-inspiring sounds
   Than our rude orchestra of hounds
   Pours o'er the listening land,
   As if the unseen sylvan powers
   Went choiring through the matin hours
   At Dian's fond command.

But, since my education in fox hunting æsthetics and lore was sadly neglected in my younger days, I most respectfully abdicate the position of historian of Pine Hill in favor of our County Commissioner, Mr. J. R. Rutter, a gentleman with heart attuned to nature's laws, and who is familiar with every bridle path in these forest recesses and for years has been personally acquainted with many of the foxes of this region. Here oft

   The challenge loud his horn rang out,
   And Reynard knew the sound;
   Not waiting for the opening pack,
   He spurned the frozen ground.

   And bounding onward far and wide,
   Left old Pine Hill behind;
   And safety sought in hasty flight
   From scenes he deemed unkind.

> The well-trained hounds, with steady bay,
> Follow fast his scented trail;
> They gain upon his flying feet,
> His speed will not avail.
>
> For hours he toils o'er hill and dale,
> Though fleetest of his kind;
> A refuge from his closing foes
> Alone in earth to find.

At the foot of the western slope of Pine Hill are found the ruins of Love's saw mill, long since abandoned. The power was derived from the East Branch. Continuing down the stream, we come to an abrupt rocky ledge on the east side. This is the site of the famous Abner Davis quarries, from which immerse flag stones are obtained, which are highly prized for building purposes. A short distance below these quarries we find the ruins of Pennock's Mills. They were built early in the present century, but the site alone is found. This was the last power on the East Branch until after the junction in Pine Grove dam. The stream only furnishes about six feet fall to the mile in this part of its course.

One-half mile south of these ruins we enter the village known as Andrews' Bridge, consisting of a half dozen dwellings, a hotel and country store, with a blacksmith and a wheelwright shop. Here is located the Octorara post-office, one among the first established by Uncle Samuel in the county, and for many years was the distributor of a weekly mail, consisting of an average of three letters and a copy of *The Dollar Newspaper.* Now it is the dispenser of a daily mail requiring a goodly-sized mail-bag. Three score and ten years ago there was a fulling mill or woolen factory on a nameless tributary in this town, owned and managed by Betsy Kent, who also was the proprietor of a country store, from which she sold free labor goods to the abolitionists of the surrounding county, who were largely in the majority, this being a Free Presbyterian and Friends settlement.

The chief feature of interest in this hamlet is the immense bridge which here spans the East Branch and is known as Andrews' Bridge No. 2, the town taking the name of the bridge, which was erected in 1814. The bridge received its name in commemoration of the Andrews family, who early settled in this locality and owned several of the surrounding farms. Andrews' Bridge is 450 feet long and the road bed is thirty feet wide. There are four archways, one of thirty-eight feet span and twelve feet high, two arches spanning twenty-four feet and ten feet high and one span twelve feet long and five feet high. It is built of solid masonry, including side and wing walls, and is one of the finest structures in Eastern Pennsylvania. The Newport road traverses this bridge. This road was originally an Indian trail, afterward appropriated by the early settlers without warrant, but about fifty years ago was regularly ordained by the Lancaster and Chester county courts.

Along the line of this road in Chester county, on the table lands, tradition points out an Indian war dance ring, and one hundred and fifty rods south of the ring the same authority locates the position of the Indian village referred to in a former paper. Immediately south of Andrews' Bridge, on the Lancaster county side, eighty years ago there was a distillery where peach brandy and apple jack were made. The building is now used as a dwelling.

One-half mile south of Andrews' Bridge we come to a farm long famous for fertility, which is deserving a place in history. It embraces land in both counties, the improvements being on the Lancaster county side. They include two sets of farm buildings, the property having at one time been in two separate tracts. The mansion house proper is a large stone structure, erected in the early part of the present century by one Black. In 1837 it became the property of Dr. Obed Baily, a gentleman who would have graced a chair in any of our leading medical colleges, notwithstanding he frequently visited his patients on foot, costumed in overalls and straw hat. In 1856 Mr. Clarkson Brosius, father of our present Congressman, purchased the property and here resided up to the time of his death, October 8, 1863. He was a thorough gentleman and devoted to his calling, that of farming. He was methodical, scientific and enterprising and was regarded as a model farmer. He was instrumental in organizing the Octorara Farmers' Club in 1856, which gave an impetus to higher farming in the community. After the death of Mr. Brosius the property passed into the hands of Wm. H. Sproul, who for years resided here, but is now a distinguished citizen of Chester, Delaware county, Pa.

During the occupancy of this historical homestead by Dr. Obed Baily, his only sons, Elisha and Joseph, entered the Medical Department of the Regular Army and rapidly gained promotion during the late unpleasantness and now rank as Colonels. Two nephews and Dr. Milner also donned their Esculapian robes while residents of "The Old Homestead." One of the nephews, Dr. Wilson Baily, late a member of the General Assembly of Pennsylvania from Chester county, distinguished himself as a major surgeon during the rebellion. This was the home of our Congressman during his boyhood, his birth place being on an adjoining farm.

Here Senator Wm. C. Sproul, now representing Delaware county in the Pennsylvania Senate, first saw the light of day, and on an adjoining farm Byron Baldwin, Surgeon in the United States Navy, was born. Two hundred and fifty rods westward our fellow citizen, Wm. F. Beyer, Esq., began his earthly career. The James Martin homestead, which furnished two doctors in medicine and one in dental surgery, was also contiguous to the Dr. Baily residence. Such an emanation of talent in one generation, from so circumscribed a rural territory, less than a square mile in extent, is seldom found.

A half mile south from "The Old Homestead" Lancaster county contributes Beyer's Run to swell the common flood. This run received its name from the late Mr. Thomas Beyer, a prominent citizen of Coleraine township. He was the father of our own Wm. F. Beyer, of the Lancaster Bar.

This stream has its source near Nine Points, in Bart township, on the farm where our distinguished fellow member, Mr. John F. Meginness, now of Williamsport, Pa., spent his early boyhood. It flows past the old Brick School House, where the veteran editor of THE NEW ERA once wielded the birch. At least three of the members of the Lancaster County Historical Society were his pupils when he presided in this temple of erudition. Three miles down the stream we find the first utilization of its waters in furnishing power to drive the machinery of William Hastings' mills, embracing clover, saw, sorghum and cider mills. They were built early in the present century by James Martin, father of the late Dr. John Martin, of Georgetown, Dr. Josiah Martin, of Strasburg, both of Lancaster county, and of Dr. Joseph Martin, of Stewartstown, York county. Mr. James Martin was a Christian gentleman in every sense of the word, and was courageous in support of his convictions. He advocated temperance, the abolition of slavery and other reformatory measures. He was one of the promoters in establishing the Free Presbyterian Church at Andrews' Bridge. He had one peculiarity, that of expressing himself in rhyme. I remember, when a small boy, of accompanying some neighboring farm hands to this mill for the purpose of making cider. In my desire for observing everything observable I noticed two cardboards conspicuously posted, one on the grinding mill and the other on the press. Not being an adept in reading script, it required some time to decipher the notices.

The first read:

"Please carry your pumice over the road,
That the next one who comes may not balk
　　with his load."

The other one gave notice

"That two men bearing upon the screw,
Are free from all damage, if any they do;
But three men bearing upon the screw
Must pay for all damage, if any accrue."

The cider mill was of the type used fifty years ago, the press being worked with a screw and wooden lever, the patrons doing the necessary work.

Near the mouth of this stream, on the farm of Howard Newcomer, a tan yard, known as Swayne's, afterward Hood's, was in active operation about forty years since.

The next industry was a pottery, now extinct, on the Chester county bank of the stream and was owned and operated by Mahlon Brosius, the grandfather of our distinguished Congressman, Hon. Marriott Brosius, whose birthplace is on the Lancaster county side of the creek, fifty rods from the pottery site. Here it was that during his early boyhood he often doffed his shoes and stockings to wade across the stream to start the hydraulic ram which furnished the water supply to the farm buildings, then little dreaming that those chubby feet were destined in after years to worthily wear the sandals of the Great Commoner. A covered bridge here provides safe dry-weather transit. One mile south we come to Bell's Mills, erected by Colonel Bell, nearly one hundred years ago, for the manufacture of paper. Three score and ten years ago Robert Hodgson converted them into flour, feed and saw mills, for which purposes they are used at the present time. Forty-three years ago the late Wi liam S. Davis became proprietor and the property continues in the Davis family. The power used to drive these mills is derived from Bell's Run, which rises in Bart township, near Bartville. Three miles from its source we find the ruins of one of the oldest grain and saw mills in this region. It was erected by Daniel Beyer, the grandfather of the present generation by this name, in Coleraine and Bart townships. He came from Montgomery county and settled on this farm in 1789. He was a millwright by trade and the mills were his own handicraft. He operated them personally up to the time of his death in 1840.

Near to Bellbank, the modern name for Bell's Mills, we find covered bridge No. 3. It is a dry-weather bridge, the Lancaster county approach being subject to inundation when the water overflows its banks.

Three-fourths of a mile down the valley the East Branch receives from the Chester county side quite an increase in volume by the accession of the waters of Muddy Run, which rises in West Fallowfield township and flows a southwesterly course through the townships of Upper and Lower Oxford to join the common flood. The water powers of this stream years ago were fully utilized. In a distance of five miles seven industries were in operation. Ascending this stream one-half mile to Cream P. O. we find a creamery. Originally this power was used to drive a grist mill. This was converted into a paper mill and, after being burnt out twice and as often rebuilt, the power was utilized in making gilt-edged butter. Ascending the stream, we come to Coates' saw and paper mill, for years on the decline. The next industrial site is the ruins of McHenry's paper mill. Up the creek we come to McCreary's flour and feed mills in good condition. The next in order are the Evans' mills, grain, saw and sorghum, to which a creamery is attached, all in fair repair. Continuing onward we find the ruins of Bentley's mills. The next enterprise was located on the head waters and shows a feat of hydraulic engineering worthy of historical notice, perhaps without a parallel in either Lancaster or Chester counties.

Sixty-five years ago an Englishman, named Parker, erected a cotton factory in a locality he named Glenville, on the head waters of this stream. He built an embankment twenty-five feet high across the valley to retain the water of two small branches, which was to be utilized in driving the factory machinery; but the great amount of evaporation from the fifteen to twenty acres of water surface during the summer months rendered the supply inadequate for the purpose intended. One hundred rods below the factory the stream was reinforced by two tributaries, one from the north, the other from the south. These streams he ascended until on a level with the factory dam and from these points ditched these brances around their respective hills until their waters flowed into the common reservoir. The power still being insufficient, he then ditched the tail race from the factory around the northern hill until he obtained sufficient fall to the bed of the stream. This waste water was then conducted onto a very high breast or pitchback water wheel, upon the outer rims of which buckets were secured, and as the wheel revolved they would fill with water from the pit and carry it to the top of the wheel where it was discharged into an aqueduct that conducted it to the upper race, from whence it flowed back into the dam, to be again used in driving the machinery of the factory. It was claimed that this hydraulic engine would raise thirty per cent. of the water flowing upon the wheel. I think twenty-five per cent. was nearer the mark. Poor Parker was fond of gaining, and, although quite rich when he came to Glenville, his associates managed to fleece him of his wealth. He sold the property to Gen. Josiah Harlan, who had served as organizer of the Turkish army in his younger days, but he suffered the factory and all the appurtenances to crumble into ruins. He afterward became Colonel of the Eleventh Pennsylvania Cavalry, and after the war returned to a brother near West Chester, where he died. The power is now used to drive a flour and feed mill.

Returning to the East Branch, 300 yards below the mouth of Muddy Run we come to the Iron Bridge, No. 4, spanning the stream, where was previous to the advent of the bridge the Long Fording. This bridge, like others on this stream, is a dry-weather bridge. The approaches to many of them on the Lancaster county side having to cross the valley of the stream, are subject to overflow when there is high water. These meadows bordering the East Branch, and through which we have passed, are annually visited in the months of March and April by goodly numbers of Wilson's Snipe (*Scolopax Wilsonii*), the most highly prized of all our game birds. These annual visitants stop during their migration northward to replenish their haversacks with the, to them, toothsome angleworm. This information is especially dedicated to that prince of Lancaster sportsmen, Captain John B. Peoples, who will doubtless don his shooting toga and hie him away to the East Branch meadows to verify the statement, taking our friend, Mr. Leidigh, of the People's Bank, with him.

The next tributary of the East Branch to claim attention is a Lancaster county stream known as Cooper's Run. It rises west of Bartville, flows east of south and empties its waters on the farm belonging to the heirs of the late Col. Andrews. Descending the stream from its source, the first tribute exacted is by a grist mill known as Morrison's. It was erected early in this Nineteenth century by Morrison, and has continued in the family until a few years since. Down the stream 150 rods we come to the ruins of Truman Coates' clover and saw mill. Mr. Coates died, without issue, a few years since, and in his testamentary document he kindly remembered the Lancaster Home for Friendless Children. One mile farther down and near the mouth of the stream we find the ruins of Col. Andrews' mill. After three score and ten years of service in grinding the grists of neighboring farmers it, fifteen years since, lapsed into desuetude. Continuing down the East Branch we come to covered bridge No. 5, known as Worth's bridge. It is also a dry weather bridge, and affords transit on the farm of Ex-County Commissioner Albert Worth. One mile down the creek on the Chester county side we come to the dilapidated village of Mount Vernon, so named, although situated in a ravine. Three score years ago it was the most populous town of the entire region, its only rival being the village of Hopewell. The cotton works are situated two miles distant in a southeasterly direction. The cotton factories and paper mills in Mount Vernon gave employment to scores of people, who in turn opened up a market for the surrounding farmers' produce. Oxford, three miles east, was then only a stage station on the through route from Philadelphia to Baltimore, but after the Baltimore Central Railroad, forty years ago, passed through Oxford new possibilities were opened up for the latter, whose growth was then remarkable and now numbers 2,000 inhabitants. Mount Vernon and Hopewell lost their prestige, industries were abandoned, enterprise ceased its wonted vigor, and degeneracy ruled supreme. The East Branch is here crossed by covered bridge No. 6. Less than a mile down the stream the junction with the West Branch is effected at a place known to local geographers as the Loop, from the fact that the East Branch and Octorara proper form a semi-circle around a Chester county hill near to the head of Pine Grove Dam. In this paper, as well as in a former one, I have briefly referred to the past and present industries located upon the Chester county tributaries of the East Branch, they properly belonging to the Valley of the Octorara. Though couventional lines separate this territory for political purposes, the people are bound together by ancestral, social and religious ties which geographical restrictions cannot efface.

And, while we to the manor born are proud of our empire county, her past history, her present standing in all that tends to make her grand and great, her unrivaled soil, her climate and general environments, together with the achievements of her sons and daughters, yet we must acknowledge and greet our mother county as a worthy rival in everything pertaining to education and the development of industrial institutions. After a residence of more than three decades along the inter-county line I, although a Lancastrian in every fibre, am glad to claim Chester county as my Alma Mater.

Here we leave the valley of the Octorara, including my native township, Coleraine, with its many cherished memories and bitter recollections, which are always thickly strewed along the pathway of him who assumes the responsibilities of the family physician.

DR. J. W. HOUSTON.

The Old Welsh Graveyard.

What is known as the Old Welsh Graveyard is in East Earl township, less than a mile west of Fairville. It has long been known by that name, and much speculating has there been as to its origin, which has always appeared enveloped in mystery. A few facts, gathered in connection with those old Welsh settlers, have lately come to my notice, which may be of interest to others as well as to myself.

The earliest mention is at a meeting of the Board of Property held April 29, 1720, when Thomas Morgan, of Haverford, and Jenkin Davis, of Radnor, appeared and desired about 1,000 acres of lard near, or at the branches of Conestoga. (See page 701, Vol. XIX., Second Series Archives.)

June 8, 1720, the Board directs a letter to the Surveyor which reads: "If the bearer, Thomas Morgan, finds any land toward the Conestoga which will please him, lay any quantity, either under or over 500 acres, and the warrant shall be ready." And Taylor, the Surveyor, under date of June 17, 1720, says: "I have agreed with Jenkin Davis for 1,000 acres on or near the Conestoga Creek." (See Taylor's Papers in Historical Society Rooms, at Philadelphia.)

Both these surveys were made, as will appear later; that of Jenkin Davis (or Davies) at the mouth of Muddy Creek, and that of Thomas Morgan near where the Welsh graveyard is now located. This Thomas Morgan is not the same person who had a warrant for land taken up where Morgantown is situated and dated October 1, 1718, and December 12, 1718, for an addition adjoining, nor do I think they were related.

Surveys were made in the Conestoga Valley as early as 1715—that of William Cloud for 300 acres near Beartown, and sold later to Nathan Evans, being of that date. Thomas Edwards had conveyed to him June 4 and 5, 1719, a tract of 1,000 acres located on both sides of Conestoga creek and east and west from the point where Cedar creek empties into it. This tract was slightly over a mile east and west and a mile and a half north and south. One half covered what is now Spring Grove, and what was formerly Weaver's mill, on the State road. On this tract Thomas Edwards and his three sons settled, and died there. At Hinkletown Jenkin Davies and his sons settled, and intermediate was Thomas Morgan. James Steel, a surveyor, agent for the Board of Property, took out a general warrant for "1,000 acres of land back among the late surveys......to be laid out in one or more parcels, and a warrant is signed, dated ye 1st September, 1718." (See page 641, Vol. XIX., Second Series, Archives). Three hundred and fifty acres of this he located adjoining the Thomas Morgan tract. This warrant for 350 acres James Steel sold to Jenkin Davies. On this tract was located the burial place for all those residing in the district from Thomas Edwards' tract, on the Cærnarvon border, west to where Jenkin Davies was located, at Hinkletown; practically all the Welsh residing in what is now Earl and East Earl. They continued to bury there until 1745, when some of them were buried in the churchyard at Bangor. A good road, leading north of the Conestoga from Churchtown to Hinkletown and passing the old graveyard, formed the ready means of communication between the extremes without crossing the Conestoga creek. The road is known as the Hinkletown road, and is still in use. The 350 acres, the warrant for which was purchased by Jenkin Davies from James Steel, remaining unimproved, under the fourth section of the agreement made between William Penn and the adventurers and purchasers, dated July 11th, 1681, was taken up by Rees Morgan. Rees Davis squatted on it, built a small house, and cleared an acre or more. A contention arose for its possession between Rees Morgan and Jenkin Davies. Thomas Edwards, having been appealed to by the Board of Property, under his decision, that it was clearly *unseated* land, a patent was granted to Rees Morgan, dated October 12th, 1742, for 215 acres, the balance going, I presume, to Rees Davis, who settled in the neighborhood. Jenkin Davies, under the same rule, was given 200 acres *further back* and was forced to be content. Thos. Morgan died before 1737, as his widow held the property at that date. (See warrant to Jenkin Davies, Taylor Papers).

Rees Morgan has so long been credited with the giving of his ground—praised for his liberality—that it seems almost criminal to disturb him and place the crown on the head of another and that a woman. The interest taken in this ground is for those there buried, and praise should be given to the one whose influence secured it against destruction, and that is Margaret, his wife, and daughter of Thomas Edwards. Rees Morgan himself could have no interest in the matter—she had, in securing to posterity the grave of her father. Rees Morgan was but clay to be molded by the hands of the proud, imperious, masterful Margaret, his wife. He, a boy, married to a woman eight years his senior, had but to do her will. She it was who directed the taking of the unseated land, and it was she also that added the words, "That Rees Morgan's wife, being my daughter, is concerned something in the interest of the affair" (see letter Thomas Edwards to Secretary Peters, Archives, page 229, Vol. VII., Second Series) and neglects to state that his son and daughter are married to a daughter and son of Jenkin Davies. The true inwardness of this is in the relationship of Thomas Edwards with the proprietors. Rees Morgan was not in good health. Fearing death, with a dissipated son to inherit his plantation, the will of the woman again prevailed to make a deed to the second son, dated October 14, 1745—fourteen years before his death, the son giving his notes for the purchase money. Thomas Edwards died May 8, 1764, and in April, 1768, Joseph Williamson was employed to enclose the ground with a stone wall two feet thick and three and a-half feet high on the inside, the enclosure being $75\frac{1}{2}$x$82\frac{1}{2}$ feet. The bill of Joseph Williamson for the labor was 17 pounds, 18 shillings and 4 pence—about twenty-five cents a perch. Eighteen pounds of nails were used to secure the covering. This and the other material used were paid as separate items by Rees Morgan. Little Bettie Morgan was interested in this work. Making several trips for nails, as the work progressed, to the store at the Blue Ball.

Rees Morgan died less than a year later (January 13, 1769). He is buried so that when Margaret dies she shall have her father on one side, her husband on the other. She procured stones for both, alike in every particular, even to the lettering, except "Thomas Edwards, Esq.," is in Italic capitals. These stones were well selected, deeply cut, and can easily last another century. Margaret's work was well done. She linked securely the name of her husband with the fame of her father, and both are preserved to this generation. If any one should not believe this let him go on the ground and see the inferior stone other hands secured for Margaret, who followed twelve years later (August 20, 1781).

Rees Morgan, in his will, bequeaths negroes and money, but no land. The legacies are paid out of the notes of his son David. The eldest son receives his £200 in instalments of £20 pounds yearly; the balance of his estate to his wife, Margaret, and son, David. He leaves 125 perches of ground to his wife, Margaret, and son, David, to be held by them and their heirs forever, in trust as a place of burial to all who may desire there to bury. As the enclosure and the ground on the outside where the negroes were buried is not more than 25 perches, there is still 100 perches left, on which there was a small house, the rent of which was to pay the quit rent (less than one cent a year) and keep the fence in repair. There are ten rows of graves, twenty-eight in each row. The first tombstones, being sandstone, have long since disappeared. Only one is left and that covers the eastern column of the gateway and reads:

Here lies the body of
JOHN DAVIS,
departed this life the 21st day of
January, 1738 A. D.
Aged 56 years.

There are only forty-four marked graves, most of which are of this century.

Rees Morgan died January 13, 1769. His will gives his son Thomas 200 pounds —to be paid 20 pounds annually, commencing within two years after his decease. The remainder of his personal estate, including seven negroes, is given to his wife

Margaret, son David and daughter Elizabeth and her children.

Elizabeth is married to John Pawling. David remained single. Margaret Morgan died August 20, 1781. She gives her property to David, Elizabeth, and Elizabeth's children.

David Morgan died 1784. He frees his negroes, gives all that remains of his real and personal estate to his sister Elizabeth and charges her with the care of his negroes, should they fail to make a living. He makes his brother-in-law, John Pawling, executor.

Elizabeth Pawling died March 4, 1786. At an Orphans' Court, held at Lancaster, December 17, 1788, Henry Pawling, of Montgomery county (the grandfather), is appointed "guardian over the estate of Margaret Pawling, Eleanor Pawling, Elizabeth Pawling and Rachel Pawling, minor children of John Pawling, during their minority."

Thus ended, I presume, the care of the trust made nineteen years before.

THE OLD WELSH GRAVEYARD.

LOCATED ONE-HALF MILE WEST OF FAIRVILLE, IN EAST EARL, LANCASTER COUNTY. SIZE 75.8'x82.6'. WALL 2'x3.5' HIGH. COLUMNS AT GATE 5' HIGH.

PLAN OF THE GRAVES.

NORTH.

WEST.   EAST.

Narrow Lane On This Side.

SOUTH.

(1.)　　　In memory of
JOHN PATTON,
born in the County of Antrim,
Ireland,
who departed this life
May 10, 1832,
in the 83d year of his
age.
He was a soldier in the Revolution, and
fought in the battles of
Germantown, Princetown and Yorktown.

(2.)　　　In memory of
MARGARET PATTON,
who died July
25th, A. D. 1849. Aged 84 years,
3 months.

(3.)　　　JAMES TREGO,
Born February 9, 1798;
Died June 6, 1880.
Aged 82 years, 3 months and 26 days.
Gathered in a good old age to the
Assembly of the Righteous.

(4.)　　　In memory of
LYDIA W. TREGO,
departed this life April 21, A. D. 1864,
Aged 54 years, 6 months
and 22 days.
She is gone, and like a pretty flower
That once in beauty bloomed,
Struck by the hand of Heavenly power,
She sleeps within the tomb.

(5.)　　　In
memory of
ISAAC DAVIS,
who departed this life
January the 5th, A. D. 1838,
Aged 85 years, 9 months
and 1 day.
Weep not for me, for here you see
My trials have been great;
But now 'tis true I bid adieu
And change my mournful state.

(6.)　　　In
memory of
LYDIA DAVIS,
who departed this life
October 5th, A. D. 1821,
aged 63 years and 11 days.
Dear friends, farewell, I go to dwell
With Jesus Christ on high,
Then for to sing, praise to my King,
To all eternity.

(7.)　　　In memory of
JOHN DAVIS, who was
born September 18, 1783,
Died January 11, 1824,
Aged 40 years, 3 months
and 24 days.
Thus much, and this is all we
Know, they're numbered
with the blessed.
Have done with sin, care and woe,

And with their Saviour rest,
On harps of gold they praise
His name, His face they always
View, then let us followers
Be of them that may
praise him too.

(8.) In memory of
ELMIRA F. DAVIS,
born September the 18th, 1829,
Died July the 21st, 1847.
Aged 17 years, 10 months and
3 days.
The years rowls round and
steals away The breath that
first it gave; What are we do
what are we be, We are
traveling to the grave.

(9.) Sacred
to the
memory of
ISAAC C.
DAVIS,
son of Richard
and Catharine
Davis,
born January
the 23d, 1821,
Died April the
23d, 1830, aged
9 year, 3
month.

(9½.) In memory of
ANDREW J. EVANS,
son of Hiram and Au
Evans, who depart-
ed this life Decem-
ber the 8th, 1828.
Aged 1 month & 8 da.

(10.) In
memory of
ISAAC D. TREGO,
aged
11 months and some
days. 1827.

(10½.) In
memory of
ELI P. TREGO,
Aged 5 months and
7 days.

(11.) In
memory of
HIRAM B. TREGO.
Aged 2 years, 3
months & 10 days.
1841.

(11½.) In
memory of
ABSALOM TREGO.
Aged 4 months
and 9 days.
1842.

(12.)
In
memory of
JOHN L. DAVIS.
Born February 10, 1850,
Died Feb. the
24, 1850.
Aged 14 days.
ON REVERSE SIDE.
Son of
Henry & Susanna
Davis.

(13.)
In
memory of
CATHARINE DAVIS,
wife of Richard Davis, SEN.,
who was born Nov. 7,
1792,
and departed this life
March 31st, 1858, aged
75 years, 4 months and
24 days.
My flesh shall slumber
In the ground Till the
last trumpet's joyful sound.

(14.)
In
memory of
RICHARD DAVIS, SEN.,
who departed this life
October the 12th, A. D. 1861,
aged 72 years, 6 months
and 13 days.
My flesh shall slumber
In the ground Till the
last trumpet's Joyful sound.

(15.)
In
memory of
LYDIA A. DAVIS,
born Dec.
21st, 1848,
Died February
the 12th, 1851,
Aged 2 years,
1 mo. and
22 days.
ON REVERSE SIDE.
Daughter of Henry
& Susanna
Davis.

(16.)
In
memory of
ELMIRA E. DAVIS,
born August
the 24th, 1847,
Died May
the 21st, 1851,
Aged 3 years,
8 mo. and
27 days.
ON REVERSE SIDE.
Daughter of Henry
and Susanna
Davis.

(17.) In
memory of
SUSANNA DAVIS,
wife of Henry S. Davis.
Daughter of Jacob & Susanna Lied.
She was born September
the 10th, 1825,
and departed this life June
the 1st, 1851,
aged 25 years, 8 months
and 16 days.

From all my friend I gone away,
And took farewell with all my heart,
To Rest in hope for that great day
When shall need and never part.

(18.) ELIZABETH DAVIS,
Born Aug. 29, 1785,
Died Oct. 15, 1872,
Aged 87 years, 1 mo. & 16
days.

(18½.) In memory of
ELIZA KAIN,
was born April 14,
1807,
Died May 9th,
1868,
Aged 61 years and
26 days.

(19.) In memory of
SARAH HAMBRIGHT,
was born November 29th, 1781,
Died September 4th,
1867,
Aged 85 year, 9 month
and 5 days.

(20.) In memory of
ELIZABETH PAWLING,
who departed this life
March 4th, 1786,
Aged 43 years
and 1 month.

(21.) In memory of
REES MORGAN,
who departed this life
Jan. 13, 1789,
Aged 59 years.

(22.) In memory of
MARGARET MORGAN,
who departed this life
August the 20th, 1781,
Aged 76 years.

(23.) In memory of
THOMAS EDWARDS, ESQ.,
who departed this life
May 8, 1764,
Aged 91 years.

(24.) Here lies the body of
ELIZABETH EDWARDS, who departed this life the 30th
day of November, 1754, in
the 76th year of her age.

ON REVERSE SIDE.
Entombed I am, in dust I lie,
Within this very place
My soul took flight with angels bright.
To see my Saviour's face.
And in the light, within a sight
Of Him above the sky,
And so shall all who believe and call
On Him before they die.

(25.) In memory of
MARY HAMBRIGHT,
Consort of
Henry Hambright, Esq.,
who departed this life
August 4th, 1825,
Aged 72 years.

(26.) In memory of
HENRY HAMBRIGHT, ESQ.,
who was born April 11th,
A. D. 1749,
and died March 2, 1835.
Aged 85 years,
10 months & 20 days.

(27.) In memory of
MARY ANN
HAMBRIGHT,
Second wife of
General Henry
Hambright,
who departed
this life April
12, 1835.

(28.) In
memory of
CHARLOTTE ANN,
daughter of Davis and
Maria Hambright,
departed this life
February 17, A. D. 1851.
Aged 14 years, 1 m., 8 d.
She saught the Lord with
all her heart, And soon
She found her sins forgiven
Cheerful with all her
friends did part In hope
to meet them all in heaven.

(29.) In
memory of
SAMUEL H.,
son of
Davis &
Maria
Hambright,
died March
4, A. D. 1851.
Aged 5 y. and 14 d.
Beloved in life,
Happy in death.

(30.) In memory of
ROBERT WALLACE,
who departed this
life the 17th day
of December, 1793.
Aged 72 years.

(31.)　　　In memory of
ZACCHEUS DAVIS, JUN.,
who departed this life
July the 4th, 1793,
In the 36th year of his age.

(32.)　　　JANE ALLEN,
a native of Ireland,
Died Oct. 9, 1826,
Aged 80 years.

(33.)　　　In
memory of
JOHN DAVIS,
who departed this life
March 21, 1774,
In the 68th year of his age.

(34.)　　　In memory of
ELIZABETH,
wife of John Davis,
who departed this
life Dec. 19, 1796,
aged 71 years
& 8 months.

(35.)　　　In memory of
ZACCHEUS DAVIS, ESQ.,
who departed this life
March the 25th, 1788,
In the 78th year of his age.

(36.)　　　In memory of
JOANNA, wife of
Zaccheus Davis, Esq.,
who departed this life
Jan. 21st, 1768,
In the 58th year of her age.

(37.)　　　　1810.

(38.)　　　　1785.

(39.)　　　F. L. DER.

(40.)　　　A. L. A. W.
1814.

(41.)　　　E. A.
1746.

Used as a cap on the eastern column of the entrance, there is a sandstone, on which are the words:

Here lies the body of
JOHN DAVIS,
departed this life the 21st day of
January, 1736 A. D. Aged 56 years.

B. F. OWEN.

GEORGE ROSS.

BORN MAY 10, 1730,
DIED JULY 14, 1779.

THE

George Ross Memorial

BEING THE PROCEEDINGS AT THE DEDICATION

OF THE

ROSS PILLAR AND TABLET

AT LANCASTER,

On JUNE 4th, 1897.

LANCASTER, PA.
REPRINTED FROM THE NEW ERA.
1897.

Frontispiece—Portrait of George Ross.
Events Leading to the Memorial, ... 376
Programme of Exercises, ... 377
Presentation Address, ... 378
Address of Acceptance, ... 380
Miss Blanche Nevin's Poem, ... 381
Illustration of Memorial Tablet, ... 387
Oration of Hon. Marriott Brosius, ... 389
Illustration of the Ross Mansion, ... 394
Ross Coat of Arms. 408

The Ross Memorial.

At the February meeting of the Lancaster County Historical Society, a communication was received from Messrs. John A. Coyle, John H. Hiemenz and Dr. M. L. Herr, the proprietors of "Rossmere," a suburb of Lancaster city on the northeast, proposing to erect a pillar and tablet, with a suitable inscription, to the memory of George Ross, a signer of the Declaration of Independence, and once the proprietor of Rossmere. It was further proposed that the Historical Society should make all the arrangements required to carry this scheme into execution, secure a design for the pillar, prepare an inscription for the bronze tablet, and finally take charge of the dedicatory services.

The society accepted the generous offer and a committee consisting of Hon. W. U. Hensel, George Steinman, F. R. Diffenderffer, S. M. Sener and Richard M. Reilly were appointed to carry out the project. With such energy was the scheme carried forward that everything was found in readiness to hold the ceremonies on June 4, 1897, the regular monthly meeting day of the Society. On that day, at 2:30 o'clock, the Lancaster County Historical Society, the High Schools of the city, and the Daughters of the Revolution, in the presence of a large concourse of people from city and country, dedicated this memorial to the only signer of the Declaration of Independence from Lancaster county. A handsome Ross memorial souvenir had been prepared, giving a portrait of Ross, a photographic representation of his mansion house which formerly stood on the site of the newly erected pillar, and a cut of the latter. These were freely distributed and formed a pleasant feature of the occasion.

There has always been a question as to the exact day of Ross' death and the place of his burial. The following paragraph from the Philadelphia *Evening Post*, of July 16, 1779, lately brought to light, seems to set both these doubts to rest:

"Last Wednesday died at his seat near this city the Hon. George Ross, esq., judge of the admiralty of this State, who justly merited it. A firm and impartial judge, and yesterday his remains were interred at Christ's church by a number of the most respectable inhabitants. He was buried from his home in this city, in North Alley, above Fifth street."

The following order of exercises was successfully carried out.

… Programme. …

2 p. m.

1. INVOCATION, ... REV. PERCY J. ROBOTTOM.

Almighty and Everlasting God, from whom cometh every good and perfect gift, we bless, thy holy name for that thou didst put it into the heart of thy servant, whose memory we now seek to honor to subscribe to the Declaration of Independence of these United States. We render unto thee most hearty thanks for the good example of thy servant, and we beseech thee to grant unto us who have entered into the inheritance of this blessing that we may show forth in our lives the blessed fruits of a Godly liberty. May we all live to consecrate our gifts for the good of thy church and the welfare of our Country. Through Jesus Christ our Lord, Amen.

2. OPENING CHORUS, By the HIGH SCHOOLS, with HIGH SCHOOL ORCHESTRA.

"Columbia, the Gem of the Ocean."—*David T. Shaw.*

"The Star Spangled Banner."—*Francis Scott Key.*

3. PRESENTATION, ... JOHN A. COYLE, ESQ.

4. MUSIC: National Airs, . . . HIGH SCHOOL ORCHESTRA.

5. ACCEPTANCE. . . . . W. U. HENSEL.

6. CHORUS, ... By the HIGH SCHOOLS.

"Hail Columbia."—*Francis Hopkinson.*

"Battle Hymn of the Republic."—*Julia Ward Howe.*

7. POEM, ... MISS BLANCHE NEVIN.

8. CHORUS, ... By the HIGH SCHOOLS.

"Our Flag is There."—*Anonymous.*

"Ark of Freedom." (Music of Austrian National Hymn.)

—*Joseph Haydn.*

9. DEDICATORY ORATION, . . HON. MARRIOTT BROSIUS.

10. CLOSING CHORUS, ... By the HIGH SCHOOLS.

"My Country, 'Tis of Thee."—*Samuel F. Smith.*

The Chorus of the High Schools under direction of PROF. CARL MATZ; the High School Orchestra under direction of PROF. CARL THORBAHN.

GEORGE ROSS MEMORIAL.

The Memorial Services.

The exercises began at two o'clock in the presence of a large concourse, the following excellent programme being rendered. The music, under the direction of Prof. Carl Matz and Prof. Carl Thorbahn, was an excellent feature and was participated in by everybody:

Mr. Coyle's Presentation Address.

The address of presentation from the donors to the Historical Society was made by John A. Coyle, Esq., who spoke as follows:

Responding to the call of the Committee of Arrangements, formal presentation to the Lancaster County Historical Society is now made of this monument to the lawyer, statesman and patriot, George Ross. Another, and an eloquent, voice will pay just tribute to his memory; the proprieties of the occasion restrict me to the mere formality of presentation, yet permit me to give public assurance, which I now do, of the accuracy of the location of this marker.

Many broad acres surrounding us on all sides, and where now there is the hum of industry and the habitations of many persons, were the farm and this the home of George Ross. Passing from him to the various owners named on your programmes, these premises became in large part the property of Michael Kelly, now deceased, in the year 1837, and remained in the ownership of himself and his children, James and Catharine M. Kelly, until 1893. So that there are living witnesses who during their lives occupied, owned and were familiar with every nook and cranny of the Ross house.

The depression in the ground, which you will see to the west of the stand, was the lane leading directly from the city to and in front of the house. At the eastern end of the pavement in front of the marker was the large spring which gushed forth in the cellar of the house until the construction of the Clay street sewer, which runs its course slightly to the north of us. The house must have been built many years ago, for an attempt to hold together the considerable portion of it not taken by the opening of Ross street was unsuccessful. All that is left of it is this pile of foundation stones turned up when excavating for the pavement, a lot of rafters, a couple of doors and window sash; one of these sashes stands aside of me. On one of the panes of glass is written the name of George Ross. It is done with a stone, corresponds with the manner in which George Ross wrote his name and has some similarity with his handwriting. There is no doubt that this name has been on the glass for over fifty years. It is believed to have been written by George Ross himself.

There is, therefore, no doubt of the identity of the spot of which your society to-day takes possession and which is marked by this shaft. If in the sight of yonder school house it shall stir the hearts of boys and girls—the coming men and women—to noble deeds not only in public station but by the fireside, also; if, built of voiceless material and answering only to the eye, it shall attract the glance of the passer-by and show him the beauty of heroism, the just pride of one's descendants in a life well lived; if it shall draw hither and thence to many other historical spots in this city—soon to be, marked, I hope—the stranger within our gates and show to him, too, that here was

the blood of which martyrs are made, a
distinct good will be done to the community, an added renown brought to this
dear old city. So may it be.

Mr. Hensel's Acceptance.

In accepting the gift of the memorial
on behalf of the Lancaster County Historical Society, Mr. W. U. Hensel referred briefly to the extraordinary growth
of Lancaster, and especially in the northwestern section of the city, where stately
mansions now occupy sites that a half
century ago were swamps and thickets,
and where millions of dollars' worth of
improvements cover lands that were,
within the period of living men, ordinary
farms. In this great material development, historical sites and incidents are
apt to be forgotten and submerged.
It is, therefore, extremely fitting
that such memorials as these should
be erected, and that this be
done under the auspices of the Historical
Society. That organization hoped to
make this simply the initial of a long
series of like events. There were a hundred spots in Lancaster made memorable
by historical events and by associations
of great and noble men, upon which tablets or pillars should record the names
and events. One of the most notable
things to a traveler in the Old World is
this custom, and even in New England
the historical spirit of the people has thus
attested itself in many places. Pennsylvania and Lancaster county need to be
more self-assertive, and the speaker hoped
to see the day when the house in which
John Andre was here a prisoner of war,
the site of the college founded by Benjamin Franklin, the houses where Henry
lived, where West painted, where Tom
Paine wrote, where Robert Fulton experimented, where Buchanan and Stevens

lived and practiced law, sites of the old revolutionary buildings, and others, would be thus marked. It is better for a community to depend upon its own public spirit and upon the individual liberality of its citizens for these than to look for municipal or legislative aid. In this regard the present occasion was likewise memorable, and the donors were entitled to the hearty thanks of the Society and the community for their public spirit and generosity.

Miss Blanche Nevin's Poem.

The following is the exquisite gem read by Miss Blanche Nevin. As will be seen, it rehearses the story of the events preceding and leading up to the Declaration of Independence, and pays a glowing tribute to the fifty-six "good men and true" who affixed their names to that immortal paper:

I.

To chafing hearts in sorest need,
To people fretting to be freed
From foreign yoke, when foreign greed
    With taxes wrung them;
God gave strong leaders, not a few,
Courageous men, upright and true,
And—Lancaster—He gave to you
    George Ross among them.

II.

Ill brooked the sons of pioneers
The sound of cowardice, and sneers
From dapper soldiery in his ears.
    It was small wonder,
Defiance was hurled back again
By irritated frontiersmen;
To tease the wild wolves in their den
    Was fatal blunder.

III.

(Ah! after many a bitter year
Each braggart boast and swaggering jeer
Cost every pretty soldier dear
    As they surrendered.
When beaten, and with downcast head,
Their hats pulled low, and eyelids red,
They followed in Cornwallis' tread,
    As swords were tendered.)

IV.

Long time it was the writhing land
Insulted felt the tyrant hand
The spark was waiting to be fanned
    On freedom's altar.
Yet, though the cause be just and right,
Long will men hesitate to fight,
If "round their necks is pressing tight
    A threatened halter."

V.

But yet we know—dear Liberty—
Man is about as true to thee
As, with his nature, he can be
    To any woman;
That very neck for thy sweet sake
At certain times he risks to break;
Nor holds his life too dear to stake,
    Nor all things human.

VI.

And Patrick Henry's passionate breath,
"Oh, give me liberty or death,"
Thrilled through the anxious land beneath
    All party faction.
Throughout the broad Atlantic States
Where brooding war, impatient, waits
The moment which precipitates
    The crash of action.

VII.

And so, when time was ripe, men came
From far and near to sign each name
Upon that proudest roll of fame,
    Our Declaration.
Facing disgrace, that patriot band,
The nervous force of all the land,
Stretched out the pen and sinewy hand
    That framed the nation.

VIII.

Now let the British lion lash
With angry tail her sides, and gnash
Her teeth and bounding forward dash
    With roaring hollow!
At last the eagle's wings have grown,
The chain is snapped which held him down;
High in the air where he has flown,
    Lions can't follow!

IX.

Good faith! That day you need not think
That Philadelphia lacked for ink;
Or men, whose fingers did not shrink
    At thought of fetters.
For well each knew that shortest shrift,
And tightest rope, and highest lift,
Might be to him stern England's gift
    For those few letters.

X.

Aye—every signer knew that war
Would follow and torment him sore.
Outlawed by it—and all his store
    Unless he hid it—
Was forfeit to the distant king,
Who held him but a chattel thing
From which another tax to wring,
    And yet—he did it.

XI.

Men made for the occasion, they,
More apt for earnest work than play.
Coined for the purpose of the day,
    From precious metal.
Men to a solemn epoch sent,
Shaped by the friction of event
To fitness for some great intent,
    New thoughts to settle.

XII.

Men of big frame and bigger heart
Which had not lost the power to smart
Of pious faith—the greater part
    Of training holy.
Who yet felt heaven in sun and sky,
And held themselves when they should die
Responsible to God on high,
    And to God solely.

XIII.

Who dreaded an avenging hell,
And honor prized too dear to sell,
Who did not love their lives too well
    To risk for others.
For a great principle of right
Willing to die, ready to fight,
Who kept their conscience clean and bright,
    And loved their brothers.

XIV.

Doubtless before his lot was cast,
Each hero struggled through a past
Of dubious fears, but, at the last,
    All vacillation
And tremor being thrust aside,
Purpose was resolute, to abide
Whatever upshot should betide
    The new-fledged nation.

XV.

Fifty-six names were written there,
In all the world's long history, where
Find ye a list which can compare
    With this in glory?
Of nobler lives; of fairer fames;
Of less self-interested aims;
Of cleaner, more untarnished names,
    There is no story.

XVI.

First, Massachusetts, stung to rage
By foolish North or fatuous Gage,
Sent five strong men to sign the page,
    From different classes.
And Hancock, gentleman, indeed,
Wrote down his name to take the lead;
"So large," he said, "the king may read
    Mine without glasses."

XVII.

Adams, the incorruptible!
Who "loved the public good too well
For private gain its rights to sell,"
    Noble in scorning.
Whose voice with no uncertain ring,
When agents came a bribe to bring,
Sent back that message to the king
    And "gave him warning."

XVIII.

Impetuous Houston, in his race
For Zubley, lost deserved place
Among the founders of his race.
    Zubley, a spying
Judas, discovered in the act
Of treachery, denied the fact,
But fled to Georgia; Houston tracked
    The traitor flying.

XIX.

And frequent was the moment, when
The casting vote which made free men
Was given by the State of Penn,
    Amid confusion.
For Morton, to our lasting pride,
Came forward when the vote was tied,
And cast his ballot on the side
    Of revolution.

XX.

Carroll—(lest people would not know)—
Added "of Carrollton" to show
Which Carroll faced the dangerous foe.
    "Now hang together
Or we'll hang separately," said he.
The die was cast, and valiantly
And long they faced a stormy sea
    Ere cleared the weather.

XXI.

We glean from the recording pen
Truth which is now, was also then,
Conspicuous—that heroic men
    Had noble mothers.
And Francis Lewis—(kindly grant
Attention to my modest vaunt)
Was "brought up by his maiden aunt,"
    And "there are others."

XXII.

The more one hears—the more one reads,
Examining their lives and deeds,
The more the critic spirit heeds
    With admiration.
Ere half their worthiness was sung,
If praises due should well be rung,
Your ears would weary of my tongue
    And its narration.

XXIII.

Among the strongest and the best
Our delegate sustained the test,
And cast his ballot with the rest,
    Brave, wise and witty,
Of broad, well educated mind;
King's advocate, and well inclined
To weigh the rights of human kind,
    Ross, of our city!

XXIV.

To-day we come, with honest pride,
From city and from country side,
To mark the spot where did abide
    This man of merit.
And make the letters deep and clear,
That they may last for many a year,
To testify that we hold dear
    What we inherit.

XXV.

It is not meet that gratitude,
Or loving memory of the good,
Should perish—for the coffin wood
    Can only cover
The dust—the vehicle of clay,
Which served the soul its passing day,
The deeds of men die not away,
    Are never over.

XXVI.

The world was better where he trod,
When George Ross rendered up to God
His soul—his body to the sod,
    Well done his duty.
The white man and the red man, too,
Full well his generous justice knew.
Bright his example shines for you,
    A thing of beauty.

XXVII.

Our town, recognizant of zeal,
And service for the common weal,
Voted him "costly plate," "genteel
    And ornamented."
But he the civic gift put by
Making magnanimous reply,
"Only what each should do did I!"
    Modest—contented.

XXVIII.
We offer to his memory's sake,
The gift he, living, would not take;
And tribute of affection make
   With hearty pleasure.
God rest his soul, where'er it be,
Safe in the peace which such as he
Deserve throughout eternity,
   In goodly measure.

XXIX.
The story of the war is fraught
With lesson, and renews the thought
That nothing great was ever wrought
   Without hard trial.
Gold cannot buy, beyond dispute,
God's highest gifts. The finest fruit
And flower of goodness take their root,
   In self-denial.

XXX.
Lancastrians, who your acres plough,
Whose fertile fields are ripening now,
In gratitude, remember how
   They were defended.
What years of suffering were borne,
How long the sharpened sword was worn;
How great the hunger, scant the corn,
   Ere war was ended.

XXXI.
See ye to it—who peaceful stand
And gather with unshackled hand
The crops that ripen in the land
   In generous bounty;
See ye to it that not in vain
Their red blood soaked the battle plain,
When men for liberty were slain,
   Oh, town and county!

XXXII.
The present guardians of your race
A little while ye fill a space,
Rise to the duties of your place!
   If care relaxes,
New forms of tyranny creep in;
Greed and corruption will begin,
Be vigilant, or they will win.
   Look to your taxes!

XXXIII.
Stand by your colors without fear,
In spite of cynic, scoff and jeer,
See that you treat "Old Glory" dear
   With reverent manner.
God help the day—God help the hour
If hearts degenerate lose the power
To thrill—to glow at sight of our
   Star Spangled Banner.
                BLANCHE NEVIN.
LANCASTER, June 4th, 1897.

THE ROSS MEMORIAL.

George Ross—born in Newcastle, Delaware, December, 1730; sometime resident of Lancaster; died in Philadelphia, July 13, 1779—was a lawyer, a statesman and a patriot. He was the only Signer of the Declaration of Independence from the city or the county of Lancaster. The pillar and tablet erected to-day commemorate his residence here and his services to the community, to the commonwealth and to his country. The story of his life is told in the words of the eloquent orator and in the verses of the gifted poetess.

While he dwelt in Lancaster his city house stood on the site of the present court house on East King Street near Duke. A considerable part of its woodwork was taken up into and is still conspicuous in the stately Lightner mansion at the southeast corner of Duke and Lemon Streets. The site marked by the memorial now erected was where his country home and farmhouse stood, then in a suburban section.

The pillar and tablet are a gift to the Lancaster County Historical Society by Dr. M. L. Herr, Mr. John W. Hiemmenz and John A. Coyle, Esq. These gentlemen have been notably prominent in the development of the northeastern part of the city, and the beautiful surroundings of the memorial are largely due to their enterprise and public spirit. The section known as "Rossmere" had this name bestowed upon it in honor of the Signer. He is also commemorated by a splendid stained glass memorial window in St. James P. E. Church, the gift of Miss Mary Ross, the only lineal descendant who bears his name. The Hopkins, Eshleman (D. G.) and Lightner families are also descended from George Ross on their maternal side.

The memorial is erected under the auspices of the Lancaster County Historical Society; its officers at present are as follows: *President*, GEORGE STEINMAN, Lancaster. *Vice-Presidents*, SAMUEL EVANS, ESQ., Columbia; JOSEPH C. WALKER, Gap. *Recording Secretary*, F. R. DIFFENDERFFER, Lancaster. *Corresponding Secretary*, W. W. GRIEST, Lancaster. *Librarian*, SAMUEL M. SENER, ESQ., Lancaster. *Treasurer*, B. C. ATLEE, ESQ., Lancaster. **Executive Committee**, W. U. HENSEL, Lancaster; HORACE L. HALDEMAN, Chickies; ADAM GEIST, Blue Ball; REV. C. B. SHULTZ, Lititz; DR. C. A. HEINITSH, Lancaster; J. W. YOCUM, ESQ., Columbia; RICHARD M. REILLY, ESQ., Lancaster; PETER C. HILLER, Conestoga; HON. ESAIAS BILLINGFELT, Adamstown; PROF. H. F. BITNER, Millersville. [The officers are also members of the Executive Committee by virtue of their offices.]

COMMITTEE OF ARRANGEMENTS:

W. U. HENSEL,   GEORGE STEINMAN,
F. R. DIFFENDERFFER,   R. M. REILLY,   S.M. SENER.

Address by Hon. Marriott Brosius

MY FELLOW CITIZENS: We are assembled to-day to keep a custom of the ages. Since Joshua commanded the stones to be piled on the banks of the Jordan as a memorial to the Children of Israel, monuments have been the customary means of commemorating great events, historic occasions and distinguished services. While our central purpose in this dedicatory service relates to the character and services of a citizen of Lancaster of Revolutionary fame, yet, as his career was associated with the illustrious events of his time, it is in a larger sense sufficiently inclusive to embrace the memorable occurence of the achievement of Colonial Independence and the birth of the Republic.

To be a citizen of a country without a peer, under a government whose cornerstones are the wisdom, virtue and patriotism of those it was appointed to govern ; to love and serve it and enjoy its protection is our singular good fortune ; but it was the extreme felicity of our Revolutionary father, our signer of the immortal Declaration, to share the glory of the achievement which made possible such a country.

George Ross was of Scotch descent, and his lineage is distinctly traceable to Malcolm, Earl of Ross, who was contemporary with Malcolm, King of the Scots, in the twelfth century. He doubtless owed his success in some measure to those effective traits of Scotch character which have been so much in evidence in our own country as to lead a distinguished American to observe: "Whenever anything good is to be done in this country you are apt to find a Scotchman on the front seat trying to do it." His father, Rev. George Ross, was educated at Edinburg, where he received the degree of A. M. in 1700. In 1705 he emigrated to America and became Rector of the Episcopal parish at Newcastle, Delaware, where his son, George, was born May 10, 1730. His mother was Catharine Van Gezel, of Delaware, a granddaughter of Gerrit Van Gezel, of Amsterdam, who was nephew and secretary to Jacob Alrichs, the Dutch Governor or Vice Director of the Dutch colony on the Delaware.

He inherited from a long line of illustrious ancestors superior endowments and at an early age laid the foundation of a liberal education. He studied law in Philadelphia with his half-brother John, a lawyer of distinguished ability, whose only rival for leadership at the Pennsylvania bar was Andrew Hamilton. Samuel Adams in his diary refers to him as a lawyer of great eloquence and extensive practice, and a great Tory. It was said of him that he loved ease and Maderia much better than liberty and strife. In the early part of the Revolutionary period he justified his neutral attitude on the ground that, "Let who would be, King, he was sure to be a subject." Before his death, however, he followed the example of his brother and became a convert to the cause of the colonies. Another brother, Rev. Æneas Ross, succeeded his father as Rector of the Parish of Newcastle. He was an earnest supporter of independence and preached patriotic sermons. His sister, Anne, married John Yeates, of Delaware, a cousin of the distinguished jurist, Jasper Yeates, a Judge of the Supreme Court of Pennsylvania, and a resident of this city. His sister, Gertrude, became the wife of George W. Read, of Delaware, a member of the Continental Congress, of the Federal Convention of 1787, United States Senator, President and Chief Justice of Delaware, and a signer of the Declaration of Independence. Another sister, Margaret, was twice married, in both instances to clergymen of the Episcopal Church. Susanna also was married to a minister of the Established Church. Catharine was married to Wm. Thompson, the commander of the famous Thompson's Battalion of Riflemen, Pennsylvania's first troops in the Revolutionary war, and the first men from any of the colonies south of New England to join the American army before Boston in the summer of 1775. This gallant officer became General of the Continental Line, and was taken prisoner at the battle of Three Rivers, near Quebec, in June, 1776. He was exchanged in 1780, and died a few months later. His sister, Elizabeth, married Colonel Edward Biddle, of Reading, a distinguished lawyer, Speaker of the Pennsylvania Assembly, and member of the Continental Congress; and Mary became the wife of Colonel Mark Bird, of Birdsboro, a prominent man of his day and an officer in the Revolutionary army. John Ross, nephew of George and son of Rev. Aeneas Ross, became the husband of Elizabeth Griscom (Betsy Ross), who made our first national flag. This recital of family connections is only important to show the character and distinction of the Ross family. It can add nothing to the lustre of the eminent personality of George Ross.

After his admission to the bar he removed to Lancaster, where he commenced his professional career in 1751. He early gave evidence of a discreet and well ordered mind. Almost the first suit he brought, and he prosecuted it with success to final judgment in his favor, was for the hand of a beautiful and accomplished lady of Scotch-Irish descent, by the name of Anne Laulor, whom he married August 17, 1751. His city residence was at the corner of East King and Duke streets, where the Court House now stands; while his suburban home was on the spot on which we are now assembled. In both places he dispensed a liberal hospitality and entertained the most eminent men of his time in law, politics, statesmanship and war.

The next scintillation of wisdom recorded of him was in devoting himself to the pursuit of his profession, eschewing politics for several years. His success at the bar brought him in a few years the appointment of prosecutor for the Crown, an office which he filled with distinguished credit.

In 1768 he was chosen a representative to the General Assembly and continued a member of that body until 1777, excepting the years 1772 and 1776. During this period the benevolence of his mind led him to study the condition of the Indians and the character of our intercourse with them. This preparation qualified him for great usefulness when he became the organ of the Colonists in their controversies with the red men and the mediator between them, making his country greatly his debtor by the judgment and wisdom with which he conducted their negotiations.

The same benevolent spirit and humane temper of mind led him to respond with promptitude to the claims of the oppressed and unfortunate from whatever cause. When the Tories became the subjects of persecution and sometimes imprisonment, and it was esteemed next to treason to defend them, he, with James Wilson and a few other eminent persons, was ever ready to plead in their behalf.

He was among the first of the Colonists to become sensible of the arbitrary acts of the English government and to feel "the sting of British tyranny." His indignation kindled at the extortionate and despotic demands of the Crown and he was prompt to co-operate in the initial movement to secure independence.

The Virginia resolutions, proposing a Congress of all the Colonies, were received in the General Assembly on the eve of its adjournment. Notwithstanding it was the opinion of many members that whatever measures might be adopted should proceed from a future Assembly fresh from their constituents, so commanding was the position of Mr. Ross among his colleagues that he was appointed a committee to draft a reply to the Speaker of the Virginia House of Delegates. In that reply he expressed with clearness and force how sensible the members of the Pennsylvania Assembly were of the importance of co-operating with the representatives of the other Colonies in every wise and prudent measure for the preservation and security of their general rights and liberties.

By the success of his services in the Assembly he plumed his wings for a higher flight of public usefulness. On the 22d of July, 1774, he was one of seven delegates chosen to represent the Province in the Continental Congress. His colleagues were Joseph Galloway, the Speaker of the Assembly, Samuel Rhodes, Thomas Mifflin, Charles Humphries, John Morton and Edward Biddle. On October 15th, on motion of Mr. Ross, it was ordered that John Dickinson be chosen an additional delegate. That Congress met on the 5th of September and adjourned on October 26th of the same year.

As George Ross shared the distinction achieved in that short session of seven

SOUTHERN FRONT.

The above is a view of the home of Honorable George Ross, which formerly stood on the site of the monumental pillar and tablet this day erected on Ross Street, between Plum and Shippen Streets, in the City of Lancaster. It was demolished in 1894 in the opening of these streets.

When the George Ross mansion was built and by whom, are among the unknown secrets of the last century which will probably never be revealed. All that is known is that on February 4, 1717, William Penn sold to John Funck the 200 acres covering the Ross estate. On February 20. 1717, Funck resold it to Michael Meyer and his wife. The latter, in turn, sold it to the Hon. James Hamilton on January 19, 1750. Hamilton sold it to George Ross on June 19, 1761. Since then it changed hands frequently.

The mansion house was probably erected long prior to the Revolution. It was a fair type of the homes of the well-to-do class of that period. Like most of them it was built of stone, that material being both abundant and good in the neighborhood. Like them, it covered an ample area of ground, and still other eighteenth century peculiarities may be seen in the gambrel roof and the small panes of glass in the windows. The location of the house was no doubt fixed by the builder by the strong spring of pure, cold water which once rose out of its very foundations. The house was in fact built over the spring, which issued bright and sparkling through the wall in the north-west corner. To the north, sloping gently downward from the house-yard, lay fields of meadow land through which the released spring made merry music as it sped along over its pebbly bed.

In every respect it was an ideal home; one to which its well-to-do owner could retreat when he returned from his duties in the Continental Congress. When the labors of the day in his town office or his legal contests in the courts were over, a twenty minutes' walk through the forest primeval took him to the quiet of this country home. One can scarcely imagine a more desirable place to which the lawyer, the scholar and the statesman could retreat for study, for recreation, or for quiet, or where he could better cast off all the perplexities of a political and professional career, if he felt so inclined.

It seems a matter for regret that this old homestead, so rich in associations of our Revolutionary period, could not have been spared to us by the resistless march of progress. It was torn down in 1894. An attempt was made to preserve the portion not taken by the street, but it was too fragile to be saved. But in thought we go back to that ancient day. Doubtless its old stone walls echoed to the quip and the jest, the sober discussion and patriotic eloquence of his fellow Congressmen, when driven to this city by Howe's capture of Philadelphia. They were men like ourselves and could unbend in moments of gladness and festivity. There were sermons in the old stones that lay in these well-built walls, but, like Memnon, their music has departed, and they are vocal in memory alone.

And now, 'tis silent all; sage, patriot, fare thee well.

weeks, it may be worth while to pause in our narrative long enough to take a glimpse of that notable Assembly, the first Continental Congress. It met in Carpenters' Hall. Its members were themselves mechanics of the highest order; masterbuilders who laid firm and strong the foundations of a Republic which recognized the right of every man to an equal chance. Its personnel was remarkable. There was Samuel Adams, the master spirit of the movement for independence; John Jay, the youngest member, in the dawn of his splendid career; Stephen Hopkins, the patriarch of the Assembly, once Chief Justice of Rhode Island ; Sherman, of Connecticut; Randolph, of Virginia, who was made chairman, and his colleague, Edward Rutledge ; Thomas McKean; John Dickinson, the learned "Pennsylvania Farmer," who gave the Colonists the potent shibboleth, "No taxation without representation;" Christopher Gadsden, whose spirited reply to the suggestion that the British world burn our seaport towns was worthy the man: "Our towns," he said, "are built of brick and wood; if they are burned down we can rebuild them, but liberty once lost is gone forever;" Patrick Henry, who crystallized the common thought of the hour that British oppression had wiped out the boundaries of the Colonies in that famous declaration, "I am not a Virginian, but an American;" and Washington, whose modesty counseled him to take a back seat, though he was to become the foremost man in all that celebrated company. Of such men and others of less note was that Congress composed. Their work was the grandest of the ages. No body of men in ten times the period had ever before achieved so much for mankind as this half hundred in two and fifty days. They surveyed and mapped the rights of man, declared that no law enacted without his consent was binding upon a British subject, that taxation without representation was tyranny, that the common law of England was every Englishman's birthright. Having defined the rights of America and solemnly declared their purpose to maintain them, they closed their work with a recital of their grievances and an earnest, calm, conciliatory and dignified appeal to the justice of the British nation for redress, for peace, liberty and security. Little wonder that the first Continental Congress extorted the admiration of the world. From the moment of their first debate, says De Tocqueville, Europe was moved. John Adams said that in point of ability, virtue and fortune they were the greatest men upon the continent. Lord Chatham in the face of the King declared: "I must aver that in all my reading of history that for solidity of reasoning, force of sagacity and wisdom of conclusion, under such a complication of circumstances, no nation or body of men can stand in preference to the General Congress assembled at Philadelphia."

But Mr. Ross was not a one term Congressman. He was re-elected on December 15, 1774, to the Congress which convened May 10, 1775. To the succeeding term he was not elected, but on July 20, 1776, he was again elected and immediately took his seat. In January, 1777, he obtained leave of absence on account of illness and never afterward returned. He thus occupied a seat in the Continental Congress from September 14 to October 26, 1774; from May 10 to November , 1775, and from July 20, 1776, to January, 1777.

While not in Congress his services were not withheld from the cause of the Colonies. He was a patriot, firmly attached to liberty and independence, and his service was always at their command. Even while a member of Congress he served in the General Assembly. The question of incompatibility of office was not raised. The pre-eminence he enjoyed among public men of his time was shown by the variety and distinction of the services to which he was called from time to time by the General Assembly. In July, 1774, he presided over a mass meeting of the citizens of Lancaster county to take into consideration the Acts of the British Parliament relative to America. At the same time he was on a committee of correspondence to cement union between the Colonies and a deputy to the Provincial Convention held at Philadelphia, July 15, 1774. In 1775, when the Assembly received a message from Governor Penn upon the unsatisfactory situation of the Colony and evidently intended to repress the ardor of those who favored the redress of grievances, a question of serious moment arose whether they should yield to the solicitation of the Governor or stand firmly by the measures of Congress. On this question there was a long debate in which Mr. Ross took a conspicuous part. He was an able debater, a persuasive and convincing speaker. The influence of his eloquence and the power of his logic prevailed. A committee of which he was a leading member was appointed to draft a reply to the Governor's message. That reply will challenge comparison with any other similar state paper on record. Jefferson himself could not have exceeded its exquisite diplomacy in form and temper. It exhibited conciliation without servility, respectful deference without obsequiousness, resolute firmness without offensive defiance. George Ross wrote it and the Assembly adopted it as their answer to the Governor's address.

When the situation became more critical and measures were required to put the Province in a suitable state of defense, he was appointed a committee to report such expedient measures as the situation required. The report recommended ways and means of defending the lives, liberty and property of the citizens and repelling any hostile invasion of British troops. It advised putting the Province on a suitable war footing, to prosecute their predetermined defense of their rights, liberty and independence. He was eminently qualified for exertions of this character, for no man better comprehended the difficulties under which the Colonists labored in their encounter with British injustice, or grappled them with a more robust spirit of determination and defiance than George Ross. This sense of the situation and his heroic spirit were accentuated when he said to his son: "We are fighting with halters around our necks, but we will win." When war was imminent he was called upon to assist in the preparation of rules and regulations for the government of the military forces that might be employed. On July 4, 1776, at the very hour the Declaration of Independence was being adopted by the Continental Congress, he was at Lancaster presiding at a meeting of the officers and members of the fifty-three Battalions of Associators of the Colony of Pennsylvania to choose two Brigadier Generals. On July 6th he wrote to Col. Gailbraith enclosing the resolves of Congress on the subject of Independence which he had just received. He was about this time President of the Lancaster Committee of Inspection, Observation and Correspondence. He was Colonel of the First Battalion of Associators of Lancaster. On July 18, 1776, he was elected Vice President of the

Pennsylvania Constitutional Convention. At different times he was a member of the Committee of Safety for Lancaster county, and on July 6, 1775, was appointed one of the inspectors of military stores. In 1777 he was associated with George Washington and Robert Morris on a committee appointed by the Continental Congress to devise a national flag. He was also appointed on a committee to prepare a declaration of rights on behalf of the State; was chairman of two other committees of importance, one to formulate rules for the government of the Convention which had superseded the Assembly, and the other to draft a law defining treason to the State and fixing a punishment for that crime. Here we note an indication of the esteem in which he was held as a lawyer. He is said to have been among the first of his profession. In the deep and intricate controversies arising in that formative period he took a conspicuous part. On occasions commanding the greatest exertions of the strongest minds he was among the foremost, never failing to acquit himself with distinguished credit.

When he retired from the Continental Congress he received an agreeable demonstration of the approbation of his constituents in the form of a resolution passed at a public meeting in the borough of Lancaster, which showed not only how sensible his constituents were of the value of his public services, but afforded him an opportunity of evincing his sensibility to the obligations which his duty to his country imposed. As this expression of appreciation and gratitude had a touch of novelty and was highly creditable to the citizens of Lancaster I will be excused for reproducing it in this connection:

"*Resolved*, That the sum of one hundred and fifty pounds out of the common stock be forthwith transmitted to George Ross, one of the members of the Assembly for this county and one of the delegates for this county in the Continental Congress, and that he be requested to accept the same as a testimony from this county of their sense of his attendance on the public business to his great private loss, and of their approbation of his conduct.

"*Resolved*, If it be more agreeable, Mr. Ross purchase with part of the said money a genteel piece of plate ornamented as he thinks proper, to remain with him as a testimony of the esteem this county has for him, by reason of his patriotic conduct in the great struggle for American liberty."

Even in our day, when this mode of requiting the services of public servants is out of fashion, we can easily understand how grateful to the feelings of Mr. Ross was this testimony of affection and gratitude. But he was as sensible of his dignity and duty as were his constituents of his services and their obligation. With a modesty characteristic of real elevation of mind, he disparaged his service to his country and declined this moderate honorarium from his fellow-citizens, protesting that in bestowing his exertions upon the cause of liberty and independence he was impelled solely by a patriotic sense of duty, and that he did no more than every man should do to advance the cause of his country without hope of pecuniary reward. Such elevation of character, lofty patriotism and disinterested devotion to the claims of duty command the homage and admiration of the world, and constitute an example worthy the emulation of mankind.

The remnant of life allowed Mr. Ross after his retirement from Congress was to be still further dignified and exalted by his elevation to the Bench of the Admiralty of the State to which he was appointed March 1, 1779. A brief service upon the Bench demonstrated the possession of great ability, dignity and tireless industry in the discharge of his judicial duties. He died on the 14th of July, 1779, of a sudden illness at his home in Philadelphia, and was buried in Christ Church burial ground. From a letter written by a member of the family at the time it appears that in his last conversation he exhibited great cheerfulness, spoke pleasantly of the long journey he was about to take and hopefully of his prospects in the haven of rest whither he was going and to which his wife had preceded him.

The pedestal and tablet we dedicate today will declare to coming generations what would remain as durably in the remembrance of mankind without the aid of brick or bronze, that George Ross was a signer of the Declaration of Independence; a fact which conferred perhaps greater distinction than any other act of his illustrious career. Next to John Hancock's, the boldest and strongest signature to that immortal instrument is that of George Ross. It has been taken for granted and commonly believed on the warrant of unveracious chroniclers for a hundred years that he was a member of the Congress that adopted the Declaration on the Fourth of July, 1776. This is not the fact, and we must not withhold the homage due the truth of history by omitting to record on this occasion absolute historic truth.

It will be seen from what I have already said that George Ross did not sit in the Continental Congress from November 3, 1775, to July 20, 1776, in which interval the vote of adoption took place. It is worthy of note that some members, not alone from Pennsylvania but from other Colonies as well, who occupied seats on the Fourth of July and voted for the adoption of the Declaration, ceased to be members before the 2nd of August when the signing took place; and on the other hand some who were not members on the Fourth of July became such before the day of signing, and while they had no agency in the adoption enjoyed the distinction of signing the Declaration. The Pennsylvania delegation underwent a radical change in that interval. Five members, viz., John Dickinson, Charles Humphries, Edward Biddle, Thomas Willing and Andrew Allen, were succeeded by George Ross, George Clymer, Benjamin Rush, James Smith and George Taylor, who took their seats on the 20th of July, and all signed the Declaration, though they had no part in its adoption.

The only signatures placed upon the instrument on the day of its adoption were those of John Hancock, President, and Charles Thompson, Secretary. The order made on the Fourth, as shown by the Journal, was "that the Declaration be authenticated and printed." On the 19th of July, however, the following resolution was passed:

"*Resolved*, That the Declaration passed on the 4th inst. be fairly engrossed on parchment with the title and style of 'The Unanimous Declaration of the Thirteen United States of America' and that the same when engrossed be signed by every member of Congress." On the 2nd of August the Journal says: "The Declaration of Independence being engrossed and compared at the table was signed by the members." The signers were thus of necessity the members at the time the instrument was submitted for signatures, all of whom with three exceptions signed at that time. Two signed later in the fall and Thomas McKean not until January, 1777.

Another circumstance invites our attention in this connection, not one that would either make or mar so great a fame as that of our Lancaster signer, but which requires an explanation to be recorded on this occasion; for the attentive student of our Colonial and Revolutionary history and the studies it has afforded for artistic representation still wonders why the face of George Ross does not appear in the celebrated painting of the "Signers" in the rotunda of the Capitol at Washington. John Trumbull was employed by the Government to execute this work. He was a painter of eminence and was employed at the same time on a number of historical studies illustrating our Revolution history, under a contract with the Government. He travelled extensively in Europe and traversed the States in search of portraits for the purpose of his paintings. His idea, as stated in his autobiography, was to secure the likenesses of the men who were the authors and signers of that memorable Declaration; and the rule he laid down for his guidance in the composition of the painting was to admit no ideal representation. He was determined in his purpose, tireless in his exertions to procure the face of every man required for the completion of his canvas. An incident given me by Mr. J. Hammond Trumbull, of Hartford, Connecticut, derived from the artist himself, illustrates the length he went to carry out his intentions. No portrait of Benjamin Harrison could be found; none was in existence. One day when the painting was nearly completed a stranger entered his studio and after looking at the picture for some time remarked: "I don't see Governor Ben. Harrison there. He signed the Declaration." "Did you know General Harrison?" asked the artist impatiently.

"Well, I ought to," was the reply. "He was my father." "Is there any likeness of him?" asked Mr. Trumbull. "No," said Mr. Harrison, "there is no picture, but my mother and the family have always told me that I was the image of my father at the same age except for the difference in color of eyes and hair." "Please stand just where you are," was the peremptory command of the painter, who caught up his pailette and brush and began to make a sketch of his visitor, making the requisite changes in eyes and hair. When the sketch was completed he showed it to Mr. Harrison, who, after studying it for a while, said : "Well, I don't believe there is a man in Virginia who ever saw Governor Harrison who would not recognize that as his likeness." And that face caught thus on the wing went on the famous canvas.

The artist found it difficult to determine who by rights should be represented. Should he admit those only who were present and voted for adoption and exclude those who voted against it, or should he recognize the title only of those who signed the instrument? On these questions he consulted Adams and Jefferson, who concurred in the advice that the signatures should be the general guide. Mr. Ross was within this rule and his face would certainly have adorned the canvas if a portrait of him had been available. Mr. Trumbull, however, in the end adopted a very liberal test and admitted to the privilege of his canvas some who adopted but did not sign, some who signed but did not adopt, and some who did both and two who did neither, viz., John Dickinson, who was an eloquent opposer of the measure, and Thomas Willing, who voted against it and being retired before the 2nd of August had no opportunity to sign.

But the mystery of the omission deepens

when we remember that there was extant a portrait of George Ross, painted by Benjamin West, of whose existence Mr. Trumbull may fairly be presumed to have had knowledge, for he was a friend of West's and a frequent visitor at his house in London during the years that the "great picture" and the persons who were to compose it were on his mind and frequently on his lips.

I find an interesting incident recorded in the life and studies of Benjamin West by John Galt, which leaves no doubt of the fact that West painted a portrait of George Ross. Young West was visiting a friend by the name of Flower, a Justice of the Peace in Chester county, who had a legal friend in Lancaster by the name of Ross. "Lancaster," says the biographer, "was remarkable for its wealth and had the reputation of possessing the best and most intelligent society to be found in America," a reputation which it is her felicity to have maintained through the intervening century and a half. Mr. Flower brought his young friend to the Ross mansion on a visit. "The wife of Mr. Ross," says the chronicler, "was greatly admired for her beauty, and her children were so remarkable in this respect as to be objects of general notice." Mr. Flower at dinner advised his friend Ross to have the portraits of his family taken, and suggested that they would be excellent subjects for young West. Application was afterwards made to West's father for permission for the young artist to go to Lancaster for the purpose of making one or more portraits of the Rosses. How many pictures were executed at that time has eluded my search; but it is certain that Mr. and Mrs. Ross' were, and it is said by members of the family that portraits of two children were also made.

Another incident narrated by the same author confirms the fact of West's visit Lancaster. Mr. Galt says: "At the time of West's visit to the Ross family he met a gunsmith by the name of William Henry, who, having something of a classical turn, proposed to the young artist to paint the death of Socrates. West had never heard of Socrates, but the gunsmith booked him up and he made a sketch which was very clever. He, however, was in doubt how to represent the slave and he said to his friend: "I have hitherto painted faces and people clothed; what am I to do with the slave who presents the poison? He ought, I think, to be naked." Henry went out to his work-shop and brought in one of his workmen, a handsome man, stripped to the waist, saying, "There is your model," and accordingly the muscular toiler went on the canvas.

A careful review of the chronology of events which cluster about the portrait of George Ross leads to the conclusion that it was executed between 1755 and 1760, when he was twenty-five or thirty years of age ; and an inspection of the picture confirms this view. A copy, made about 1875, by Philip Wharton, I am advised, now hangs in Independence Hall. It is not a little singular that anyone in possession of a portrait of so eminent a person at a time when a group of figures to whose companionship he had so just a title was being painted by order of the Government, did not produce it even without request. The only admissible explanation is that from 1810 to 1824, when Mr. Trumbull was in quest of portraits for his historical studies, the Ross picture was stored away in somebody's closet, out of sight and therefore out of mind, and the artist's search failed to reach its hiding-place. It thus happened that the celebrated painting of the "Signers" which cost the Government $8,000 received the artist's benediction without the face of Lancaster's illustrious signer.

But the fame, of George Ross is not conditioned by the accident of an effigy or the circumstance of an artist's unavailing search. Immortal wreaths in this world of ours will ever crown immortal deeds. A Roman orator, to stimulate the heroism of his countrymen, placed before them the vision of a heaven of never-ending repose and happiness for those who defended their country. So is there a heaven of never-ending repose for the honest fame of the good and great in the remembrance of mankind. The memory of this eminent citizen, upright judge, and sterling patriot, as well as that of his illustrious contemporaries who led the Colonies through the Red Sea of Revolution to the Canaan of Independence, can never lose its perennial green; for their fame is indissolubly linked with and imperishably enshrined in the history of that memorable and heroic struggle to secure the inalienable rights of man, place government on the moveless base of liberty and justice, and establish in the New World the supremacy of principles as inextinguishable as the stars and a civilization as shining as the sun.

My fellow citizens, our task ends. As we have spoken, the hour and the occasion have passed. Sad indeed would it be were we to miss the lesson they teach. To secure the fruit of the achievements of the past we must emulate its high examples. They point the way to patriotism, courage, faith, fortitude and rectitude. Veneration for the examples of the heroic dead found a tongue in the young Greek who exclaimed: "The trophies of Miltiades will not let me sleep." So a high sense of the achievements of the masters who laid our keel and wrought our ribs of steel may lift us to the high level of their excellence, until like Hector's son we catch heroic fire from the memory of illustrious sires and by our exertions make our country as immortal as the memory of its founders.

ROSS
COAT-OF-ARMS

The Ross Arms blazoned above are taken from a silver tankard in possession of G. Ross Eshleman, Esq., of this city. The tankard belonged to George Ross, the Signer, and came to him from his father. According to "Burke's Peerage," pages 1181-82, the arms were created February 28, 1672, and are blazoned as follows: "gules; three lions rampant; argent. Crest, a hand holding a garland of laurel, proper." In a copy of an early blazonry of the arms there appear "Supporters—two savages, wreathed about the head and middle with laurel and holding clubs in their exterior hands, all proper." The motto is: "*Spem, Successus, Alit.*"

www.ingramcontent.com/pod-product-compliance
Lightning Source LLC
Chambersburg PA
CBHW032011300426
44117CB00008B/985